Martin Yan's
Asian Favorites

Martin Yan's
Asian Favorites

FROM HONG KONG, TAIWAN, AND THAILAND

Martin Yan

Food photography by Maren Caruso

Location photography by Stephanie Jan

Ten Speed Press

BERKELEY   TORONTO

10

Ten Speed Press
PO Box 7123
Berkeley, California 94707
www.tenspeed.com

Distributed in Australia by Simon and Schuster Australia,
in Canada by Ten Speed Press Canada, in New Zealand by
Southern Publishers Group, in South Africa by Real Books,
in Southeast Asia by Berkeley Books, and in the United
Kingdom and Europe by Airlift Book Company.

Library of Congress Cataloging-in-Publication Data
Yan, Martin, 1948–
    [Asian favorites]
    Martin Yan's Asian favorites : from Hong Kong, Taiwan,
and Thailand / Martin Yan.
            p. cm.
Includes index.
    ISBN 1-58008-370-6 (pbk.)
    ISBN 1-58008-371-4 (hardcover)
1. Cookery, Asian. I. Title: Asian favorites. II. Title.
    TX724.5.A1 Y37 2002
    641.595—dc21   2001003890

Project Manager: Tina Salter
Design: Catherine Jacobes Design
Editor: Holly Taines White
Food Photographer's Assistant: Faiza Ali
Food Styling: Kim Konecny and Erin Quon
Food Specialist: Sophie Hou
Prop Stylist: Carol Hacker
Copy Editor: Carolyn Krebs

First printing, 2001
Printed in China

1 2 3 4 5 6 7 8 9 10 — 05 04 03 02 01

contents

Acknowledgments

EVERY BOOK PROJECT I'VE UNDERTAKEN has convinced me that, like The Beatles, I couldn't get by without a little help from my friends. The many hands that guided this project to completion belong to some of the most talented, creative, and dedicated people I know, and, as always, it was a pleasure and honor to work with them. So let me take a little time to give them their due credit, although the accolades they deserve far surpass the size of this page.

Putting a cookbook together isn't just a matter of sitting down at a word processor and typing it up. You've first got to develop and test the recipes, and without the technique and expertise of our kitchen crew, we would never have gotten even that far. Sandra Rust, Jan Nix, and Julie Tan Salazar have been indispensable additions to my test kitchen on this, as well as many other projects, along with chefs Sophie Hou, William Chow, Eva Kwong, David Skrzypek, and John Valencia as well as Stephanie Jan, Frankie Poon, Winnie Lee, Leena Hung, Jennifer Louie, and a bevy of promising culinary students from Cosumnes River College in Sacramento, California.

When it came down to coordinating all aspects of creating this book, Jeannie Cuan, as always, was a dependable, diplomatic, and eternally competent project coordinator. With grace under pressure, she kept things running, and did so with a smile. The researching and creative writing skills of Ivan Lai, Kim Decker, and Leena Hung helped turn my wandering thoughts and memories into text that's both fun to read and informative. Margaret McKinnon, Susan Yoshimura, and Drew Gillaspie all provided eagle-eye proofreading help.

At Ten Speed Press, a professional crew came together under the direction of Kristy Melville, publisher and vice president, and every one of them deserves thanks and praise. Holly Taines White, senior editor, was supportive, insightful, patient, and fast. Carolyn Krebs, as copy editor, and Brigit Binns, as proofreader, did exemplary work, as you'll see when you delve into these pages.

A cookbook is much more than the sum of its recipes. The on-location photographs that spice up the pages are thanks to the artful eye of Stephanie Jan. The lush photographs that accompany the recipes—and really make the book shine—are the handiwork of photographer Maren Caruso as well as her assistant, Faiza Ali, food stylists Kim Konecny and Erin Quon, food specialist Sophie Hou, and prop stylist Carol Hacker. It took designer Catherine Jacobes to showcase everyone's work in the contemporary design of this book. Kudos to all!

Once again, Tina Salter was a wellspring of publishing savvy, and her friendship, support, and hard work were the secret ingredients that make this finished book such a treat. She's a true professional, and if she doesn't know that already, this book should make it abundantly clear. Thank you so much, Tina.

Back at the office, Ginny Bast provided critical professional backup that kept everything functioning in our absence. And Drew Gillaspie came through with last-minute help in finishing the cookbook.

Of course, I'm forever in debt to my wife, Sue. Whenever the delays, flight cancellations, eighteen-hour workdays, and brief, sleepless nights start to wear on me, I need only think of you and I'm rejuvenated.

Introduction

THERE IS A GURGLING STREAM THAT FLOWS into a small pond just a quick stroll from the house where I was born. I still have vivid memories of the first time I stumbled upon it—I was so small, and the tiny brook seemed big enough to be the Yangtze River.

Years after leaving my ancestral home, I still carry the image of that special place with me, and whenever I visit China, I make a point to return there for peace of mind, for inspiration, and for getting in touch with my roots. And no matter how many times I visit, the peaceful waters always have new secrets to reveal.

I feel the same way every time I go back to Asia. No matter how many times I have criss-crossed this magnificent continent, I know in my heart that on my next trip, the journey will reveal new secrets that I had not known before. There will be new surprises and new discoveries on every corner.

It matters little how many years I have lived in North America. I will forever feel at home in Asia, where I can wander down to any street vendor's food cart or neighborhood restaurant and grab a bite of the same snacks or meals that fed my body and my soul while I was growing up. So for me, a trip to Asia proves that what's old is new again. And that what's new very often echoes a bit of the past.

This whole process of discovery—and rediscovery—excites me so much that I just had to return to my old stomping grounds for another recipe-collecting spin. And I was so sure that the culinary and cultural treasures I unearthed would inspire you just as much they did me, that I had to put them in a new television series of *Yan Can Cook,* and into this book, for you to re-create at home.

My crew and I made our first stop at my old stomping grounds, Hong Kong. This is where it all started for me as a thirteen-year-old restaurant apprentice. During those years in this city

Martin welcomes viewers while filming at Wat Phra Kaew and the Grand Palace: Bangkok.

of life—a city that never stops—I packed my "toolbox" with the tricks of the trade by studying with some of the most creative chefs in the world.

There are more restaurants in Hong Kong than there are neon signs hanging over her narrow streets and with so many great chefs hard at work there, I often wonder who's holding down the restaurant kitchens in the rest of the world. You can find Hong Kong's top toques in hotels, fine-dining establishments, and even on the streets, manning a curbside snack cart or food stall. And with such an embarrassment of culinary riches, the residents of Hong Kong brook no mediocrity when it comes to their daily dining—they don't have to.

Hong Kong is an international crossroads as well as a culinary hotspot. Many of the best chefs in the world have made Hong Kong their home because of the ample opportunities for culinary creativity it affords. On this last visit, we filmed and cooked alongside many of Hong Kong's leading chefs. Their years of experience in top restaurant kitchens worldwide translate to a magical display of wizardry that never ceases to impress, even to those who thought they had seen it all (such as yours truly). When people love eating out as much as they do in Hong

Kong, famous chefs enjoy the status of rock and sports superstars. But no matter how "out of this world" the food gets, I can count on it having the firm Chinese foundation that keeps me, and many of the talented chefs in this glitzy culinary mecca, well grounded.

After the sheer decadence of Hong Kong, we visited Taiwan. Picture a microcosm of all of Chinese cuisine and culture on one island, and you have a good image of Taiwan. Much of it began when people from every corner of mainland China descended upon the island in the first half of this century. They brought with them their local dialects, customs, and, of course, their recipes.

And we're lucky they did! Just the street foods and snacks alone could keep a hungry traveler like me occupied for weeks on end. And sure enough, each goodie I tried reminded me of some corner of mainland China. Even though you might not have grown up in China, I'll bet some of the recipes I brought back from this "China-in-miniature" will make you feel like you did.

While in Taiwan, I also had the great privilege to witness the strength and spirit of the Taiwanese community. On September 21, 1999, a 7.6 earthquake hit the island; my crew and I were on hand to experience the historic temblor. Many homes, businesses, and several historical landmarks that we had filmed only days before were either destroyed or severely damaged. When we returned to complete the on-location filming, I was amazed by how quickly the people and the businesses had recovered. A natural disaster of such magnitude didn't weaken Taiwan. Instead, it strengthened the resolve of these courageous people.

After Taiwan, it was off to somewhere totally different: Thailand. This country never ceases to be a revelation to me, with its boundless hospitality, natural beauty, and its people's ability to withstand amazing amounts of heat in their food! But fiery feasts—as fun as they may be—aren't all Thailand has to offer.

You don't just visit Thailand, you experience it. Thanks to the good office of the Tourism Authority of Thailand, my crew and I did just that. But more than smoothing out our production schedule, the folks at TAT were invaluable guides who opened our eyes to many of the wonderful sights and sounds that a newcomer like me could easily miss. Thailand evokes the Garden of Eden, but at the same time, it quivers with the excitement and anticipation of a nation that has just about plunged headlong into the twenty-first century. Thailand is going

Opposite: **Martin assisting with net repair in a local fishing village.**

places, and it's taking its proud history and rich culture along with it, blending old and new with the grace and good nature that has become its trademark.

Filming took us from Chiang Mai in the North, to Bangkok—the country's heart—and down to the blue lagoons and spectacular beaches of the South. At each stop, we got a taste of lifestyles both ancient and modern. At one end of the spectrum are the hill tribes of the North, who live much as they did before there was an official Thailand; at the other end Bangkok's practically non-negotiable traffic reminds us that no matter where you go these days, you never quite escape that horrible commute.

The range of experiences we encountered up and down the country reflected the ingenuity and diversity of the cuisine, which, simply put, is like nothing else in the world. It may borrow culinary concepts and conventions from its neighbors, but even in Thailand's conspicuously Chinese communities, the flavors and aromas I remember so clearly from childhood were woven with colorful silk threads that were uniquely Thai. The whole experience made me feel right at home nonetheless. I was free to revel in the dishes, the flavors, and the friendly culture responsible for them.

So I guess I've learned that you *can* go home again, whether "home" is the village in southern China where you grew up, a bowl of the rice soup you had every morning, or in Siam, where the peoples' smiles make you feel like you're family wherever you go.

Don't be surprised if your trip back "home" takes you to places that seem unfamiliar; after all, you too have certainly changed over the years. That's what I love so much about returning, again and again, to my culinary roots: each new experience changes my perspective on the past, and my outlook for the future. Even if your roots are planted nowhere near Asia, all it takes is this little culinary compendium to make you feel at home at our Asian table.

Tools, Techniques, and Tips

Whether you are preparing a spicy Thai curry or a classic Hong Kong–style stir-fry, all you need are a few simple tools. The recipes in this book keep this in mind. You won't need much more in the way of specialized equipment than a wok or stir-fry pan, a steamer, and a good trusty knife.

The Wok

In most Southeast Asian kitchens, the most essential and versatile piece of cookware is the wok. Almost every Asian dish can be made with the wok, and once you discover just how versatile the wok is, it will become your most-used kitchen tool.

The wok distributes heat evenly, is easy to clean, and can be used for many different cooking techniques. Besides stir-frying, you can do practically anything in a wok. You can use it for braising, deep-frying, stewing, steaming, and poaching. You can even smoke meats with this wonderful piece of cookware!

Finding a wok that suits your needs is easy. There's a wide selection of woks on the market. The three most important things about the wok you choose are shape, size, and material.

The Shape

Clearly, all woks are round, but what makes the difference is the bottom shape of the wok: round-bottomed or flat-bottomed.

Round-bottomed: In the old days, you could only find round-bottomed woks, which were designed for cooking over wood or charcoal burners in the Chinese kitchen. Today, this shape work well on gas burners with the help of a perforated, ring-shaped metal stand that sits over the burner, holding the round-bottomed wok in place.

Flat-bottomed: These relatively new woks can be used on both gas and electric burners, and you don't need a wok stand. Keep in mind that when using electric burners, it's a bit harder to control the heat. You must always heat any wok first before putting in the ingredients.

The Size

Wok sizes range from 8 to 36 inches in diameter. It is important to choose the right size to perform a variety of your cooking needs. Usually, a 14-inch wok is the best for an average kitchen, for a family of four to six people. If you are cooking for two, a 12-inch wok will do. You'll find much larger ones in Chinese restaurant kitchens.

The Material

In the old days, traditional Chinese woks were made of unpolished cast iron which absorbed a lot of heat quickly. Today, you can find woks made of a variety of materials.

Cast-iron or carbon steel woks are the most time-honored because they retain heat well. They should be "seasoned" before using. To season a carbon steel wok, wash the wok well and place it over medium heat to dry. While drying the wok, use paper towels with a small amount of cooking oil to wipe the inside surface. Change the towels and continue to wipe until no more residue is removed. Then clean with hot water and little or no soap while still hot, and dry over high heat.

Woks and stir-fry pans made of hard-anodized aluminum, which is a great conductor of heat, have become very popular these days. There's no need to season them like cast-iron woks, and they often have a nonstick cooking surface.

High-wattage electric woks are almost as versatile as regular woks. They are good for deep-frying, braising, and steaming. Electric woks have a built-in thermostat control, allowing you to set and maintain proper cooking temperatures.

Cleaning Your Wok

It is best to clean your wok while it is still hot: using little or no soap, wash it gently with hot water. After cleaning and rinsing, dry cast-iron and carbon steel woks over high heat to prevent rusting.

Stir-Frying

Stir-frying is the cooking method most associated with the wok. It cooks bite-size food in a small amount of oil, over intense high heat while you stir constantly. Stir-frying is simple and easy; follow these tips, and you can make a perfect stir-fry every time!

STIR-FRYING TIPS

Prepare ahead. Stir-frying is fast. The dish can be done before you even blink! So make sure you have everything cut up, measured, and have any marinated ingredients ready and close at hand. And don't forget the serving plate!

Uniform sizes. To cook more evenly, cut all meats and vegetables into uniform sizes.

Heat first, oil second. First, heat the empty wok over high heat for 1 to 2 minutes. Lower your hand slightly over the surface, and once you can feel the heat, you're ready to add the oil. Swirl the oil around to coat the cooking surface, then add the first ingredients.

Work in order. Not all ingredients take the same amount of cooking time. To ensure that everything is cooked properly, the sequence of adding ingredients is important. Usually, aromatic seasonings like garlic and ginger go in first, then the proteins, such as meat, seafood, or poultry. And lastly, the vegetables—the heartier and denser ones are added before the softer and leafier ones.

Keep it moving. Don't forget to stir food around with a spatula or a pair of wooden chopsticks occasionally. High heat is what makes stir-frying fast. Keep everything moving in the wok or it'll burn quickly.

Give it space. If there is too much food in the wok, the ingredients won't cook evenly and meat won't brown properly. To prevent this, meats and vegetables are sometimes cooked separately: meat is cooked first, then removed, and then the vegetables are added.

Stir in the shine. Most Chinese dishes that call for extra liquid at the end are thickened with a cornstarch solution to give a beautiful shine and consistency. Normally, I recommend 1 teaspoon of cornstarch dissolved in 2 teaspoons of cold water for every ¼ cup of liquid in the wok. You can adjust the ratio according to the recipe. Always mix the cornstarch with cold liquid before adding it. Once it goes into the wok, keep stirring until the liquid boils and thickens.

Taste. Don't forget to taste the dish before you put it on the serving plate. Adjust the seasonings, if needed.

Deep-Frying

Your wok is great for deep-frying. Deep-frying is all about temperature control. If you deep-fry food at the right temperature, it will be light and crispy without being greasy. Normally, oil temperatures range from 325° to 375°, depending on what is being deep-fried. If the oil is not hot enough, the food will soak up too much oil and be greasy. If the oil is too hot, then the outside of the food will burn before the inside is cooked. If you don't have a deep-frying thermometer, don't worry! There are many other ways to test if the oil has reached the right temperature. The traditional Chinese method is to stick one end of a wooden or bamboo chopstick deep into the hot oil, bubbles rise up from the chopstick immediately. Another easier and more reliable method is to take a little piece of what you are about to deep-fry, and pop it into the hot oil. If it sizzles immediately, the oil is ready for deep-frying.

DEEP-FRYING TIPS

Make sure the wok is solidly positioned to avoid tipping. Pour oil into the wok to a depth of 2 to 3 inches. Heat the oil to the temperature called for in the recipe, checking it with a deep-frying thermometer. Pat ingredients dry before deep-frying or the oil will spatter. To better control the oil temperature, bring ingredients to room temperature before adding them into the oil. Deep-fry in small batches to keep the oil temperature from fluctuating too wildly. Use a pair of long wooden chopsticks or a wire strainer to turn and separate the food occasionally, so it will brown evenly. After deep-frying, let the oil cool completely. Strain it and store in an airtight container and place in the refrigerator. You can reuse the oil for deep-frying as long as it's kept clean. But once it begins to bubble when heated, discard it.

The Steamer

In the traditional Chinese home kitchen, there was no oven. Even today, many families in China still do not have ovens. So, steaming food became an important technique. Steamed seafood, rice, dumplings, and cakes are common in Chinese cuisine, but I also steam a lot of vegetables and meats.

The most common steamer is made with bamboo. It has gaps in-between the slats at the bottom to let the steam through. You can stack them up to cook several dishes all at one time. Bamboo steamers come in different sizes. Normally, a 12-inch steamer fits perfectly in a 14-inch wok; an 8-inch steamer is just right for a 10-inch wok. Stainless steel and aluminum steamers are also available in stores.

You can transform your wok into a steamer. Just fill your wok with water to a depth of 2 to 3 inches. Place a steam rack over the water, making sure there is 1 inch of space between the water and the rack, and cover with a lid. Placing 4 chopsticks tic-tac-toe above the water will do for a rack, then place a plate over the rack, leaving at least 1 inch of space all around.

STEAMING TIPS

Place a steam rack over boiling water in a wok. Make sure the rack sits 1 inch above the water. Any glass heatproof pie dish will work well for steaming. To keep dumplings from sticking, line the steamer with a damp cloth, a piece of parchment paper, or with fresh greens, such as napa cabbage or lettuce. Remember to check the water level at the bottom of the steamer occasionally. If the water level is low, add boiling water to prevent drying up. Be careful with the steam; always lift the lid away from you to let the steam escape before adding water or removing the dish.

The Knife

Besides the wok, you'll find that a Chinese chef knife is also a magical tool! With just one knife, you can slice, mince, chop, crush, tenderize, and transfer ingredients from surface to pan. You can even use the end of the handle to crush garlic and spices. The cleaver is a multipurpose kitchen tool.

Finding the Right Cleaver

In Asian stores, you will find the traditional Chinese chef knives made from carbon steel. They are easy to sharpen, but rust easily. Another disadvantage of carbon steel knives is that they can discolor acidic foods like onions and lemons on contact. Although an ordinary stainless steel knife can solve these problems, they are hard to sharpen. I recommend a quality high-carbon stainless steel Chinese knife; it has the best of both worlds. It won't discolor foods, and it maintains a fine, sharp edge for a good length of time.

All you need in an Asian kitchen are two knives: a heavy one for hacking bones and butchering meats, and a lighter one for practically everything else.

Simple Cleaver Cuts

Most Asian cooks use different cutting techniques for different dishes. Here are the ones you can learn at home. With a little practice, you'll be able to make perfect cuts in no time and every time!

Slicing. When slicing, the knife is held either vertical or horizontal to the cutting board and the cut is made straight across the ingredient.

Julienne and Shredding. Both these terms mean to cut into sticks. First, you have to slice the ingredient into a roughly $1/8$ inch thickness, then stack 2 to 3 pieces together and cut them again into $1/8$-inch sticks. Some recipes in this book ask for "slivers." To do this, you'll need to start with paper-thin slices, use the same shredding technique, and cut them into very thin sticks.

Dicing. "Dice" means to cut into cubes. Once you slice the ingredient and shred it into sticks, line the sticks up perpendicular to the blade and cut straight down across to create dice. The sizes of the cubes are different according to each recipe. For fast cooking such as stir-frying $1/4$- to $1/2$-inch cubes work well.

Mincing. This term means to finely cut ingredient into very small bits. Start with slicing or dicing the ingredient into small pieces. Then, using the tip of the knife as a pivot, move only the lower blade in a chopping motion, from side to side across the ingredient until it is evenly and finely chopped.

Roll-cutting. Vegetables that are long or conical in shape, such as carrots and zucchini, are best for this cutting method. Holding the knife perpendicular to the cutting board, cut straight down on a diagonal. Then roll the vegetable for a quarter-turn, and cut again at the same angle, creating a bite-size piece. Keep on rolling the vegetable, a quarter-turn at a time, maintaining the same knife angle and cutting all the way through the vegetable.

Crushing. This technique is especially popular with Asian ingredients such as ginger, garlic, and lemongrass. Just place the knife flat on top of the ingredient with the blade facing away from you. Press down hard over the blade a few times with your palm, until the ingredient is smashed.

Mortar and Pestle

In many parts of Asia, particularly in Thailand, the mortar and pestle are widely used to make all kinds of spices and curry pastes. A mortar is shaped like a round bowl with a short stand to provide a firm base, and a pestle looks just like a small baseball bat. They are usually made from wood and/or stone, but you can also find them made out of marble or baked clay. If you love Thai cuisine, an inexpensive mortar and pestle set is a handy tool to have in the kitchen. Although they are heavy and labor intensive, they do a better job of pounding than the food processor. Besides, the quantities of the ingredients that most recipes call for are usually too small for a mincer or blender to work efficiently. If you cannot find one, just use the handle of your trusty cleaver as a pestle to pound ingredients in a bowl.

Making Thai Curry Pastes

- Dry spices are combined and toasted in a small skillet to bring out the aroma and the taste. Keep the heat low and stir constantly; watch carefully or they'll burn *fast!*

- Fresh ingredients such as garlic, galangal, and lemongrass should first be cut into small pieces for easier pounding. Then the fresh ingredients are pounded to a paste and combined with the dry ingredients.

- Once the paste is made, store in an airtight container in the refrigerator for up to 3 weeks. Or you can freeze small portions in an ice-cube tray and use whenever needed; just remember to bring it to room temperature before using. Pastes keep for up to 4 months in the freezer.

HONG KONG

The Global Eating Place

FROM A DISTANCE. IT COULD BE ANY OTHER MODERN SKYLINE: bright lights, glass, concrete, and neck-straining skyscrapers, with a liberal sprinkling of billboards at their feet. But move a little closer, and the whole scene will come into sharper focus.

See the green "Nine Dragon" mountain range, from which the Kowloon Peninsula got its name, rising behind the manmade mountains of glass and steel? You won't see that in Chicago or Manhattan. And what about the little fishing boats and houseboats trolling the harbor in the foreground? Their old-fashioned simplicity makes a stark contrast with the modern cityscape. Come to think of it, the very harbor itself, teeming with life and the unmistakable fragrance of my youth, proves that this, in fact, is a place like no other in the modern world.

Hong Kong, a place—a state of mind, some would say—that completely redefines our notion of the modern urban center. At first sight, that rearrangement seems a little chaotic but, trust me, it's a controlled chaos. After all, in Hong Kong, control and chaos are just two sides of the same coin. To the outsider, much of Hong Kong seems a mishmash of conflicting elements. It can even be a little head-spinning for me, and I've spent a good chunk of my life here! The frantic pace and the subatomic energy vibrating everywhere are emblematic of the island's day-to-day existence, and this intensity applies to all aspects of Hong Kong life: commerce, work, and, of course, dining.

Crab festival, cooking competition.

View from the roof of the Mandarin Hotel on Hong Kong Island.

Here you'll find great-tasting food on every corner. Hong Kong is crawling with the world's greatest chefs—in the fine-dining restaurants, elegant international hotels, and especially in the street-snack stalls and hole-in-the-wall eateries that are the foundations of the city's culinary heritage.

Where the Unworkable Works—and Plays

As much as it seems that this mixed bag couldn't possibly "work," it does. Hong Kong works hard. How else could this small, cramped island have risen to its status as an internationally renowned capital of trade and business? Its Hang Seng stock market is beginning to rival those of Wall Street and the Nikkei, and its corporate conference rooms are packed with "suits" whose decisions shape economies around the world.

Meanwhile, Hong Kong knows what "all work and no play" does to a person, and to a city. As one evening out on the town will tell you, this territory is just as good at playing as it is at working. After all, it's not only a business hub, but also a wildly popular travel destination and a jewel in Asia's cultural crown. There's a reason why millions of tourists visit Hong Kong each year. Quite simply, it's the irresistible lure of a place where

Boat Club—Hong Kong Island.

people are always on the move, where the action runs on a nonstop loop, and where restaurants and streets are just as bustling at midnight as they are at noon. Hong Kong is a city of life, and like any other living thing, its heart beats twenty-four hours a day. And its seven million inhabitants—the city's true life force—are poised and ready to go!

Seven million people. That's a lot of shoes, books, and CD collections to pack into such a small place. The only way to accommodate them all is …up—a philosophy that more or less shapes the skyline of Hong Kong. And while each new layer of building may add a little to the overall congestion, it also adds a new layer of life and character to Hong Kong's unique structure.

The people in Hong Kong take the hustle and bustle in stride, one-upping even New Yorkers when it comes to maintaining a true "urban cool." So how do they make it all work, bringing together the old and the new, the peaceful and the frantic, the buttoned-up and the busting loose? *T'ai chi*, for one thing. But I credit the ancient Chinese concept of yin-yang balance. After all, no matter how international Hong Kong's face becomes, its heart and soul are still unquestionably Chinese.

The International Intersection: Where the Four Corners of the Globe Meet to Eat

I consider it a testimony to how deeply Chinese Hong Kong's psyche is that it can accommodate so many people, so much change, and such powerful international influence without losing its own character.

Hong Kong has a complex history of interacting with the "outside" world, taking the fruits of those interactions, and incorporating them in a unique way into the fiber of its culture. And nowhere is that interplay more evident than in the cuisine. I never get bored eating in Hong Kong, and not just because it has so many restaurants that I could eat in a different one every day of my life and still not have the same thing twice.

Hong Kong's food really keeps me on my toes, because it's an ever-evolving cuisine—just as Hong Kong is a living, breathing, changing city. Hong Kong has always been a crossroads, a gathering place for all manner of Europeans, North Americans, Middle Easterners, and other Asians. Its colonial history has left an international stamp on its cultural and culinary face, as evidenced by how the Hong Kong hotels blend the daily rituals of *yum cha* and *dim sum* with the British fancy for tea and crumpets. These forces from the past and present keep the cuisine from growing stale.

As a magnet for international trend and style, Hong Kong, the "Fragrant Harbour," continues to attract creative culinary energy from all corners of the globe. While many visitors stay only temporarily, some make Hong Kong their home, leading to an expatriate population that culls its members from all the continents of the world.

Part of the current acceptance of all foods foreign may be an attempt to accommodate the homesick tastes of some of these new residents and visitors. But if you ask me, that's a superficial explanation. Many Hong Kong natives are affluent and they travel all over the world. Naturally they soon develop likings for "exotic" dishes ranging from Italian panini, made with focaccia, to Buffalo chicken wings to Norwegian smoked salmon to Moroccan couscous.

When you get down to it, the people of Hong Kong simply love to eat. We fixate on food. Remember, the island was originally settled by Cantonese, and we Cantonese are known for our never-ending quest for the next great food idea.

The Lap of Luxury

For the best in Hong Kong's international flavor, join me at the city's most luxurious hotels, where many of its most respected restaurants are located. Hong Kong's elegant eateries are often the laboratories where dishes that blend Western cooking techniques with Chinese ingredients and flavors—and vice versa—are conjured up. It's a true melding of the culinary arts with international diplomacy—a hybrid of Escoffier and Kissinger.

If you're feeling like a high-roller after enjoying some worldly wining and dining, don't forget to take advantage of Hong Kong's other global luxuries. I'm talking about the international boutiques, the shopping centers, the cars, and the commerce that make living the good life in Hong Kong a snap.

A Night in the Life of Hong Kong

Old Blue Eyes may have been thinking about New York when he sang about the city that doesn't sleep, but he could just as easily have been talking about Hong Kong, another city that pulls more all-nighters than a college student during finals week. And judging from the number of tables in Hong Kong's twenty-four hour eateries that are still packed hours after the conventional dinner rush has ended, many of Hong Kong's citizens don't do much sleeping either.

It's likely that no matter what you do during the witching hours, you won't forget to eat. Hong Kong's inhabitants sure don't. They feed whenever passion—rather than the clock—

Martin serenading passersby in Lan Kwai Fong, Hong Kong's Soho District.

strikes. They're obsessed with food at any time of the day, and the happy sounds of slurping, munching, and chomping heard throughout the night are proof. Even the morning rituals of *yum cha* (taking tea) and *dim sum* dining are available to all-night eaters. As much as I enjoy all of Hong Kong's other night temptations, I think I'd be just as happy spending my evenings tethered to a table full of its edible treats.

Fine Fare for the Common Man

Fancy hotel dining and highfalutin, Hong Kong nightlife are all well and good. But if you really want to experience the city's sights, sounds, and flavors, then, do as the Hong Kong residents do. That means mingling among the people as they grab a quick bite on the way to work, or meeting friends at a tea house for early morning *dim sum*.

The best way to explore "Everyman's" (or "Everywoman's") Hong Kong is to do it on foot. The streets may seem noisy and chaotic at first, but your ears will quickly turn the blaring horns and the street vendors' shouts into an almost pleasant background din.

Pay a visit to Temple Street Market. It's a curbside cafeteria with rows of wandering hawkers serving a mind-boggling list of options. For starters, there are fish balls, fried tofu, roast pork, steamed chicken-and-vegetable buns, sweet red bean jelly, and sliced red-cooked duck.

Can't make up your mind? Join the club! I just point at whatever looks good and enjoy. Don't be shy; you can always ask for recommendations. Being part of the street-food crowd makes meeting people easy, and it gives you a little picture of the whole Hong Kong community to boot. Class distinctions are irrelevant here; professionals slurp their soup alongside day laborers without batting an eyelash. After all, everyone here has the same thing in mind: good food in a hurry.

To truly experience the breadth of Hong Kong's food, you can't just hit the streets. You've got to go home, too. For me, real dining in Hong Kong wouldn't be the same without a few meals like the kind my mother makes. I can think of no better way to take myself back to a simpler, slower time than sitting down to a table of simply-prepared foods with my Hong Kong friends and family. No matter how international, cosmopolitan, or fast-paced things get here, Chinese traditions and family ties remain a part of everyday life.

Fitting the realities of modern-day Hong Kong with the simple pleasures of its past isn't as impossible as it seems. If I know anything about Hong Kong, I know that this unique place can make it work. You can make it work in your own kitchen, too. All you need are the following recipes. They incorporate the best of international accents, cutting-edge culinary style, and down-home Chinese sensibility in the same flavorful mix that makes Hong Kong worth coming back to time and again.

Yam and Potato Pancakes

This is my take on the tried and true breakfast hash brown: little pancakes of shredded potato and sweet yam fused with the robust flavor of shiitake mushrooms, onions, and chives. Cook to perfection—crispy on the outside, soft and moist on the inside.

MAKES 16 PANCAKES, SERVES 4 TO 6

1/2 **pound yam**

1/2 **pound russet potatoes**

1 **cup all-purpose flour**

1 **cup water**

1 **egg, lightly beaten**

4 **fresh shiitake mushrooms, stems discarded, caps thinly sliced**

1/2 **cup chopped onion**

2 **tablespoons minced Chinese chives or green onions, green part only**

2 **teaspoons soy sauce**

1 1/2 **teaspoons salt**

1/8 **teaspoon white pepper**

About 1/3 **cup vegetable oil**

1. Peel yam; shred in a food processor or with a box grater.

2. Peel and shred potato; roll in tea towel and twist the ends hard to remove excess liquid.

3. Combine flour, water, and egg in a bowl. Mix to form a thick paste. Add yam, potato, mushrooms, onion, chives, soy sauce, salt, and white pepper; mix well.

4. Place a wide frying pan over medium heat until hot. Add 2 tablespoons oil, swirling to coat sides. For each pancake, spoon 1/4 cup batter into pan to form a 4- to 6-inch circle, about 1/4 inch thick. Cook, turning once, until golden brown and crispy, 8 to 9 minutes on each side. Repeat with remaining batter, adding oil as needed. Serve hot.

T'ai Chi, not T'ai Bo

You'll often find early risers in this city-that-never-sleeps practicing the slow, fluid, and relaxing moves of *t'ai chi*. Forget the "no pain, no gain" mantra of Western exercise here; with *t'ai chi*, "if it hurts, be alert." Many of Hong Kong's senior citizenry credit their regular practice of *t'ai chi* with keeping them nimble and healthy. We would all do well to follow their lead. And it's not just popular with older folks; many young people have also discovered that *t'ai chi* can work wonders in increasing their flexibility and fitness.

Steamed Shrimp Dumplings

A Superstar Chef

Being a great chef takes nerves of steel. Just ask Chef Kuen Cung Chow, of Hong Kong's Superstar Restaurant. Recently he earned the title of "Iron Chef" in the popular Japanese culinary show of the same name. In these cooking duels, two highly esteemed chefs are pitted against each other. The contestants must create a sample of dishes based on a theme ingredient, the identity of which is a well-kept secret until show time. The show's outspoken judges evaluate the dishes and award the "Iron Chef" title to the winner. To make it more entertaining, the contest is timed, televised, and commented upon with a scrutiny befitting the Super Bowl. And my good friend Chef Chow made it through with championship colors! I'm honored to include his recipe for Steamed Shrimp Dumplings here.

The key to success for these tender little dumplings is the the wrappers! They are made of rice flour, which turns translucent when cooked, showing off the shrimp inside.

MAKES 14 DUMPLINGS, SERVES 6

Wrappers

$1/2$ **cup wheat starch**

$1/2$ **cup glutinous rice flour**

$1/4$ **cup cornstarch**

$1^1/2$ **teaspoons vegetable oil**

$1/2$ **cup plus 2 tablespoons boiling water**

14 large raw shrimp (about $1/2$ pound)

$1/4$ **teaspoon salt**

$1/8$ **teaspoon white pepper**

Ginger Vinegar

2 tablespoons rice vinegar

2 tablespoons water

2 tablespoons grated ginger

$3/4$ **teaspoon sugar**

$1/4$ **teaspoon soy sauce**

$1/4$ **teaspoon sesame oil**

About 1 tablespoon vegetable oil

3 large lettuce leaves

1. To make wrappers, combine wheat starch, glutinous rice flour, and cornstarch in a bowl. Add oil and boiling water, stirring with chopsticks or a fork, until dough is evenly moistened. Knead dough into large ball. Cover and let rest for 20 minutes.

2. Shell, devein, and butterfly shrimp, leaving tails intact. Place in a bowl with salt and white pepper; let stand for 10 minutes.

3. To make ginger vinegar, combine rice vinegar, water, ginger, sugar, soy sauce, and sesame oil in a small bowl. Set aside.

4. Shape each dumpling: On a lightly floured board, knead dough until smooth. Roll dough into a cylinder about 12 inches long; cut crosswise to make 14 pieces. Cover dough to prevent drying. Dip a paper towel in oil; wipe towel over work surface and blade of a cleaver to lightly oil. Place one portion of dough on work surface; with cleaver blade smear dough into a thin circle about 3 inches in diameter. Lift the thin circle of dough and drape over back of a shrimp, leaving tail exposed. Pinch edges together under shrimp to seal. Cover while shaping remaining dumplings. Re-oil work surface and cleaver blade as needed.

5. Prepare a wok for steaming (see page 6). Line bottom of steamer with lettuce. Place dumplings on lettuce without crowding. Cover and steam until shrimp turn pink and wrappers are translucent, 3 to 4 minutes. Serve hot with ginger vinegar for dipping.

Pan–Fried Vegetable Ham Rolls

The elegant simplicity of this dish makes these rolls a classic on the menu of the Dynasty Restaurant at the New World Hotel. Tender pork loin, ham, and leafy green spinach are rolled and pan-fried. Who says a great dish has to be a complicated one?

MAKES 12 ROLLS, SERVES 4 TO 6

Sauce

3 tablespoons chicken stock (see page 38)

2 tablespoons Chinese black vinegar

2 tablespoons Chinese rice wine or dry sherry

1 tablespoon dark soy sauce

1 tablespoon soy sauce

2 teaspoons sesame oil

2 teaspoons minced garlic

1 teaspoon sugar

1 pound spinach, cleaned, stems removed

2 teaspoons sesame oil

1/2 teaspoon salt

1/8 teaspoon white pepper

1/2 pound boneless pork loin

12 thin slices ham

3 tablespoons vegetable oil

1. To make sauce, combine stock, vinegar, rice wine, soy sauces, sesame oil, garlic, and sugar in a saucepan; set aside.

2. Bring a pot of water to a boil. Add spinach and cook for 2 minutes. Drain, rinse with cold water, and drain again. Squeeze to remove excess liquid. Roughly chop spinach into 2-inch pieces. Add sesame oil, salt, and white pepper; toss lightly to mix.

3. Cut pork loin into 12 thin slices. To assemble each roll, place a slice of ham over a pork slice and trim to same size. Place about 2 tablespoons spinach along one end of ham slice. Roll up and secure with a wooden toothpick.

4. Place a wide frying pan over medium-high heat. Add oil, swirling to coat sides. Add rolls and pan-fry on all sides until browned, 8 to 10 minutes. Transfer rolls to a serving platter.

5. Heat sauce to boiling. Pour over rolls and serve.

What's Old Is New Again

The chance to sample elegant four-star cuisine keeps pulling me back to Hong Kong like a magnet. But sometimes I get a hankering for those homey, Chinese classics I find at snack stalls, from street vendors, and in the little mom-and-pop restaurants that are the city's heritage. When I can't decide which culinary road to take, I head to the kitchen of my good friend Chef Tan Sek-lun. In his restaurant, Dynasty, at the New World Hotel. Chef Tan serves the best of both worlds by putting an upscale spin on the things my mother makes. Regional specialties like southern Chinese clay pot dishes, the freshest seafood, and straight-from-the-farm vegetables are his stock in trade—but they've always got his refined, updated stamp.

Shrimp Purse

What do you keep in your purse? I like to keep shrimp in mine. These elegant shrimp satchels take a while to create, but for my money, they're well worth the time and effort. **SERVES 4**

1 dried black mushroom
12 medium raw shrimp
1/4 cup fish paste
1 1/2 teaspoons minced water chestnuts
12 *siu mai* or potsticker wrappers
Banana or cabbage leaves, for lining steamer

Dipping Sauce

3 tablespoons red vinegar or vinegar of choice
1 1/2 tablespoons soy sauce
1 tablespoon fine chile sauce
1 tablespoon sesame oil

1. Soak mushroom in warm water to cover until softened, about 20 minutes; drain. Discard stem and dice cap. Shell and devein shrimp, leaving tails intact.

2. Place fish paste, water chestnuts, and mushroom in a bowl; mix well.

3. Make each purse: Place 1 teaspoon fish paste mixture in center of a *siu mai* wrapper; keep remaining wrappers covered to prevent drying. Place a shrimp, tail side up, on top of fish mixture. Gather up and pleat wrapper around filling to form an open-topped pouch with shrimp tail exposed. Pinch firmly to seal. Place purses on a lightly floured plate. Cover purses with a damp cloth while filling remaining wrappers.

4. Prepare a wok for steaming (see page 6). Line a steamer basket with banana or cabbage leaves and arrange purses on top. Cover and steam for 5 to 6 minutes.

5. To make dipping sauce, combine vinegar, soy sauce, chile sauce, and sesame oil in a small bowl: mix well.

6. Place purses on a serving plate. Serve warm with dipping sauce on the side.

A Temple to the God of Shopping

Any bargain hunter would do well with a visit to the Temple Street Night Market, a collection of hundreds of open-air stalls that turns into a shopper's paradise when the sun goes down. Temple Street is not about department stores or fancy boutiques. Most of the "shops" are about the size of a magazine kiosk. Merchants display their entire stock on folding counters and TV trays. Given the small selling quarters, it's amazing how much variety you'll find: anything from gaudy plastic chopsticks and Rolexes of questionable origin to items made with genuine craftsmanship. If you can't find it at Temple Street's Night Market, it probably doesn't exist. And of course, where there are shoppers, there's food! All the classic Hong Kong snacks—noodle soups, wontons, *jook*—are here for the taking.

Crispy Sesame Rice Dumplings

Do we have desserts at a dim sum *brunch? Well, not exactly, but these crispy glutinous rice balls come close. Bite into one of these wonderfully chewy rounds filled with red bean and lotus root paste and you will want to whip up another batch to enjoy with your afternoon tea.* **MAKES 14 DUMPLINGS, SERVES 6**

Wrappers

2 cups glutinous rice flour

1/2 cup boiling water

Filling

1/3 cup red bean paste

1/3 cup lotus seed paste

3 tablespoons finely chopped roasted peanuts

Vegetable oil, for deep-frying

1 egg, lightly beaten

1/2 cup sesame seeds

1. To make wrappers, place glutinous rice flour in a bowl. Add boiling water, stirring with chopsticks or a fork, until dough is evenly moistened. Knead dough into large ball. Cover and let rest for 20 minutes.

2. To make filling, combine red bean paste, lotus seed paste, and peanuts in a bowl; mix well.

3. Shape each dumpling: On a board lightly dusted with rice flour, knead dough until smooth. Roll dough into a cylinder about 12 inches long; cut crosswise to make 14 pieces. Cover dough to prevent drying. With flour-dusted hands, make an indentation in center of a piece of dough; place about 1 tablespoon of filling in hole and pinch edges to seal and shape into balls. Cover while shaping remaining dumplings.

4. In a wok or 2-quart saucepan, heat oil for deep-frying to 350°. Dip dumplings in beaten egg, drain briefly, then coat with sesame seeds. Deep-fry dumplings, a few at a time, turning once, until they puff slightly and float, 2 1/2 to 3 minutes. After dumplings rise to the surface, cook until golden brown, about 30 seconds more. Remove with a slotted spoon and drain on paper towels. Serve warm or at room temperature.

A Sneak Technique for a Sweet Treat

Let me give you a hint for making these crispy little bubbles of sweetness that are favorite snacks all over Hong Kong: don't roll out the dough. If you roll it out and then try to wrap it around the filling, the hairline seams where you've sealed the dough will burst open into gaping, laughing cracks when you deep-fry the balls. Instead, cup the dough in the palm of your hand and use the thumb of the opposite hand to push a little well into the dough's center. At the same time, using the fingers of the hand that's holding the dough, gently draw up the "walls" of the well. They'll thin out some, but that's okay. Now place the filling into the well, gather the thin top edges of dough together, and press tightly to create a seal. This safely sealed glutinous rice ball won't let out its secrets until you take a bite.

Raw Tuna and Vegetables Wrapped in Rice Paper

Here's an inventive take on the sushi roll, courtesy of Vong Restaurant at the Mandarin Oriental Hotel. Raw ahi tuna, avocado, cucumber, carrot, and green onion are wrapped in translucent rice paper and accented with a ginger-lime wasabi dipping sauce. One bite and you will join me in a chorus of "sushi is sensational!" **MAKES 6 WRAPS, SERVES 3**

Filling

2 ounces dried bean thread noodles

³/₄ pound tuna fillet, cut into long strips ¹/₂ inch wide and ¹/₂ inch thick

1 carrot, cut into 7-inch lengths, finely julienned, and blanched 1 minute

¹/₂ English cucumber, finely julienned

6 green onions, finely julienned

1 small avocado, thinly sliced

6 mint leaves, slivered

6 cilantro sprigs

6 (9-inch) dried rice paper wrappers

Dipping Sauce

2 tablespoons fresh lime juice

1 tablespoon fish sauce

2 teaspoons grated ginger

1 teaspoon sugar

1 tablespoon slivered jalapeño chile

¹/₄ teaspoon wasabi paste

1. Soak bean thread noodles in warm water to cover until softened, about 5 minutes; drain. In a large pot of boiling water, cook noodles for 1 minute; drain, rinse with cold water, and drain again. Cut into 7-inch lengths; divide into 6 equal portions.

2. Make each wrap: Brush rice paper wrapper lightly with warm water. Let stand until it becomes soft and pliable, about 30 seconds. Layer one-sixth of the tuna, carrot, cucumber, green onion, avocado, mint, and cilantro fillings in center of wrapper and top with 1 portion of bean threads. Fold bottom third of wrapper over filling, fold in sides, then roll to enclose filling. If making ahead, wrap each roll in plastic wrap and refrigerate for up to 4 hours.

3. To make dipping sauce, combine lime juice, fish sauce, ginger, sugar, chile, and wasabi in a bowl; stir until sugar dissolves.

4. To serve, cut rolls into 1¹/₂-inch lengths; stand rolls on a serving plate so filling shows. Serve with dipping sauce.

The Vong Show

Jean-Georges Vongerichten has the Midas touch when it comes to restaurants. The dining concept he offers at the Vong locations in New York, Chicago, and London has kept their reservation books full since they first fired up their stoves. The same is happening at the latest Vong in Hong Kong's Mandarin Oriental Hotel. The Asian-influenced contemporary French cuisine and upscale pan-Asian *dim sum* that earned Vong such acclaim in the West has found a willing audience in Hong Kong. Vong's chef de cuisine and native son Lee Tak Sum demonstrates his talent for combining the flavors of the Pacific Rim in this recipe for Raw Tuna and Vegetables Wrapped in Rice Paper. It takes the Chinese concept of the egg roll to Japan, where it picks up some raw tuna from that country's delicious sashimi tradition, and wraps it all up in the rice paper skin that's at home in any Vietnamese kitchen.

Star–Studded Toasts

Here's something that deserves star billing on any menu: star-shaped bread topped with tangy shrimp paste, deep-fried until golden brown. I love the lemony shrimp flavor and crisp texture, and so will your guests. **SERVES 4 TO 6**

12 to 14 slices day-old sandwich bread

Shrimp Paste

1/2 pound medium raw shrimp, shelled and deveined
2 walnut-size shallots, coarsely chopped
1 clove garlic, minced
1 egg white, lightly beaten
1 teaspoon jalapeño chile, seeded and chopped
1 teaspoon minced lemongrass
1 teaspoon fish sauce
1 teaspoon fresh lime juice
1 tablespoon chopped cilantro
1/2 teaspoon grated lime zest

2 tablespoons sesame seeds
Vegetable oil, for deep-frying

1. With a star-shaped cookie cutter about 2¹/₂ inches across, cut a star from each bread slice; save trimmings for other uses.

2. To make shrimp paste, combine shrimp, shallots, garlic, egg white, chile, lemongrass, fish sauce, and lime juice in a food processor. Process until smooth. Transfer to a bowl; stir in cilantro and lime zest.

3. Spread shrimp paste about ¹/₄ inch thick on one side of each bread star. Sprinkle with sesame seeds and press gently onto shrimp mixture.

4. In a wok, heat oil for deep-frying to 350°. Deep-fry stars, shrimp sides down, a few at a time until golden brown, about 1 minute . Turn over and fry 30 seconds longer. Drain on paper towels and serve.

Move over Hollywood! Hong Kong movies are taking on the world. Homegrown talents like Jackie Chan, Chow Yun-Fat, and Jet Li are now big-name headliners in the West; they follow the path laid decades earlier by the iconic Bruce Lee. The nonstop action Hong Kong movie is now an artistic film genre that directors the world over both admire and imitate. So if your idea of Hong Kong cinema is a low-budget chop-fest with bad dubbing, you need to rethink, then sit back and enjoy.

Fun See Crab Cakes

Watch out Maryland—Hong Kong may take over as the world's crab cake capital. Chewy-textured bean thread noodles and fragrant curry paste give these crab cakes a uniquely Asian twist. **MAKES 6 CAKES, SERVES 3**

Filling

¹/₂ ounce dried bean thread noodles
¹/₂ pound fish paste
¹/₄ pound cooked shelled crabmeat, flaked
¹/₂ cup Japanese-style bread crumbs (panko)
¹/₄ cup chopped onion
2 tablespoons chopped cilantro
1 tablespoon red curry paste (see page 133)
1 tablespoon fish sauce
2 teaspoons cornstarch

Japanese-style bread crumbs (panko), for coating
About ¹/₄ cup vegetable oil
Flying fish roe (tobiko), for garnish (optional)

1. Soak bean thread noodles in warm water to cover until softened, about 15 minutes; drain. Cut into 2-inch lengths.

2. To prepare filling, place bean thread noodles in a bowl with fish paste, crabmeat, bread crumbs, onion, cilantro, red curry paste, fish sauce, and cornstarch; mix well. Divide filling into 6 portions. Shape each portion into a patty about 2¹/₂ inches wide and ¹/₂ inch thick. Coat with bread crumbs; shake to remove excess.

3. Place a wide frying pan over medium heat until hot. Add oil; when oil is hot, add 3 patties and pan-fry, until golden brown, turning once, 3 to 4 minutes on each side. Remove and drain on paper towels. Repeat with remaining patties.

4. Arrange crab cakes on a serving platter and garnish with fish roe.

Paste Makes Taste

If your neighborhood market does not afford you the luxury of ready-made fish paste, you can make your own quite easily. Just pulse cooked firm, boneless white fish fillets (such as halibut or sea bass) in a food processor until the flesh is the smooth consistency of a paste. For a smoother texture, have the fish chilled to a cool temperature—it's not only wise in terms of food safety, but it prevents the fish from turning too mushy and pasty, too. If you don't have a food processor, use a cleaver. With a little elbow grease, you can mince the fish into a paste the old-fashioned way.

Money Bags

These savory, meat-filled bags are double cooked, for double luck. You deep-fry them first for a crispy texture, then braise them in a flavorful stock. If you don't have chives handy, use green onions. Pick a long strand so it will be easier to tie. **SERVES 6**

Filling

1/3 **pound boneless, skinless chicken, diced**

1/3 **cup drained canned corn**

1/4 **cup finely diced jicama**

3 tablespoons finely diced red bell pepper

1 tablespoon chopped green onion

2 tablespoons soy sauce

2 teaspoons sesame oil

1 tablespoon cornstarch

1/4 **teaspoon Chinese five-spice powder**

6 egg roll wrappers

6 Chinese chives or green onion tops, blanched

Vegetable oil, for deep-frying

Braising Liquid

1 cup chicken stock (see page 38)

3 tablespoons Chinese rice wine or dry sherry

1 tablespoon oyster-flavored sauce

1 teaspoon cornstarch dissolved in 2 teaspoons water

1. To prepare filling, combine chicken, corn, jicama, red bell pepper, green onion, soy sauce, sesame oil, cornstarch, and five-spice in a bowl; mix well.

2. To make each bag, place an egg roll wrapper on a work surface. Place 2 heaping tablespoons of filling in center of wrapper. Gather up edges to form a bag shape. Tie a blanched chive around neck of bag to secure.

3. In a wok, heat oil for deep-frying to 375°. Deep-fry bags, two at a time, turning occasionally, until golden brown on all sides, 2 to 3 minutes total. Remove and drain on paper towels.

4. To prepare braising liquid, combine stock, rice wine, and oyster sauce in a wide shallow pan. Bring to a boil. Add bags so that only the bottom third of bag is immersed in liquid; decrease heat and simmer, uncovered, for 4 to 5 minutes. Carefully transfer bags to a serving platter. Increase heat to high and add cornstarch solution to braising liquid. Cook, stirring, until sauce boils and thickens. Pour sauce around money bags and serve.

A Day at the Races

If horse racing is the sport of kings, then Hong Kong is a city of royalty—playing the ponies is as popular here as it is at Churchill Downs. At the Happy Valley Race Course, they've been lining up horses and riders at the starting gates for over 150 years. A day at the races is equal parts social event and sporting event. On my last visit, I was invited to hobnob with Hong Kong's who's-who at the Jockey Club. A club membership in this swanky spot is the true ticket to the city's social registry. More than a historical institution, the Jockey Club is well regarded for its many charity projects. Now, that's my idea of sharing the wealth!

The Whole World in a Hotel

In Hong Kong, the elegant five-star hotels are destination spots in themselves. That's especially true for culinary travelers like me. Hong Kong's hotels boast some of the best restaurants on the island. Locals are just as likely as tourists to head to them for food that ranges from cutting-edge fusion and international cuisines to traditional Chinese and Asian fare, and from formal prix-fixe meals to casual poolside snacks. In my favorite Hong Kong hotel I can enjoy *dim sum* at a 1930s-style Cantonese tea house, dine in a Milanese palazzo, sip *saké* in a Tokyo sushi bar, meet for tea and scones as if the British never left, or feast on a rib eye steak and mashed spuds, American style—all within an elevator ride of my hotel room!

Hong Kong's nightime skyline.   29

Asparagus Beef Rolls

Spears of asparagus, long-stemmed enoki mushrooms, and julienned red bell pepper wrapped with thinly sliced beef and bacon make a beautiful, edible bouquet and an elegant starter to any meal. **MAKES 12 ROLLS, SERVES 6 TO 8**

Marinade
2 tablespoons soy sauce
1 tablespoon minced garlic
2 teaspoons packed brown sugar
1 teaspoon sesame oil

³/₄ pound beef eye of round
6 slices smoked lean bacon
12 large asparagus spears, trimmed to 5 inches long
1 ounce enoki mushrooms, ends trimmed
¹/₂ small red bell pepper, seeded and julienned
2 tablespoons vegetable oil
¹/₃ cup chicken stock (see page 38)
¹/₂ teaspoon cornstarch dissolved in 1 teaspoon water

1. To make marinade, combine soy sauce, garlic, brown sugar, and sesame oil in a medium bowl.

2. Cut beef into twelve 3 by 4-inch rectangular slices, each ¹/₈ inch thick. Add beef to marinade and stir to coat. Let stand for 10 minutes. Cut bacon in half crosswise to make 12 pieces.

3. Make each roll: Place a slice of beef on a work surface. Place an asparagus spear, several enoki mushrooms, and a julienned bell pepper strip along one long end of beef slice. Roll beef over vegetables into a cylinder. Wrap bacon around beef roll and secure with a wooden toothpick.

4. Place a wide frying pan over high heat until hot. Add oil; when oil is hot, add rolls and pan-fry until browned on all sides, 2 to 3 minutes. Add stock and bring to a boil. Decrease heat, cover, and simmer for 3 minutes. Add cornstarch solution and cook, stirring, until sauce boils and thickens.

5. Remove toothpicks and arrange rolls on a serving platter. Pour pan juices over, and serve.

Spicy Mint Garlic Spareribs

Don't wait until after dinner to have a little mint—try some with these ribs. A touch of honey adds further complexity to this sophisticated dish. **SERVES 4**

2 pounds pork spareribs
2 cups water
1 cup pineapple juice

Marinade

¼ cup hoisin sauce
2 tablespoons Chinese rice wine or dry sherry
2 tablespoons fresh lime juice
2 tablespoons dark soy sauce
2 tablespoons soy sauce
2 tablespoons chopped garlic
1 tablespoon chopped fresh mint leaves
1 tablespoon chile garlic sauce
1 tablespoon sugar

3 tablespoons honey
Mint leaves, for garnish

1. Cut ribs between every second or third bone to make serving-size pieces. Place in large pan with water and pineapple juice. Bring to a boil over high heat. Decrease heat, cover, and simmer until meat is barely tender, about 30 minutes. Drain.

2. To make marinade, combine hoisin sauce, rice wine, lime juice, soy sauces, garlic, mint, chile sauce, and sugar in a large bowl; mix well. Add ribs and turn to coat. Cover and refrigerate for 2 to 3 hours.

3. Preheat broiler with rack placed 4 to 5 inches from heating element.

4. Lift ribs from marinade and place on a rack in a foil-lined pan. Stir honey into remaining marinade and reserve.

5. Broil ribs, basting occasionally with reserved marinade, until well glazed, 2 to 3 minutes on each side. Serve hot garnished with mint leaves.

Mint Condition

If you haven't discovered the role that mint plays in Asian kitchens, you're in for a refreshing surprise. For Vietnamese cooks, fresh mint is just as important to their colorful salads and spring rolls as greens and vegetables. In Thailand, mint adds a distinctly mild pungency to the classic green curry herb mix. And thanks to India's contact with the Middle East—mint's original home turf—its cooks use the fresh herb in chutneys and the dried herb in ground meat mixtures that they form into kebabs or patties called *kofta*. Hong Kong's cuisine reflects this pan-Asian aesthetic, so it's only natural to find mint sprouting up in dishes all over the city.

Eight Treasures Squash Soup

Kabocha? You Betcha!

More than falling leaves and a biting wind, what signals summer's last gasp to me is the changing inventory at my local farmers' market. Once the produce tables start filling up with pumpkins, I get ready to pull out my winter coat—and my chef's knife. And I'm not talking about just jack-o'-lantern pumpkins, either. Take kabocha, for instance. This lumpy, turban-shaped gourd has a thin, waxy green skin splotched with yellow and orange. Beauty, of course, is in the eye of the beholder—and on the palate of the taster, as you'll find out the minute you experience kabocha's mildly sweet, tender orange flesh. It's a favorite in Japan, where cooks prepare it with a little brown sugar or dunk chunks in tempura batter and deep-fry. Because of its round shape and ample size, I think a hollowed-out kabocha squash makes a great soup tureen.

Why eight treasures? In Chinese culture, the number eight is associated with gold and fortune. So, this soup is not only delicious, it's precious as well. In this recipe, the kabocha squash makes a creative serving vessel, but if you're not cooking for a party, serve the soup in a regular bowl and luck will still come your way. **SERVES 4**

1 whole kabocha squash, 2 to 3 pounds
$^1/_4$ pound medium raw shrimp, shelled, deveined, and butterflied
$^1/_4$ pound boneless, skinless chicken, diced
$^1/_4$ pound Virginia ham, diced
3 fresh shiitake mushrooms, stems discarded, caps diced
1 small carrot, diced
$^1/_4$ cup frozen peas, thawed
3 to 4 cups chicken stock (see page 38)
3 tablespoons Chinese rice wine or dry sherry
1 green onion, thinly sliced, for garnish

1. Bring a large pot of water to a boil. Lower squash into water so that it is completely covered and cook for 10 minutes; drain. Let stand until cool enough to handle. Cut top off squash and reserve as lid; scoop out and discard seeds.

2. Place shrimp, chicken, ham, mushrooms, carrot, and peas in squash. Place filled squash in a large pot.

3. Combine stock and rice wine in a bowl; pour into filled squash so liquid comes to within 1 inch of the top. Pour remaining liquid into pot around squash. Place reserved squash lid over filled squash.

4. Cover pot and bring to a boil over high heat. Decrease heat and simmer until flesh of squash is tender when pierced, 30 to 35 minutes.

5. Ladle soup into four bowls. With a spoon, scoop flesh from squash and divide among soup bowls. Garnish with green onion.

Shrimp and Roast Pork Noodle Soup

If you can't get to your local dai pai dong *street vendor, it takes only a short time to make this satisfying and addictive noodle soup. The memory of it is something that you'll savor for hours afterward... well, at least until your next bowl of noodle soup.*

SERVES 4

8 ounces dried thin Chinese noodles or angel hair pasta

4 cups chicken stock (see page 38)

2 tablespoons soy sauce

1 leek, white part only, thinly sliced on the diagonal

1/4 pound medium raw shrimp, shelled and deveined

1 teaspoon chile sauce

1/8 teaspoon white pepper

1/4 pound Chinese barbecued pork or ham, thinly sliced

1/4 teaspoon black sesame seeds, for garnish

Thinly sliced red and green chile, for garnish

1. In a large pot of boiling water, cook noodles according to package directions. Drain, rinse with cold water, and drain again. Divide noodles among 4 soup bowls.

2. Place stock and soy sauce in a pan and bring to a boil. Add leek and cook for 2 minutes. Decrease heat to medium; add shrimp and cook until they turn pink, about 2 minutes. Add chile sauce and white pepper.

3. Ladle hot soup over noodles in bowls. Arrange barbecued pork over noodles, sprinkle with sesame seeds and chile, and serve.

In the Throng of the Dai Pai Dongs

For the ultimate in Hong Kong street food, head for the nearest *dai pai dong.* (*Dong* means "street stall" and *dai pai* refers to the licenses the stalls need to sell food legally.) These roadside kitchens evolved from roving vendors' carts. Imagine a semi-permanent counter surrounded by little stools. Add a bare-bones kitchen with a few pantry staples and an electric burner fed by an outlet loaded to near-ignition. Top the whole thing off with a makeshift tent or sheet of zinc, and you have a classic *dai pai dong.* Sure, they don't exactly earn five stars for their atmosphere, but for steamy dumpling soup, a bite of noodles, a bracing cup of tea, or the "house specialty" *jook*—the spirit of *dai pai dong* in a bowl—these stalls can't be beat. And you can't beat the price either—the *dai pai dong* really is the eatery for the humble masses.

Country Veggie Stir-Fry

This stir-fry is a snap to make, typical of the fast and delicious food enjoyed by families in Hong Kong or anywhere, for that matter, after a hard day's work.

SERVES 4 TO 6

2 tablespoons vegetable oil
2 cloves garlic, sliced
1 red jalapeño chile, thinly sliced
6 stalks asparagus, cut diagonally into 1-inch lengths
1/2 cup peeled and diced jicama
1/2 cup drained canned baby corn
1/2 cup peeled and sliced lotus root or water chestnuts
1/4 pound snow peas or sugar snap peas, strings removed
1/2 cup chicken stock (see page 38)
1/4 cup *sa cha* sauce
1 tablespoon soy sauce
1 teaspoon cornstarch dissolved in 2 teaspoons water

1. Place a wok over medium-high heat until hot. Add oil, swirling to coat sides. Add garlic and chile; cook, stirring, until fragrant, about 10 seconds. Add asparagus, jicama, baby corn, lotus root, and snow peas; stir-fry for 3 minutes.

2. Add stock, *sa cha* sauce, and soy sauce; bring to a boil. Add cornstarch solution and cook, stirring, until sauce boils and thickens.

3. Transfer to serving plate and serve.

The futuristic skyline of today's Hong Kong makes it easy for us to forget that only a century ago, this island was nothing more than a collection of tranquil farms and fishing villages. With the inevitable march of progress, sleepy rural townships turned into "satellite cities"—emerging urban areas that seem to have sprouted up overnight. Many of the fastest-growing satellite cities are in the New Territories, and all the creature comforts of the modern age are here for the taking: shopping, hotels, cultural events, and food, food, food! Dig a little deeper behind the bustling commercial scenes, however, and you'll discover that not all of the past is lost. Be it a plucky little vegetable patch surviving in the shadows of a high-rise, or a self-sufficient farm, surprises are everywhere in the satellite cities, new and old.

Seafood Noodle Soup

In the chic eateries of Hong Kong's Lan Kwai Fong area, you will likely find inventive dishes like this creamy seafood noodle soup garnished with caviar—one of the famed creations of Jean Pierre Bagnato, executive chef at Café des Artistes. Cream-based soups are not traditional in Hong Kong, but with the rising popularity of fusion foods, ingredients from the West have become world travelers and can be found setting new trends in dishes like this. **SERVES 4**

1/4 **pound dried flat rice noodles, about** 1/4 **inch wide**

1/2 **teaspoon salt**

1/8 **teaspoon white pepper**

1 **tablespoon vegetable oil**

1 **tablespoon julienned ginger**

1 **carrot, julienned**

1 **leek, white part only, julienned**

1 **zucchini, julienned**

1/2 **red bell pepper, seeded and julienned**

1/2 **rib celery, julienned**

1 1/2 **cups seafood stock (see page 44)**

3 **whole star anise pods**

4 **small raw shrimp**

4 **small sea scallops**

1 1/4 **cups whipping cream or half-and-half**

Caviar (or fish eggs), for garnish

Cilantro sprigs, for garnish

1. Soak rice noodles in warm water to cover until softened, about 15 minutes; drain. Bring a pot of water to a boil. Add noodles and cook for 2 minutes. Drain, rinse with cold water, and drain again. Transfer to a bowl and season with salt and white pepper.

2. Place a wok over high heat until hot. Add oil, swirling to coat sides. Add ginger and cook, stirring, until fragrant, about 10 seconds. Add carrot, leek, zucchini, bell pepper, and celery; stir-fry for about 4 minutes. Remove wok from heat.

3. In a pan, bring seafood stock and star anise to a simmer. Add shrimp and cook for 1 minute. Add scallops and cook for 2 minutes. Add cream and heat to simmering (do not allow mixture to boil).

4. Remove star anise and divide noodles and vegetable mixture among 4 soup bowls. Place 1 shrimp and 1 scallop over each serving. Ladle hot stock over all, garnish with caviar and cilantro sprigs, and serve.

All Night Long in Lan Kwai Fong

Where do Hong Kong's trendsetters go to see and be seen? Lan Kwai Fong, that's where. Amidst these narrow streets gourmands and club-hoppers are out merrymaking until the wee hours. If you're curious about the latest "theme" restaurants and the city's best selection of global cuisine, come and spend the evening (and your money) here in Hong Kong's Soho district. Open kitchens in sleek new restaurants provide dinner-as-theater, with celebrity chefs playing the starring roles. Whether you're after West Coast flair in a coolly casual pizza kitchen or a dance club that throbs to a European techno beat until dawn, Lan Kwai Fong is worth staying up for.

Shrimp on Asparagus Skewers

This recipe is from my good friend Chef Chan at the Rainbow Seafood Restaurant on Lamma Island. Asparagus stalks serve as delightful skewers for tender shrimp—you'll enjoy the taste of both with each bite. If asparagus is not in season, use any type of slender vegetable stalk, such as Chinese broccoli. **SERVES 4**

Taking Stock with Chicken Bones

Homemade chicken stock really makes a difference in any recipe and it's so easy to make. It keeps well in the refrigerator for up to a week or in the freezer for 3 months. To make 1¹/₂ quarts of stock, I use a large pot and bring 8 cups water and 3 pounds chicken bones to a boil, skimming off any scum that forms on the top. Decrease the heat and simmer for 1¹/₂ hours. Add 3 green onions, 8 slices ginger (about the size of a quarter), and a pinch each of salt and pepper and simmer for 30 minutes more. Strain stock, discarding bones and seasonings. Finally, skim and discard any fat that rises to the surface of the stock. Now you have a delicious base for soups, sauces, and braises right in your refrigerator.

Marinade
1 teaspoon salt
¹/₈ teaspoon white pepper
¹/₂ teaspoon cornstarch

Seasoning
¹/₂ teaspoon Chinese five-spice powder
¹/₄ teaspoon salt
¹/₄ teaspoon black pepper

Sauce
3 tablespoons chicken stock (see sidebar)
1 tablespoon hoisin sauce
1 tablespoon ketchup
1 tablespoon soy sauce
¹/₂ teaspoon rice vinegar
1 teaspoon sugar

16 to 18 medium raw shrimp, heads and tails intact
16 to 18 slender asparagus spears

Vegetable oil, for deep-frying
3 slices ginger, julienned
2 teaspoons minced garlic
1 green onion, cut into 1-inch pieces

1. To make marinade, combine salt, white pepper, and cornstarch in a bowl. To make seasoning, combine five-spice, salt, and black pepper in a bowl. To make sauce, combine stock, hoisin sauce, ketchup, soy sauce, vinegar, and sugar in another bowl. Mix the contents of each bowl well and set aside.

2. Remove heads from shrimp and reserve. Shell and devein shrimp, leaving tails intact. Butterfly shrimp lengthwise. Lay each shrimp flat, then fold in half so that end touches tail. Make a cut through each center large enough to thread asparagus through. Add shrimp to marinade; coat well. Let stand for 10 minutes.

3. Bring a pot of water to boil. Blanch asparagus spears for 30 seconds. Drain, rinse in cold water, and drain again.

4. To assemble "skewers," carefully push asparagus spear through the slit in center of shrimp.

5. In a wok, heat oil for deep-frying to 375°. Add shrimp heads and deep-fry until they turn pink, about 2 minutes. Remove and drain on paper towels. Sprinkle with seasoning mixture.

6. Carefully drain all but 2 tablespoons oil from wok. Return to high heat until hot. Add ginger, garlic, and green onion; cook, stirring, until fragrant, about 10 seconds. Add shrimp-asparagus skewers and cook for 2½ minutes, stirring gently. Add sauce and cook until heated through.

7. Place shrimp skewers in center of a serving platter. Arrange shrimp heads around skewers, drizzle over sauce, and serve.

Lemme Go to Lamma Island!

As Hong Kong's fishing industry grows more industrial, the small fishing communities on Hong Kong's Lamma Island are a refreshing reminder of days past. I like to wander among the docked fishing boats so I can greet my dinner the minute it arrives. Lamma Island is also a great place for hiking trips. I was there in December, when the island's protected wildlife reserves fill with graceful white cranes heading to their southern winter home. At first sight, the birds appear on the horizon as nothing more than a mass of black dots. But as they glide closer, they magically become the lithe, aerial acrobats of art and poetic tradition. For me, Lamma Island is the real "Fantasy Island."

Stir-Fried Vegetables with Gingko Nuts

Don't Forget the
Gingko Nuts!

I heard that gingko nuts help boost memory, but I can't remember why. Guess I should be eating more gingko nuts! Oh yeah, now I remember: Studies have shown that substances in the *Gingko biloba* tree's byproducts—including its seeds, or "nuts"—increase the flow of oxygen to the brain, enhancing memory and mental alertness. Millions in China take these slightly bittersweet treats for relief from indigestion, hangovers, bacterial and fungal infections, wheezing, and kidney disorders, too. With benefits like that, it's easy to remember to take these culinary cures.

This vegetable stir-fry is neither plain nor boring. That's because Chef Choice Chan of Kung Tak Lam Vegetarian Restaurant tosses a few gingko nuts into the fray. They not only add contrasting texture but also a healthy and beneficial dose of Chinese herbal medicine. **SERVES 4**

6 dried black mushrooms
1 teaspoon dried shrimp

Sauce
1¹/₂ tablespoons oyster-flavored sauce
1 teaspoon sesame oil

2 tablespoons vegetable oil
1 to 2 teaspoons sliced fresh chile (jalapeño or serrano)
2 ribs celery, thinly sliced
1 carrot, roll-cut into 1-inch pieces
6 fresh or canned baby corn, cut in half diagonally
¹/₂ cup fresh or canned gingko nuts
¹/₃ cup chicken stock (see page 38)

1. In separate bowls, soak dried mushrooms and dried shrimp in warm water to cover until softened, about 20 minutes; drain. Discard mushroom stems and slice caps.

2. To make sauce, combine oyster sauce and sesame oil in a bowl.

3. Place a wok over high heat until hot. Add oil, swirling to coat sides. Add chile; cook, stirring, until fragrant, about 10 seconds. Add mushrooms, shrimp, celery, and carrot; stir-fry for 1 minute. Add baby corn, gingko nuts, and stock; bring to a boil. Decrease heat to low and simmer until carrot is tender, about 4 minutes. Add sauce and cook, stirring, until heated through.

Dancing Shrimp and Squid

Here's a dish that's as fanciful as its title suggests. Just a few scores with the knife and voila; your seafood will be dancing. Don't over-blanch the squid or they will become tough—tougher than dancing with two left feet! **SERVES 4**

Ginger–Vinegar Sauce

¹/₄ **cup rice vinegar**

3 **tablespoons soy sauce**

2 **tablespoons grated ginger**

2 **teaspoons sesame oil**

2 **teaspoons sugar**

Hot and Spicy Sauce

¹/₄ **cup chile garlic sauce**

¹/₄ **cup fresh lemon juice**

2 **tablespoons chopped green onion**

2 **tablespoons soy sauce**

1 **tablespoon sesame oil**

1 **tablespoon sugar**

1 **large squid (about ¹/₂ pound), cleaned**

12 **large raw shrimp**

4 **cups water**

2 **tablespoons Chinese rice wine or dry sherry**

3 **slices ginger, lightly crushed**

1 **green onion, cut in half and lightly crushed**

1. To prepare ginger-vinegar sauce, in a bowl combine vinegar, soy sauce, ginger, sesame oil, and sugar. In another bowl prepare hot and spicy sauce: Combine chile garlic sauce, lemon juice, green onion, soy sauce, sesame oil, and sugar. Mix well and set both sauces aside.

2. Cut squid hood into rectangles about 1¹/₂ inches by 3 inches. Lightly score half of the pieces with crosshatching marks about ¹/₂ inch apart. On the other squid pieces, cut slits 1 inch long and ¹/₄ inch apart along one short edge of each piece to create a fringe effect.

3. Shell, devein, and butterfly shrimp, leaving tails intact.

4. Combine water, rice wine, ginger, and green onion in a pan; bring to a boil. Add squid and cook until pieces curl, about 2 minutes. Remove squid with a slotted spoon; drain. Add shrimp and cook until pink, 4 to 5 minutes; drain.

5. Arrange squid and shrimp on a serving platter. Serve warm with sauces on the side.

Boogying with the Big Cats

In China, any time is the right time for a Lion Dance: weddings, New Year's celebrations, graduations, even the grand opening of a business. But how did this traditional Chinese festival dance of good fortune get its start? Just blame it on the Chinese Lion King, a real clown with a habit of playing jokes. One day, he decided to have a little fun at the expense of the Jade Emperor by faking an injury, and when the Jade Emperor came to his aid, the Lion King popped up and scared the wits out of him. The Emperor was not amused, going so far as to cut off the Lion King's head. But the Goddess of Mercy took pity on the poor lion and tied his head to a long, colorful ribbon, bringing him back to life. The Lion King was so grateful that he promised to dedicate his life to helping others. To this day, we still do the dance of the Lion King to chase away evil spirits and usher in the good ones any time a celebration is called for.

Three-Flavor Shrimp

Why settle for one flavor when you can have three? This shrimp stir-fry is the perfect choice for your next dinner party; with shrimp in three separate seasonings—spicy pepper, curry, and chile—you're bound to satisfy every palate around the table. Be sure not to let the wok get too hot or you will burn the sauces. **SERVES 4**

Spicy Pepper Salt

$1/2$ teaspoon Sichuan peppercorns

$1/4$ teaspoon crushed red pepper flakes

$1\,3/4$ teaspoons salt

$1/2$ teaspoon Chinese five-spice powder

$1/8$ teaspoon white pepper

Curry Sauce

2 teaspoons curry powder

$1/2$ teaspoon salt

$1/8$ teaspoon white pepper

1 teaspoon sesame oil

Chile Sauce

$1/3$ cup sweet chile sauce

1 tablespoon minced ginger

1 tablespoon minced green onion

$3/4$ pound medium raw shrimp

3 tablespoons vegetable oil

$1/4$ English cucumber, peeled and thinly sliced

1. To prepare spicy pepper salt, place peppercorns in a small frying pan over low heat; cook, shaking pan frequently, until aromatic, about 5 minutes. Immediately remove from pan to cool. Coarsely grind peppercorns and pepper flakes in a spice grinder. In a small bowl combine with salt, five-spice powder, and white pepper.

2. To prepare curry sauce, combine curry powder, salt, pepper, and sesame oil in a small bowl. To prepare chile sauce, combine sweet chile sauce, ginger, and green onion in another bowl. Mix sauces and set aside.

3. Shell, devein, and butterfly shrimp; divide into 3 portions.

4. Place a wok over high heat until hot. Add 1 tablespoon oil, swirling to coat sides. Add 1 portion of shrimp and stir-fry until pink, 2 to 3 minutes. Add $3/4$ teaspoon of spicy pepper salt (save remainder for other uses), and mix well. Remove shrimp from wok; wipe wok clean.

5. Return wok to medium heat. Add 1 tablespoon oil, swirling to coat sides. Add chile sauce; cook for 1 minute. Add second portion of shrimp and stir-fry until pink, 2 to 3 minutes. Remove from wok and wipe wok clean.

6. Return wok to medium heat. Add the remaining 1 tablespoon oil, swirling to coat sides. Add curry sauce; cook for 1 minute. Add remaining portion of shrimp and stir-fry until pink, about 2 minutes.

7. Arrange spicy pepper shrimp, chile shrimp, and curried shrimp on a serving platter, separating each flavor of shrimp with cucumber slices.

Shopping for Shrimp

How can you find shrimp that are well qualified to carry the lead in your culinary production? First, buy only shrimp that have a firm feel. Look for clean, translucent shells with a minimum of black spots. The shrimp should be moist but not swimming in a pool of liquid. Store fresh shrimp in a refrigerator set no higher than 40° and use it within two to three days unless you plan to freeze it. As for cooking shrimp to perfection, it doesn't take too long—just a few minutes of stir-frying will do. Once they turn pink, curl a bit, and become firm, they're ready.

Steamed Seafood with Glass Noodles

Stock from the Sea

Fish and seafood stocks are simple to make and store well in either the refrigerator, for 3 days, or the freezer, for up to 3 months. To make fish stock, use a large pot and cover 2½ pounds white fish bones with 8 cups water; bring to a boil and cook for 10 minutes, skimming off any foam that forms on the top. Decrease the heat and simmer for 10 minutes. Add 3 green onions, 6 slices ginger (each about the size of a quarter), and a pinch each of salt and pepper and simmer for 30 minutes more. Strain stock, discarding the bones and seasonings. Skim and discard any fat that rises to the surface of the stock. This recipe makes 1½ quarts fish stock. Fish bones are available at your local fish market. If you have leftover shrimp, crab, or lobster shells, they can be substituted for some or all of the fish bones and the stock will become a seafood stock. Fish and seafood stocks are interchangeable in most recipes.

This dish was inspired by a Tonka fishing family with whom I spent some time. Envision mini-towers of scallops, salmon, and tofu on a sea of glass noodles. Use a cookie cutter to make these perfect pillars of seafood. Don't waste the leftover scraps of tofu and salmon. Use them in a soup or stir-fry. **SERVES 6**

2 ounces dried bean thread noodles
1 (14-ounce) package regular tofu, drained
½ pound salmon fillet
3 sea scallops, halved horizontally
1 tablespoon cornstarch
¼ teaspoon salt
⅛ teaspoon white pepper

Sauce

¼ cup seafood stock (see sidebar)
1 tablespoon soy sauce
1 tablespoon Chinese rice wine or dry sherry
1 teaspoon cornstarch dissolved in 2 teaspoons water

Chopped Chinese chives or green onions, for garnish

1. Soak bean thread noodles in warm water to cover until softened, about 5 minutes; drain noodles and cut in half. Set aside.

2. Cut tofu in half horizontally to make 2 pieces, each about 1-inch thick. With a 2-inch-diameter cookie cutter, cut 6 rounds of tofu. With the same cutter, cut 6 rounds of salmon. (Save trimmings for other uses, such as soup.)

3. Place tofu, salmon, and scallops in a wide shallow bowl. Sprinkle with cornstarch, salt, and white pepper. Let stand for 10 minutes.

4. Place tofu rounds on work surface. Top each with a round of salmon, then place a piece of scallop on each. Place bean thread noodles in a heatproof dish. With a wide spatula, lift seafood stacks and nestle in noodles.

5. Prepare a wok for steaming (see page 6). Place dish in steamer. Cover and steam over medium heat until salmon and scallops turn opaque, 10 to 15 minutes.

6. To prepare sauce, combine stock, soy sauce, and rice wine in a small saucepan. Bring to a boil over medium heat. Add cornstarch solution and cook, stirring, until sauce boils and thickens.

7. To serve, spoon sauce over seafood stacks and garnish with chives.

Baked Egg with Crabmeat

This is one of my favorite baked dishes—silky egg custard and succulent crab, topped with a cheesy layer of Parmesan, and baked to homey perfection. Although I use a Dungeness crab because the shell makes a dramatic vessel for the custard, you can use any variety of cooked crabmeat—just make sure it's very fresh—and a standard baking dish. **SERVES 4**

Custard

2 eggs, lightly beaten

1/4 cup chicken stock (see page 38)

1 tablespoon minced cilantro or green onion

1 tablespoon Chinese rice wine or dry sherry

1 tablespoon oyster-flavored sauce

1 teaspoon minced ginger

1 tablespoon cornstarch

1/8 teaspoon white pepper

1 1/2 cups cooked shelled crabmeat, flaked

Shell from back of Dungeness crab, cleaned (optional)

1 tablespoon grated Parmesan cheese

1. Preheat oven to 375°.

2. To make custard, combine eggs, stock, cilantro, rice wine, oyster sauce, ginger, cornstarch, and white pepper in a bowl. Whisk until evenly blended but not foamy. Stir in crabmeat.

3. Pour custard into crab shell or a 5-inch-diameter shallow baking dish. Sprinkle cheese over the top.

4. Place custard in oven and bake until golden brown and a knife inserted into the center comes out clean, 20 to 25 minutes. Serve warm.

Taking a Stab at the Hairy Crab

Few culinary events in Hong Kong are anticipated with as much excitement as the Shanghai hairy crab season. Beginning in September and lasting through most of November, Hong Kong's ports, restaurants, and markets kick into festival mode as trains, planes, and boats haul in this freshwater delicacy from China's Shanghai region. Obsessed connoisseurs wait in line to pay hundreds of dollars per pound for fresh hairy crabs, or *dai jarp hai*. They gladly pay even more when the crustaceans get the star treatment from Hong Kong's talented chefs. And if you're wondering why all the fuss over a crab, you'll just have to taste the pure, fresh flavor of a single nugget of meat or the creamy texture of a nubbin of roe to find out for yourself.

Fish in a Fish Basket

These stir-fried fish chunks arrive inside a basket of a tasty deep-fried fish. Whole fish symbolize prosperity and plentitude, making this a favorable offering at temples.

SERVES 4 TO 6

1 (2- to 3-pound) whole fish, such as sea bass or red snapper, cleaned

1 tablespoon soy sauce

1/8 teaspoon white pepper

Sauce

1/4 cup chicken stock (see page 38)

1/4 cup Chinese rice wine or dry sherry

2 teaspoons fermented soybean paste

1 teaspoon chile garlic sauce

1 teaspoon sugar

3/4 pound firm white fish fillet, such as sea bass or red snapper

Vegetable oil, for deep-frying

1/2 cup cornstarch, for coating fish

2 tablespoons minced shallots

1/2 green bell pepper, seeded and cut into 3/4-inch diamonds

1/2 red bell pepper, seeded and cut into 3/4-inch diamonds

1/2 cup diced bamboo shoots

1 teaspoon cornstarch dissolved in 2 teaspoons water

1. Place whole fish on a clean cutting board. Debone fish by making a cut along the spine on both sides of fish; remove and discard spine and entrails; leave head and tail attached. Rinse with cold water and pat dry. Combine soy sauce and white pepper in a bowl; rub whole fish inside and out with mixture. Let stand for 10 minutes.

2. To make sauce, combine stock, rice wine, soybean paste, chile garlic sauce, and sugar in a bowl. Mix well and set aside.

3. Cut fish fillet into 1-inch pieces. In a wok, heat oil for deep-frying to 375°. Coat whole fish, inside and out, with cornstarch; shake to remove excess. Place fish on a large wire strainer; open up fish from the top and place a slightly smaller wire strainer inside. Press together both strainers to hold fish open like a basket. Deep-fry fish until golden brown, 12 to 15 minutes. Remove and drain on paper towels.

4. Carefully drain all but 1 tablespoon oil from wok. Place wok over high heat until hot. Add shallots and cook, stirring, until fragrant, about 10 seconds. Add fish pieces and stir-fry for 1 minute. Add bell peppers and bamboo shoots; stir-fry for 1 minute. Add sauce and bring to a boil. Add cornstarch solution and cook, stirring, until sauce boils and thickens. Place whole fried fish on a platter. Spoon stir-fried fish fillet into interior and serve.

Steamed Slices of Grouper and Salmon

I got the idea for this recipe from a dish I sampled at the Hyatt Regency's Hoi Yut Heen Restaurant in Hong Kong. Tender pieces of white fish and thinly sliced salmon are rolled to resemble budding roses, artfully arranged on a plate, and steamed into an edible seafood bouquet. **SERVES 6**

³/₄ pound firm white fish fillets, such as grouper or sea bass
¹/₄ pound boneless, skinless salmon, or 1 (3-ounce) package cold-smoked salmon
2 green onions, cut into 1-inch pieces

Sauce

¹/₂ cup seafood stock (see page 44)
1¹/₂ teaspoons Chinese rice wine or dry sherry
1 teaspoon fresh lime juice
¹/₈ teaspoon salt
¹/₈ teaspoon white pepper
1 tablespoon cornstarch dissolved in 2 tablespoons water

1. Cut white fish into pieces about 4 inches long, 1¹/₂ inches wide, and ¹/₈ inch thick. Thinly slice salmon. Place a piece of white fish on work surface, then center a strip of salmon on top. Roll fish into loose bundles so they resemble a tomato rose. Scatter green onions in a heatproof dish. Stand fish rolls on green onions.

2. Prepare a wok for steaming (see page 6). Place dish in steamer and steam over medium heat until fish is opaque throughout, 7 to 8 minutes.

3. To prepare sauce, combine stock, rice wine, lime juice, salt, and white pepper in a small pan over medium heat and bring to a boil. Add cornstarch solution and cook, stirring, until sauce boils and thickens.

4. Place fish rolls on a serving plate. Pour sauce over top and serve.

Barbecued Fish with Spicy Vegetables

It didn't take long for Executive Chef Christof M. Syre, at the Regent Hong Kong, to pick up on an important Chinese culinary commandment: Thou shalt not waste food. This thrifty sensibility is reflected in this dish, which makes excellent use of a whole fish.

SERVES 4

1 (1¹/₂- to 2-pound) whole fish, such as sea
    bass or red snapper, cleaned

¹/₂ teaspoon salt

Seasoning

2 tablespoons chile sauce

1 tablespoon vegetable oil

2 stalks lemongrass (bottom 5 to 6
    inches only), split in half
    lengthwise, lightly crushed

2 green onions, cut into 2-inch lengths

¹/₂ cup diced tomatoes

¹/₄ cup thinly sliced shallots

6 sprigs cilantro

1 teaspoon seeded and shredded
    jalapeño chile

2 tablespoons Thai chile sauce

1. Prepare a fire in a charcoal grill or preheat a gas grill.

2. On each side of fish, cut 3 diagonal slices across body, cutting deep enough to hit the bones. Sprinkle fish with salt; let stand for 5 minutes. Rinse fish and pat dry with paper towels.

3. To make seasoning, combine chile sauce and oil in a small bowl; rub over fish.

4. Preheat oven to 400°. Place fish on well-oiled grill 4 to 6 inches above a solid bed of medium-hot glowing coals. Grill fish, turning once, until golden brown, about 5 minutes on each side (fish will be only partially cooked). Carefully lift fish from grill and let cool briefly.

5. Place a piece of aluminum foil large enough to wrap around fish on work surface. Place half of lemongrass, green onions, tomatoes, shallots, cilantro, and chile in center of foil. Brush fish on both sides with chile sauce and set on top of vegetables. Place the remaining lemongrass, green onions, tomatoes, shallots, cilantro, and chile over fish. Fold foil over fish to enclose. Place wrapped fish on a baking sheet.

6. Bake until fish turns opaque and juices have formed inside packet, 8 to 10 minutes.

7. Place fish packet on a serving platter. Open foil and turn it back and under fish. Spoon out juices inside packet for dipping.

Barbecued Fish in Banana Leaves

Hong Kong is a wonderful melting pot of world cuisines. Europe-born Joseph Budde, chef at the Grand Hyatt Hong Kong, fuses the flavors of Hong Kong and Thailand in this recipe for barbecued fish. Distinctive Thai spices liven up its flavor, creating a big, bold taste. **SERVES 4**

8 dried black mushrooms

1/4 cup dried wood ears

Seasoning

2 tablespoons fresh lime juice

1/2 teaspoon salt

1/4 teaspoon black pepper

1/4 teaspoon curry powder

1 to 2 teaspoons thinly sliced jalapeño chile

1 1/4 pounds firm white fish fillets, such as sea bass or red snapper, each about 3/4 inch thick

2 (8 by 12-inch) pieces banana leaf or aluminum foil

1 large tomato, sliced

1. Prepare a fire in a charcoal grill or preheat a gas grill.

2. In separate bowls, soak mushrooms and wood ears in warm water to cover until softened, about 20 minutes; drain. Discard mushroom stems and thinly slice caps. Thinly slice wood ears.

3. To prepare seasoning, combine lime juice, salt, pepper, curry powder, and chile in a bowl. Cut fish into 4 equal portions; rub with seasoning. Let stand for 10 minutes.

4. Dip banana leaves in a pot of boiling water for 3 to 4 seconds to soften; wipe dry.

5. Assemble each packet: Place a leaf or piece of foil, shiny side down, on work surface. Place half of the fish in single layer in center of leaf. Top with half of the mushrooms, wood ears, and tomato slices. Bring 2 long sides of leaf together and double-fold to seal. Fold ends of leaf and fasten with wooden toothpicks.

6. Place packets on an oiled grill 4 to 6 inches above a solid bed of medium-hot, glowing coals. Grill, turning packets frequently, until fish turns opaque, about 15 minutes total.

7. Place packets on a serving platter. Cut open with scissors and serve.

Grandma's Chicken in Rice Cooker

In China, a chicken (or game hen) in every rice cooker is a sure sign of prosperity and of a great dinner to come. These game hens are rubbed with ground Sichuan peppercorns and stuffed with fragrant spices. The result? Deliciously tender meat infused with mouthwatering flavor. **SERVES 4**

1¹/₂ **teaspoons salt**

¹/₂ **teaspoon ground toasted Sichuan peppercorns**

2 (1¹/₂-**pound) Rock Cornish game hens, cleaned**

2 (2¹/₂-**inch-square) pieces dried tangerine peel or fresh tangerine or lemon peel**

6 **cloves garlic, lightly crushed**

6 **slices ginger, lightly crushed**

2 **whole star anise pods**

¹/₄ **cup Chinese rice wine or dry sherry**

1 **teaspoon soy sauce**

3 **tablespoons water**

1 **tablespoon vegetable oil**

2 **green onions, cut into 1-inch lengths**

1. Combine salt and ground Sichuan peppercorns in a bowl.

2. Rinse game hens and pat dry. Rub hens inside and out with salt mixture. Let stand for 30 minutes.

3. If using dried tangerine peel, soak in warm water to cover until softened, about 20 minutes; drain.

4. Place tangerine peel, garlic, ginger, and star anise in a bowl; stir to combine. Place one-half of seasoning mixture inside each game hen.

5. Combine rice wine and soy sauce in a bowl. Brush wine mixture over game hens.

6. Place water, oil, and green onions in a 6-cup (or larger) electric rice cooker. Place game hens, breast sides up, in rice cooker. Press dial to cook; cook until meat near thighbone is no longer pink when pierced, about 15 to 20 minutes.

7. Cut game hens into halves or quarters, place on a platter, and serve.

The Many Faces of the Electric Rice Cooker

Step into any kitchen in Hong Kong—doesn't matter if it's in a restaurant or a home—and you're bound to spot at least one electric rice cooker. These modern conveniences are indispensable in fast-paced Hong Kong kitchens, where having plenty of perfectly cooked rice on hand at the touch of a button isn't a luxury but a necessity. Even if you don't prepare rice every day (there are people who don't eat rice daily?), an electric rice cooker is a worthy investment. For one, you can steam other foods in it, from vegetables and whole chickens to a plate of leftovers that needs reheating. You can even make soup in a rice cooker when you want to give the soup pot a day off. When you do use the cooker for rice, it can do double-duty as a chafing dish by keeping the rice warm and moist after it's fully steamed. Now, if I could only get it to do the dishes. . . .

Getting Around—
and Above—Hong Kong

It's a bird! It's a plane! No, it's just me flopping my way around Hong Kong. For such a small island, the transportation options are head spinning. With its six and a half million inhabitants, and millions more visitors landing at its snazzy new airport each year, Hong Kong needs many ways to shuttle busy bodies around. For decades, the Star Ferry has been making hundreds of daily trips across Victoria Harbour. If you're a landlubber, stick with trains, taxis, buses, trams, the spiffy new underground, or even pedal-powered rickshaws. On the other hand, if it's a view you're looking for, heading up Hong Kong's mountain peak trams takes you to the top of the island. And for really high altitudes (at a high-altitude fee), fly like an eagle on one of Hong Kong's commercial helicopter services. Around here, there's no such thing as standby.

Clockwise: The best way to beat Hong Kong's traffic is by helicopter. Martin relaxing on Hong Kong's antique cable car. Back seat sailing to Cheung Chau Island.

Double–Boiled Chicken with Ginseng

Culinary Cures

The line between food and medicine is a thin one in the Chinese culinary tradition. In Hong Kong, herbal medicine shops are as popular as juice bars in the United States. It's sometimes hard to tell whether the leaves, berries, roots, and strips of bark in these shops—carefully catalogued and stowed in row upon row of drawers—are for clearing up a sore throat or flavoring tonight's meal. It is a moot point, really. For centuries, Chinese have been taking herbs as both ingredients and medicines—and without the help of a spoonful of sugar—unless, of course, it was part of the recipe.

Nothing beats the restorative powers of chicken soup. There are at least a dozen recipes in every culture. My mom has twice that many, and for special occasions she adds ginseng, which enhances both the flavor and healing qualities of this soup. **SERVES 4**

1 pound chicken legs and thighs
5 slices ginger, lightly crushed
4 fresh shiitake mushrooms, stems discarded, caps halved
3 green onions, cut into 2-inch pieces
1 dried ginseng root, about 1 ounce
2¹/₂ cups water
¹/₂ cup Chinese rice wine or dry sherry
1 teaspoon salt

1. Bring a pot of water to a boil. Remove skin and excess fat from chicken. Add chicken to pot and return to a boil. Cook for 1 minute; drain.

2. Place chicken in a 2-quart casserole. Add ginger, mushrooms, green onions, ginseng, water, rice wine, and salt; cover casserole.

3. Prepare a large wok for steaming (see page 6). Place covered casserole on steaming rack. Cover wok and steam over medium-high heat, adding water to steamer as needed, until chicken is tender, about 2 hours.

4. Skim fat from stock and serve.

Hong Kong Soft Beef Tacos

East meets south-of-the-border with this grab-and-go snack. When time is of the essence, what's better than a fast and easy taco? The tasty filling for this version is made with marinated beef stir-fried with crunchy wood ear and flavorful shiitake mushrooms. Just roll it all up in a tortilla and off you go! **SERVES 4 TO 6**

Marinade

2 tablespoons dark soy sauce

1 teaspoon minced garlic

2 tablespoons cornstarch

$^3/_4$ pound beef flank steak, thinly sliced across the grain

Sauce

$^1/_3$ cup hoisin sauce

2 tablespoons chile sauce

3 tablespoons vegetable oil

$^1/_2$ pound white button mushrooms, julienned

$^1/_4$ pound fresh shiitake mushrooms, stems discarded, caps julienned

$^1/_4$ cup fresh wood ear mushrooms, trimmed and julienned (optional)

5 Chinese chives or green onions, cut into 2-inch pieces

$^1/_2$ cup julienned carrot

$^1/_4$ cup chicken stock (see page 38)

2 teaspoons cornstarch dissolved in 1 tablespoon water

6 (8-inch) flour tortillas, warmed

1. To prepare marinade, combine soy sauce, garlic, and cornstarch in a bowl. Add beef and stir to coat. Let stand for 10 minutes.

2. To prepare sauce, combine hoisin and chile sauces in a small bowl. Set aside.

3. Place a wok over high heat until hot. Add 2 tablespoons oil, swirling to coat sides. Add beef and stir-fry until no longer pink, about $1^1/_2$ minutes. Remove meat from wok.

4. Add remaining 1 tablespoon oil to wok, swirling to coat sides. Add both mushrooms, chives, and carrot; stir-fry for $2^1/_2$ minutes. Add stock and bring to a boil. Decrease heat to low and simmer for 1 minute. Return beef to pan and add cornstarch solution. Cook, stirring, until mixture boils and thickens.

5. Place meat mixture in a serving bowl. Serve tortillas and sauce alongside. To eat, spread about 2 teaspoons of sauce on a warm tortilla, top with $^1/_4$ cup meat filling. Fold tortilla in half, and eat out of hand.

Beef and Pickled Vegetable Patty in a Clay Pot

Here's an edible bit of Hong Kong history for your kitchen: clay pot cooking! This traditional cooking vessel makes fabulous one-pot meals. If you don't have a clay pot, use a 1-quart saucepan with a lid. Either way, you are re-creating culinary history with this classic recipe variation contributed by my friend Stephen Hak-Ming Yeung, East Ocean Restaurant's executive chef. **SERVES 4**

Meat Patty

1/2 **pound ground beef**

1/4 **cup chopped green onion**

2 **tablespoons chopped pickled daikon**

1 **tablespoon oyster-flavored sauce**

1 **tablespoon soy sauce**

2 **teaspoons sesame oil**

1 1/2 **teaspoons sugar**

1/8 **teaspoon white pepper**

1/2 **cup chicken stock (see page 38)**

1 **cup long-grain rice**

1 1/2 **cups water**

1 **egg**

1. To make meat patty, combine beef, green onion, pickled daikon, oyster sauce, soy sauce, sesame oil, sugar, and white pepper in a bowl; mix well. Add stock and mix mixture by hand until it is smooth. Shape mixture into a patty, 6 to 7 inches in diameter; press center of patty with a spoon to make an indentation.

2. Wash and drain rice. Place rice and 1 1/2 cups water in a 2-quart clay pot or saucepan. Bring to a boil (over medium heat if using clay pot); decrease heat to very low, cover, and simmer until some water evaporates, 7 to 8 minutes.

3. Place patty over rice. Crack an egg into indentation. Cover and continue to cook until rice is tender and beef is barely pink in center, 10 to 15 minutes.

4. Turn off heat and let stand for 10 minutes before serving.

The Way of Clay

If it ain't broke, don't fix it, right? The age-old technology behind making clay pots certainly doesn't need fixing. These traditional glazed, sand-and-clay pots, often encased in a protective wire mesh, are just as handy in our gadget-driven age as they have been for centuries. For making slow-cooked braised or stewed dishes, you can't beat them. You can take the rustic pots straight from stove to table, and they're oven-safe too. Look for clay pots in Chinese markets and well-stocked Chinese groceries. To keep it from cracking, never place your clay pot over direct heat while it's empty, and let it cool completely before setting it in cold water or on a cool surface.

Cabbage Meatballs

Steaming is a healthier alternative to pan-frying, even for meatballs. For this dish, I steam meatballs, made from pork, nestled in napa cabbage and served on portobella mushroom caps and bean thread noodles. **SERVES 4**

Meatballs

¼ cup dried shrimp

½ pound ground pork or chicken

⅓ cup chicken stock (see page 38)

1 tablespoon chopped water chestnuts

1 tablespoon chopped green onion

1 tablespoon coarsely chopped Sichuan preserved vegetables

1 tablespoon cornstarch

1 tablespoon dark soy sauce

1 tablespoon oyster-flavored sauce

2 teaspoons sesame oil

2 ounces dried bean thread noodles

2 small napa cabbages

4 medium portobella mushrooms, stems discarded

Blanched chives, for garnish

Thinly sliced red bell pepper, for garnish

1. Soak dried shrimp in warm water to cover until softened, about 20 minutes; drain. Coarsely chop.

2. To make meatballs, combine shrimp, pork, stock, water chestnuts, green onion, preserved vegetables, cornstarch, soy sauce, oyster sauce, and sesame oil in a large bowl; mix well. Cover and refrigerate for about 30 minutes.

3. Soak bean thread noodles in warm water to cover until softened, about 5 minutes; drain. Cut in half.

4. Remove outer leaves of cabbages until their diameters are 2½ to 3 inches. Trim bases to flatten. Cut top leaves off to makes cases 2½ to 3 inches high. Remove inner leaves to create an area for stuffing. (Save trimmings for another use.) Spoon half of meatball filling into each cabbage case. Tie kitchen twine around cases to secure.

5. Prepare a wok for steaming (see page 6). Place noodles in a heatproof dish. Place mushrooms, gill sides up, on noodles. Stand stuffed cabbages on dish on steaming rack. Cover and steam until cabbage is tender and filling is barely pink, about 30 minutes. Remove twine and replace with blanched chives before serving. Garnish with bell pepper.

Char Siu Rack of Lamb

This dish came from Chef Chiang Shing-Kung at the Long Tong Loa Beijing restaurant. Nothing could be more Chinese than char siu, but this recipe—using the lamb rack, paired with a fruit salsa—reflects the international flair of Hong Kong. **SERVES 4**

Marinade

1 tablespoon minced fresh rosemary

1 tablespoon minced garlic

1 teaspoon ground toasted Sichuan peppercorns

2 tablespoons dark soy sauce

2 tablespoons soy sauce

1 teaspoon salt

1 tablespoon vegetable oil

1 rack of lamb, trimmed of fat, about 2 pounds

Glaze

1/3 cup hoisin sauce

1/3 cup soy sauce

3 tablespoons honey

Salsa

1 mango, peeled and diced

2 tablespoons chopped red bell pepper

2 tablespoons chopped onion

1 tablespoon minced fresh mint leaves

2 tablespoons dark soy sauce

2 tablespoons soy sauce

2 tablespoons honey

2 tablespoons fresh lemon juice

1 tablespoon plum sauce

Hot cooked rice

Mint leaves, for garnish

1. To prepare marinade, combine rosemary, garlic, peppercorns, soy sauces, salt, and oil in a large bowl. Add lamb and turn to coat. Cover and refrigerate for 2 to 3 hours.

2. To prepare glaze, combine hoisin sauce, soy sauce, and honey in a bowl. Mix and set aside.

3. To prepare salsa, combine mango sauce, bell pepper, onion, mint, soy sauces, honey, lemon juice, and plum sauce in a bowl, mix well. Cover and refrigerate until ready to serve.

4. Preheat broiler with rack placed 4 to 5 inches from heating element. Place lamb, meat side up, in a foil-lined baking pan. Broil lamb, meat side up, for 10 to 12 minutes. Turn, brush with glaze, and broil for 5 to 7 minutes more. Turn meat again, brush with glaze, and broil for another 3 to 4 minutes.

5. Slice rack between ribs. Serve with rice and salsa and garnish with mint leaves.

Bag It!

I may come to Hong Kong for the food, but many others come with another goal in mind: whoever returns home with the most shopping bags, wins. In Hong Kong, shopping is a competitive sport. But there's no need for cheating, because this city has enough merchandise to go around. Stroll Wellington Street or Kimberley Road for custom-designed jewelry, and check out Cat Street for handmade Chinese furniture. As for Hollywood Road, it's got knick-knacks and antiques galore. And foodies like me can shop 'til we drop at international markets packed with Italian pastas, Spanish olives, Californian wines, and French truffles—as well as Chinese tea and moon cakes. I've shopped and gone to heaven!

Jook

Practical Jook?

Anyone who grew up in Hong Kong and Southern China must have fond memories of *jook*, the ultimate in Chinese comfort food. This classic porridge—also called rice *congee*—captures the essence of Chinese cooking in a bowl. It's based on rice, and nothing says "Chinese food" quite like rice. And since you use very little raw rice in making *jook* (in the old days they even added day-old rice to the pot) it's frugal, too—another hallmark of Chinese cooking. In fact, the condiments that give *jook* its flavor are often leftovers from the night before or items you're trying to clear out of your refrigerator or pantry: roast pork, sausages, bits of seafood, preserved duck eggs, mushrooms, slivered green onions, shredded ginger, chopped cilantro, and peanuts, for starters. More than a breakfast treat, *jook* is a soothing snack to slurp at any hour, making it as versatile and adaptable as the very best of Chinese cooking.

No, it's not a mistake that this recipe calls for 15 cups of liquid and only 1 cup of rice. That's because a little rice goes a long way when making jook. *The rice is simmered until individual grains are indistinguishable, creating a wonderfully silky texture. I can't think of a more perfect treat for breakfast, or any time of the day, for that matter.*

SERVES 4 TO 6

1 cup long-grain rice
9 cups water
6 cups chicken stock (see page 38)
3 ounces salmon fillet, thinly sliced
3 ounces sea bass fillet, thinly sliced
3 ounces small raw shrimp, shelled and deveined
2 ounces boneless beef, thinly sliced

Toppings

$^1/_3$ cup minced Sichuan preserved vegetables (see page 58)
3 preserved eggs, peeled and cut into wedges (optional)

Condiments

Soy sauce
Julienned ginger
$^1/_8$ teaspoon white pepper

1. Wash and drain rice. Place rice with water and stock in a large pot. Bring to a boil over high heat. Decrease heat to medium-low and cook, uncovered, stirring occasionally, until thick and creamy, 1$^1/_2$ to 2 hours. Remove from heat.

2. Just before serving, stir salmon, sea bass, shrimp, and beef into hot *jook*. Ladle into individual soup bowls. Serve with toppings and condiments on the side.

Glutinous Rice Pancakes

You won't find this at your local pancake house unless it also happens to be a dim sum *tea house. These savory pancakes are made with sticky glutinous rice, which forms into pancakes without falling apart. The crispy outer shells and chewy centers will make these a favorite in your house.* **MAKES 4 PANCAKES, SERVES 4**

1²/₃ **cups white glutinous rice**

Filling

2 dried black mushrooms
¹/₄ cup diced bamboo shoots
¹/₄ cup sliced fresh button mushrooms
¹/₄ cup chopped glazed walnuts (see page 117)
3 tablespoons chopped cilantro
1 green onion, chopped
1 tablespoon chopped pickled daikon (optional)
3 tablespoons oyster-flavored sauce
1 tablespoon sesame oil

About 2 tablespoons vegetable oil

1. Soak glutinous rice in water to cover, at least 4 hours or overnight; drain.

2. Prepare a wok for steaming (see page 6). Spread rice in a heatproof dish and place on steaming rack. Cover wok and steam over high heat, sprinkling water over rice every 10 minutes, until it is tender and translucent, about 25 minutes.

3. Soak dried mushrooms in warm water to cover until softened, about 20 minutes; drain. Discard stems and dice caps.

4. To prepare filling, scoop warm rice into a bowl. Add black mushrooms, bamboo shoots, fresh mushrooms, walnuts, cilantro, green onion, daikon, oyster sauce, and sesame oil. Mix well and let cool. Divide rice mixture into 4 equal portions; shape each portion into a pancake 3 to 4 inches wide and ¹/₄ inch thick.

5. Place a wide frying pan over medium-high heat until hot. Add 1 tablespoon of the oil, swirling to coat sides. Add 2 pancakes and cook, until golden brown, turning once, 5 to 6 minutes total. Cook remaining pancakes, adding oil as needed. Serve warm.

Let's Do the Cha Cha

People in Hong Kong *yum cha,* or "drink tea," morning, noon, and night. And where there's tea, there's *dim sum*—sweet or savory morsels that are the perfect partner for China's national brew. Some of my favorites include *har gao* (steamed dumplings of tender shrimp wrapped in a crystalline wheat starch dough), *char siu bao* (puffy white buns filled with sweet barbecued pork), and *har dor see* (deep-fried toast points topped with shrimp paste). *Dim sum* means "touches the heart," and nothing could be more heart-touching than spending a few hours sipping tea and nibbling on delicate dumplings, buns, and other *dim sum* treats.

Yin-Yang Pizza

I have to hand it to the chefs at the Royal Garden Hotel, who manage to fuse the classic Italian pizza with such Asian ingredients as shiitake mushrooms, Chinese sausage, and Japanese eggplant. This pizza is not only delicious, it's a feast for the eyes. The toppings shape the pizza into a yin-yang symbol, and you can't get any more balanced than that. **SERVES 4**

Eggplant Sauce

1 Asian eggplant

3 tablespoons hoisin sauce

2 teaspoons sesame oil

Pesto

1 cup packed cilantro leaves

1/4 cup pine nuts

4 cloves garlic, thinly sliced

1 teaspoon sesame oil

1/2 cup olive oil

1/4 teaspoon salt

1/8 teaspoon white pepper

2 tablespoons vegetable oil

1 small red onion, thinly sliced

1 crookneck squash, sliced

2 fresh shiitake mushrooms, stems discarded, caps sliced

1 (12-inch) ready-made prebaked pizza crust

1 cup (4 ounces) shredded mozzarella cheese

1/4 cup sliced ham or Chinese sausage

1/4 cup drained canned pineapple chunks

1 teaspoon sliced jalapeño chile

1. To make eggplant sauce, preheat oven to 350°. Place eggplant in a shallow pan and bake until soft, 10 to 15 minutes. Cut eggplant into 1/2-inch dice and place in a bowl with hoisin sauce and sesame oil; mix lightly.

2. To make pesto, place cilantro, pine nuts, garlic, and sesame oil in a food processor. Process until finely chopped. With motor running, slowly add olive oil. Add salt and white pepper; set aside.

3. Place a wide frying pan over medium heat until hot. Add 1 tablespoon vegetable oil, swirling to coat sides. Add onion and cook until golden brown and caramelized, 10 to 15 minutes. Remove onion from pan.

4. Preheat oven to 400°. Add remaining 1 tablespoon oil to pan, swirling to coat sides. Add squash and mushrooms; cook, stirring, until squash is tender, 7 to 8 minutes.

5. Place crust on work surface. Cover one-half with eggplant sauce and one-half with pesto.

6. Sprinkle one-third of the cheese on eggplant side, then top with squash, mushrooms, and one-half of the onion. Sprinkle another third of the cheese on pesto side and top with ham, pineapple, and remaining onion. Sprinkle remaining cheese and the chile over the top.

7. Bake pizza until cheese melts, about 15 minutes.

Soho Is So Hot

With a name like Soho, it's got to be hip, right? Soho New York and Soho London are both hotbeds of up-and-coming art, fashion, and international flavors, and the same's true for Hong Kong's own Soho— south of Hollywood Road. Its recent cultural and culinary renaissance parallels that of its Western cousins. The narrow lanes and alleys have blossomed into a gourmand's garden of delights. Here we find quaint Alsatian charcuteries, amiably noisy tapas bars, trattorias specializing in rustic Tuscan fare, and enough highbrow coffee spots to keep even a seasoned Seattlite wide awake and sipping. So, when you're in the mood for food with an international flair, Soho is right up your alley.

Chinese Five–Spice Cookies

Here is a toothsome treat that will go perfectly with your tea. These almond-flavored cookies are enhanced with Chinese five-spice, a pungent mixture of ground cinnamon, cloves, fennel seeds, star anise, and peppercorns. The results are so buttery and delicious, they're sure to pull a disappearing act the minute you serve them. Better make a double batch if you expect company. **MAKES 24 COOKIES**

1 cup (¹/₂ pound) unsalted butter, at room temperature
¹/₂ cup sugar
2 teaspoons almond extract
2¹/₂ cups all-purpose flour
¹/₄ teaspoon Chinese five-spice powder

1. In the bowl of an electric mixer, beat butter until creamy. Beat in sugar and almond extract.

2. In another bowl, stir together flour and five-spice. With motor running, gradually add to butter mixture, blending thoroughly. Shape dough into a patty, wrap in plastic wrap, and refrigerate until firm, about 30 minutes.

3. Preheat oven to 325°. Press dough into lightly floured cookie molds or place dough on a lightly floured surface. Roll into a sheet about ¹/₃ inch thick. With a 2-inch-round cookie cutter, cut dough into circles, or cut with a sharp knife into strips 2¹/₂ inches long and ¹/₂ inch wide.

4. Place cookies 2 inches apart on an ungreased baking sheet. Bake until lightly browned, 25 to 30 minutes.

5. Let cool on baking sheet for 5 minutes, then transfer to a rack and let cool completely. Store in an airtight container.

Meet me at the Pen!

As it turns out, the British and Hong Kong's Chinese have a lot in common, especially their love of tea. Both cultures have a knack for turning tea time into a bustling social engagement. The lobby of the Peninsula Hotel is the favorite destination to meet up for a spot of Earl Grey with crumpets at tea time. Or, if you're in the mood for a Chinese experience, drop by the hotel's Spring Moon tea house, where you can enjoy steamed pork buns and other *dim sum* treats, and wash it all down with a fresh pot of Lapsang Souchong. No matter which style you choose, tea at the "Pen" is both a culinary and a cultural experience.

Papaya and Snow Fungus in Syrup

It's Snowing Fungus!

You may not think of fungus as an exciting dessert ingredient, but throughout China, snow fungus (also called white fungus) is no stranger to the cuisine's mildly sweet desserts. Beige and stiffly sponge-like when dry, snow fungus turns silvery-white and takes on a pleasing, gelatinous texture when cooked. While it doesn't have much taste of its own, snow fungus absorbs the flavors of whatever else you cook with it. Soak snow fungus in warm water until softened, remove the rigid core from its underside—snipping it with a pair of scissors does the trick—and then cut the fungus into whatever size pieces you'd like. Since it tends to expand with rehydration and cooking (it can grow up to three times its dried size), remember that a little goes a long way.

I never feel guilty about eating dessert, especially when I make this low-fat soupy treat: sweet scented papaya and pieces of delicate snow fungus in a sugary almond syrup. A guilt-free delight! **SERVES 4**

$^1/_2$ **ounce dried snow fungus (white fungus)**
1 ripe papaya (about 1 pound), skinned and seeds removed
3 cups water
6 ounces rock sugar
$^1/_4$ **cup Chinese almonds**

1. Soak snow fungus in warm water to cover for 30 minutes; drain. Remove and discard hard core and tear into bite-size pieces.

2. Cut papaya in half lengthwise, then cut into 1-inch chunks.

3. Place water in a saucepan; bring to a boil. Add rock sugar and stir until dissolved. Add snow fungus and Chinese almonds. Decrease heat to low and simmer for 5 minutes. Add papaya and stir to coat.

4. Prepare a wok for steaming (see page 6). Pour papaya mixture into a heatproof bowl with lid. Place in steamer; cover wok and steam for 5 minutes.

5. Transfer to a serving bowl and serve hot, or refrigerate and serve chilled.

TAIWAN

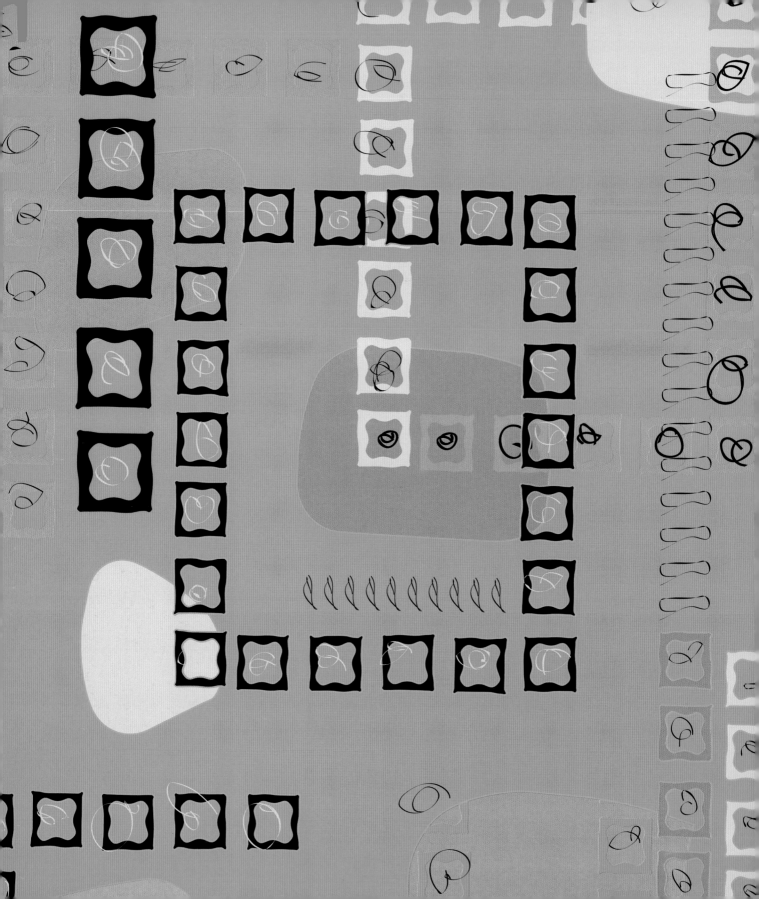

TAIWAN

A Culinary Crossroad

OR MANY, TAIWAN MEANS LITTLE MORE than the "Made in . . ." labels on their clothes, but for others, and I include myself in this group, the island of Formosa is a place buzzing with vigor and creative energy. And what makes Taiwan truly unique is that it can thrive alongside a rich Chinese culture that dates back thousands of years. Today's Taiwan is a close link in the long, powerful chain of China's past and a symbol of its promising future.

What strikes me most about Taiwan, and its fabulous cuisine, is how it contains within its shores the whole of Chinese culture, in microcosm. Spread over a space of just fourteen thousand square miles, much of China's regional distinctions, dialects, varied lifestyles, and culinary traditions are represented and condensed into something uniquely Taiwanese.

Much of this windfall collection of all things Chinese can be attributed to the 1949 migration of nearly two million mainland Chinese to the island. The mainlanders—who followed their leader, Chiang Kai-shek, the "Father of Taiwan"—hailed from all corners of China. By and large, they've managed to maintain their distinctive regional ties. Hence Taiwan is like the lazy susan on the tables in its own restaurants: Take a quick spin, and you can experience all the delights China has to offer!

Open air cooking atop Taiwan's mountainous terrain.   To feed the growing cities, every inch of arable land is used.

Taiwan: An Edible Patchwork

If it is eaten on the mainland, it is eaten in Taiwan, too. All the standards of Beijing, Sichuan, Shanghai, and Cantonese cuisines are in plentiful supply, not only in restaurants and at street food stalls—and Taiwan has plenty of those—but also in millions of home kitchens. It reminds me of the culinary patchwork in my adopted home, San Francisco: neighborhoods like Italian North Beach and Chinatown are homes to countless ethnic restaurants that lend their character to the city at large.

But as is the case on the mainland, there's a lot more in store for true gourmands than the four main Chinese regional cuisines. China is a huge country of a billion-plus people, made up of many distinctive regional cultures and foods. It frustrates me that, for simplicity's sake, Chinese cuisine is pigeonholed into the convenient foursome. There is much to praise about regional cuisines whose names aren't so likely to appear on your neighborhood Chinese restaurant menus: Chiu Chow, Yunnan, Hakka, Tanka, Hoklo, Shangdong, and Fukien cuisines, for starters.

Gathering greens for market.

With so many of these regional and even subregional cuisines flourishing in Taiwan, is there really any such thing as a true Taiwanese cuisine? Fortunately for lovers of simple, rustic, often one-pot dishes made from the freshest local ingredients, there is. Taiwanese cuisine rises from the dictates of nature: the island's geography, climate, and native ingredients, as well as from culture: the cross-fertilization of imported regional styles once they've come into close contact in Taiwan.

Taiwan doesn't have a lot of arable land. The island is mountainous, and this not only squeezes the population into a relatively cramped space, it also makes raising land-hungry livestock such as cattle a losing proposition. Enter seafood, and lots of it. From biggies like grouper and tuna down to tiny sardines no bigger than a paperclip, the Taiwanese dinner table is truly blessed. I never leave Taiwan without sampling the freshest catch of clams, scallops, and—my favorite duo—squid and shrimp. I find them totally irresistible, and so will you.

National Fu Hsing Dramatic Arts Academy, Teipi City.

But Taiwan's food supply hasn't always been quite so flush. In times of hardship, even scraping up enough rice was a challenge, so people used roots such as sweet potatoes and taro to make their own sort of Taiwanese "root" *jook*. Today, you can still find all-night restaurants throughout Taipei serving the humble porridge in classic Taiwanese style: with a selection of side dishes and, now that there's plenty to go around, rice. Stroll into these casual *jook* joints (if there aren't any empty seats, just grab a spot at the counter), order your root *jook*, and take your pick of all the side dishes available. Some favorites include oyster omelets, bean curd in any way imaginable, pickled vegetables with a mildly spicy bite, eggs with preserved radish greens, and bite-sized fish stir-fried with nuts. Considering that some of the eateries boast upwards of one hundred side dish options, give yourself enough time to make your choice.

Taiwanese *jook* may be a simple dish, but it symbolizes the creativity and innovation that Taiwanese cooks can muster up under difficult circumstances. Pork bones, bitter melons, simple river greens: they may seem like ugly ducklings to the average cook, but in the Taiwanese kitchen, they're transformed into true culinary swans. No wonder even prosperous Taiwanese still look with nostalgia and pride upon these comfort foods from uncomfortable times.

Take an inventory of a Taiwanese pantry and you'll find all the usual staples that mainland settlers brought over from their ancestral homes: soy sauce, rice wine, chile sauce flavored with garlic, and sesame oil. But then there are the local favorites too: Taiwanese-style preserved radishes, chiles, peanuts, black beans, and a type of Taiwanese basil known as "nine-story tower." In the skilled hands of a gifted Taiwanese cook, they add layers of complexity to the island's otherwise no-nonsense cuisine.

Taipei: An Undiscovered Culinary Paradise

With so many regional representatives of Chinese cuisine holding a culinary summit in Taiwan, it's little wonder that the restaurants of Taipei offer a grand panoramic buffet of China all within a few miles' radius. And while it's tough to beat a Taiwanese home-cook's knack with a wok or a clay pot, busy urban lifestyles are beginning to cut into the home kitchen's supremacy.

Interestingly enough, many notable Taipei chefs are specializing in the type of home-style food that is characteristically Taiwanese. Rustic-themed restaurants are making a comeback, but with a trendy twist. You can be a trendsetter by visiting quirky spots such as Black Brother Dog Restaurant (the name is Taiwanese slang for "a group of young hooligans"). Appropriately enough, it was started by five such "hooligans" who settled down enough to open a restaurant. They've furnished it with eclectically mismatched dinnerware and vintage chairs, benches, and tables.

Similar in their youthful, hip atmosphere are the city's brew houses, or *pejiu wus*—some of the most happening

Ma Zhu Temple on Taiwan's East Coast.

places to spend a fun evening with friends. Formal and quiet, they're not. To get the most out of the experience, wear your grubbies and be prepared to shout over noise at the bar. But they're great places for casual, home-style Taiwanese cooking and for flowing taps of Asian and international beers.

If you're looking for five-star dining, Taipei certainly has its fair share of elegance, too. Look to international hotels and well-established restaurants such as Green Leaf for the same kind of upscale food, polished service, and rarefied surroundings that you'd find in the finest restaurants anywhere in the world.

Yet what impressed me most about Taiwanese cuisine is what I found in the streets. In my book, night market food stalls and street hawkers are what make the Taiwanese dining experience truly unique. Drop by Huahsi Street, or the Shihlin night market in the northwest corner of Taipei, and take your pick among dozens of Chinese delicacies. For a decidedly Taiwanese treat, try a *jen ping*: a wheat-flour wrapper encasing bean sprouts, cabbage, mushrooms, pork, parsley, or perhaps a little of that "nine-story tower," topped with finely ground peanuts. They're eaten just like that—wrapped, but unfried, like a burrito—and they're out of this world. At less than two U.S. dollars each, you can't afford to miss them.

Bean curd in all its guises is so popular in Taiwan that they actually have a street named Tofu Street. Taiwanese particularly like it pressed and drained of its liquid until it reaches a meaty consistency—perfect for meat abstainers. Find a street stall that sells pressed bean curd simmered in broth with soy sauce and tea, and if that flavored broth also has some shell-on eggs bobbing in it—they're another Taiwanese street-snack favorite—you are in the presence of one of the island's classics! So follow your nose and drop by Taipei for a pleasant culinary surprise.

But if the travel bug is not biting, just grab this book and head into the kitchen. I collected recipes during my most recent visit to this microcosm of Chinese cuisine and culture, wheedling kitchen secrets from street-snack vendors, friends and relatives, and renowned chefs alike. The results await on the following pages; before long, "Made in Taiwan" will soon be replaced by "Made in My Kitchen."

Precious Pearly Rice Balls

The Hakkas are famous for their savory glutinous rice cakes. Traditionally they pack the insides of the rice cakes with red bean paste, pickled vegetables, or savory meats. My version of pearly rice balls are filled with ground pork, water chestnuts, and chunks of shrimp. Same great idea, with a different twist. **MAKES 6 TO 8 RICE BALLS, SERVES 4 TO 6**

$^3/_4$ **cup black glutinous rice**

$^3/_4$ **cup white glutinous rice**

Filling

$^3/_4$ **pound ground pork**

$^3/_4$ **pound raw shrimp, shelled, deveined, and coarsely chopped**

1 egg, lightly beaten

2 tablespoons chopped water chestnuts

1 tablespoon chopped Chinese chives

1 tablespoon soy sauce

2 teaspoons minced ginger

2 teaspoons cornstarch

$^1/_2$ **teaspoon salt**

$^1/_8$ **teaspoon white pepper**

1. In separate bowls, soak both kinds of glutinous rice in water to cover for 2 to 3 hours. Drain each rice separately and set aside.

2. Prepare a wok for steaming (see page 6). Spread black glutinous rice evenly over half of a heatproof plate; spread white glutinous rice on other half and steam until tender, about 20 minutes.

3. To make filling, in a medium bowl combine pork, shrimp, egg, water chestnuts, chives, soy sauce, ginger, cornstarch, salt, and white pepper; mix well. With wet hands, roll mixture into balls, using 1 heaping tablespoon for each. Roll half the balls in black glutinous rice, coating completely. Roll the remaining balls in white glutinous rice, coating completely. Arrange balls, without crowding, on a heatproof plate.

4. Prepare a wok for steaming (see page 6). Cover and steam balls over high heat about 25 minutes. Serve hot.

The Perfect Guest

In Taiwan, there's a lot more to Chinese cuisine than the four classics: Beijing, Shanghai, Cantonese, and Sichuan. Take Hakka cooking, for example. But don't take too much—leave some for me! While not exactly a household name in North America, the cuisine of these "sea gypsies," as they're often called, is popular throughout Asia. *Hakka* means "guest," and as their name indicates, Hakka people get around—they were among the first mainland Chinese to settle in Taiwan about a thousand years ago. Wherever they go, their scrumptious foods earn fans. These traditional farmers and fishermen are known for earthy dishes rich with seafood and produce. As far as I'm concerned, these guests can have cookovers as often as they'd like!

Bean Curd Seaweed Wraps

Although wrapped food has recently become all the rage in the West, Chinese have been serving food "wrap" style for centuries. Bean curd sheets make excellent wrappers for baby corn, mushrooms, and ham. Just tie them with a strand of seaweed. You can buy fresh or dried bean curd sheets at most Asian grocery stores. To rehydrate, soak in warm water until sheets become pliable. **MAKES 16 SEAWEED WRAPS, SERVES 6 TO 8**

16 dried black mushrooms
¹/₄ pound fresh bean curd sheet, cut into 16 (2 by 3-inch) pieces
8 drained canned baby corn, halved lengthwise
2 green onions, julienned
¹/₄ pound Chinese ham, julienned
1 sheet Japanese seaweed (nori), cut into 16 (1 by 5-inch) pieces
Vegetable oil, for deep-frying

Sauce

¹/₂ cup prepared teriyaki sauce
2 tablespoons chicken stock (see page 38)

1. Soak mushrooms in warm water to cover until softened, about 20 minutes; drain. Discard stems and slice caps.

2. Make each wrap: Place a piece of bean curd sheet on a work surface. Place a piece of baby corn, several slices of mushrooms, green onions, and ham on top. From long side, roll up into a cylinder and wrap with a seaweed strip; moisten ends with water and press to seal.

3. In a wok, heat oil for deep-frying to 375°. Add bean curd wraps and deep-fry until golden brown, 2 to 3 minutes. Drain on paper towels.

4. To make sauce, in a small saucepan combine teriyaki sauce and stock; stir and cook over medium heat until heated through.

5. Arrange wraps on a serving platter and serve with sauce on the side.

Serious Snacking

If your idea of the perfect snack is a bag of chips, you've never snacked in Taiwan. It may be a small island, but its snacking capacity stretches the imagination—and the stomach. People line up around the block for their share of local specialties, like giant steamed meat-filled dumplings that one family-run shop has served to hungry queues for four generations. And there are always *jungz,* a.k.a. Chinese tamales, a mass of sticky glutinous rice surrounding a rich filling of pork sausages, mushrooms, and preserved vegetables, all wrapped in a bamboo leaf. And don't forget the noodles. Taiwan is full of noodle shops, and my favorites serve *dan-tsu* noodles, rich with stewed pork. Take a seat on the squat benches and let the dim glow of the overhead lamps set the mood for this slurpy snack.

Crispy Squid Rings

You can find these delectable treats at sidewalk food stalls all over Taiwan. Sprinkled with salt, pepper, and five-spice powder—a popular way to season deep-fried seafood snacks—these rings are more popular than wedding rings. Well, almost. **SERVES 4**

3/4 **pound fresh baby squid, cleaned**

Marinade

2 teaspoons Chinese rice wine or dry sherry

1 teaspoon minced garlic

1/2 **teaspoon sugar**

1/4 **teaspoon salt**

1/8 **teaspoon white pepper**

Batter

1/2 **cup all-purpose flour**

1/3 **cup cornstarch**

1 egg yolk

3/4 **cup water**

1 tablespoon vegetable oil

1 teaspoon baking powder

Spiced Salt

1 tablespoon salt

1/2 **teaspoon sugar**

1/4 **teaspoon Chinese five-spice powder**

1/8 **teaspoon white pepper**

Vegetable oil, for deep-frying

Sliced red bell peppers or red jalapeño chiles, for garnish

1. Separate squid bodies from tentacles. Cut bodies into rings; leave tentacles whole.

2. To prepare marinade, in a medium bowl combine rice wine, garlic, sugar, salt, and white pepper. Add squid and stir to coat. Let stand for 10 minutes.

3. To prepare batter, in a medium bowl combine flour, cornstarch, egg yolk, water, oil, and baking powder. Whisk until smooth.

4. To prepare spiced salt, in a small bowl combine salt, sugar, five-spice, and white pepper. Mix and set aside.

5. In a wok, heat oil for deep-frying to 375°. In small batches, dip squid into the batter and, using a wire mesh basket, add carefully to the oil. Deep-fry until golden brown, 1 1/2 to 2 minutes. Remove and drain on paper towels. Repeat until all squid is cooked. Arrange squid on a serving platter. Sprinkle spiced salt over and garnish with sliced peppers or chiles.

Squid Pro Quo

Don't let cleaning squid scare you away from using it in recipes. Follow these steps and you'll have your squid ship-shape: Peel the see-through, speckled membrane from the squid's hollow, bullet-shaped hood. Then locate the clear, spiny shell inside it and gently tug the shell out. Holding the hood in one hand and the tentacles in the other, gently pull the tentacles to separate them from the hood. Rinse the tentacles and carefully remove the ink sack; discard or save it to use as a natural food coloring for pastas or sauces. Rinse out the inside of the hood. If using the tentacles, lay them upside down so they radiate outward, and squeeze them gently to pop out the hard structure known as the "beak." Now the squid is ready for whatever the chef has in store.

Cookie–Cutter Fish

Now here's a sneakily simple treat; these appetizers may look like elaborate edible miniature sculptures, but when you get down to the 1-2-3s of making them, they're incredibly simple. **SERVES 4**

¹/₂ pound skinless salmon fillet

8 large fresh shiitake mushrooms, stems discarded

8 slices Chinese eggplant, ¹/₂ inch thick

2 tablespoons vegetable oil

¹/₂ teaspoon salt

¹/₈ teaspoon white pepper

Sauce

2 tablespoons black bean sauce

1 teaspoon sesame oil

1 teaspoon rice vinegar

Vegetable oil, for deep-frying

8 slices taro root or sweet potato, ¹/₂ inch thick

Julienned green onion, for garnish

Plum sauce, for dipping

1. With a 1¹/₂-inch cookie cutter, cut 8 rounds each from salmon fillet, mushrooms, and eggplant slices. (Save the trimmings for later use in a soup.)

2. Place salmon, mushrooms, and eggplant in a medium bowl. Drizzle with oil, sprinkle with salt and white pepper, and turn to coat. Let stand for 10 minutes.

3. To make sauce, in a medium bowl combine black bean sauce, sesame oil, and rice vinegar. Mix well and set aside.

4. In a wok, heat oil for deep-frying to 375°. Add taro slices and deep-fry until golden brown, about 4 minutes. Remove and drain on paper towels.

5. Place a grill pan over medium-high heat until hot. Arrange salmon, mushrooms, and eggplant slices on pan; cook, turning once, until salmon is opaque and mushrooms and eggplant are tender, about 2 minutes on each side.

6. To form stacks: Layer slices of taro, eggplant, salmon, and mushroom. Arrange stacks, taro side down, on a serving platter and garnish with green onion. Place black bean sauce and plum sauce on the side for dipping.

Consulting the Taro

If you think the taro is only good for predicting the future, you're not playing with a full deck! I'm not talking about tarot *cards*, but taro root, a tuber with a rough, brownish exterior and grayish-purple, starchy flesh. Chinese cooks love its versatility and sweet, nutty flavor. Once you remove its hairy peel (wear rubber gloves to protect your skin from the raw root's irritating juices), treat taro the same way you would a potato: shred it, fry it, boil it, mash it, bake it. . . . Use it in your favorite potato recipes for a flavorful, colorful twist. Of course, you can make the opposite substitution—potato for taro—if taro is tough to find in your area. Use taro soon after you buy it; unlike potatoes, these tubers only last for two to three weeks when stored in a cool, dry place.

Soft Tofu in Green Leaves Soup

This elegant soup is fit for a formal banquet, with spinach that is puréed and then deep-fried, looking like a sea of little green leaves suspended in the soup. Add shrimp and tofu slices and you have a masterpiece in a bowl. **SERVES 4**

6 ounces spinach

2 large egg whites (1/4 cup)

1/2 teaspoon salt

1/8 teaspoon white pepper

1 (1-pound) package soft tofu, drained

Vegetable oil, for deep-frying

3 cups chicken stock (see page 38)

1 tablespoon soy sauce

1/2 teaspoon sesame oil

1/4 pound medium raw shrimp, shelled, deveined, and chopped

2 tablespoons minced carrot

2 tablespoons cornstarch dissolved in 3 tablespoons water

1. Wash spinach and remove coarse stems. Place spinach, egg whites, salt, and white pepper in food processor; purée until smooth. Set aside.

2. Cut tofu into thirds horizontally, then julienne into strips 1/4 inch thick. Carefully transfer to paper towels to drain thoroughly.

3. In a wok, heat oil for deep-frying to 375°. Deep-fry spinach purée for 1 to 2 minutes, stirring continuously. Remove with a fine mesh strainer and place into an ice water bath; let cool for 2 to 3 minutes. Drain on plate lined with paper towels and set aside.

4. In a medium saucepan, combine stock, soy sauce, and sesame oil; bring to a boil over medium-high heat. Add shrimp and carrot; cook for 1 to 2 minutes. Add cornstarch solution and stir until slightly thickened. Add spinach purée and mix well.

5. Ladle soup into a serving bowl; place tofu in the soup and serve.

What to Do with Soft Tofu?

If tofu is the workhorse of Chinese and Japanese kitchens, soft, or "silken," tofu is an especially graceful, elegant thoroughbred. Its smooth, silky texture and easy blendability allow it to play a number of roles that hardier, firm tofu just can't. For instance, if you're dairy-sensitive, blend soft tofu into smoothies as a replacement for yogurt or milk. It also makes a great nondairy thickener in sauces. I like to cut soft tofu into cubes and add them to soups for a pleasing textural contrast, and I even serve it on its own as a pudding-like dessert topped with fruit and light syrup. Just don't try to stir-fry or braise soft tofu, because the delicate curds will easily fall apart. Such tender tofu deserves a soft touch.

Tofu—ready for snacking.

Tofu shaping.

Tofu Street

Hollywood has the Walk of Fame, New York has Wall Street, and Paris has the Champs-Elysées. But I'd trade a stroll along any of these famous thoroughfares for a quick jaunt down Taiwan's Tofu Street. This is bean curd paradise, and a fitting tribute to Taiwan's love for the soybean in all its many guises. Where else can you find an entire street dedicated to the pursuit of tofu treats? And judging from the popularity of tender tofu dumplings, braised bean curd in spicy sauce, golden fried tofu, and dozens of other savory tofu dishes, some smart growth may be in Tofu Street's future. Next up: Tofu City! That's *my* idea of civic planning.

Tofu Street

Tofu Diamonds in Savory Jade Broth

Delicate tiles of tofu sandwiched with thin slices of ham, sprinkled with sesame seeds and pine nuts, and served atop spinach and broth, this dish is impressive yet simple to create. Traditionally made with Yunnan ham—a highly-flavored smoked ham from Southwest China—you can substitute easier-to-find Virginia ham. **SERVES 4**

1 (1-pound) package soft tofu, drained

8 thin slices ham

1/4 pound spinach, stems removed

1 teaspoon black sesame seeds, toasted

1 teaspoon white sesame seeds, toasted

1 tablespoon pine nuts, toasted

Broth

3/4 cup chicken stock (see page 38)

1 teaspoon sesame oil

1 teaspoon cornstarch

1 teaspoon sugar

1/4 teaspoon salt

1. Cut tofu in half horizontally to make 2 pieces, each about 1-inch thick. Cut each piece into 6 rectangles. Trim each rectangle into a diamond shape to obtain 12 pieces. Cut ham slices into the same-sized diamond shape. (Save trimmings for soup.)

2. To form stacks: Place a piece of tofu on a heatproof dish. Layer with a slice of ham, a second piece of tofu, a second slice of ham, and finish up with a third piece of tofu. Make 3 more stacks with the remaining tofu and ham.

3. Bring a pot of water to a boil. Add spinach and cook for 1 minute; drain. Wrap spinach in a clean towel and squeeze to extract excess liquid. Chop spinach and set aside.

4. Prepare a wok for steaming (see page 6). Steam tofu stacks over medium-low heat for 8 minutes.

5. To prepare broth, in a small saucepan combine stock, sesame oil, cornstarch, sugar, and salt. Bring to a boil over medium heat. Add spinach and stir; cook for 1 minute. With a wide spatula, transfer tofu stacks carefully to 4 individual bowls. Pour in the broth from the side of the bowl. Sprinkle with sesame seeds and pine nuts and serve.

Fish Fillet Soup

You'll have fewer lids to wash with this recipe. That's because you "cover" the soup bowls with the fish fillets instead! They not only save you from dishpan hands, they also season the broth and make a tasty treat themselves. **SERVES 4**

4 (¼-pound) firm white fish fillets, such as sea bass or red snapper,
    each about ¾ inch thick
4 baby bok choy, trimmed
4 medium raw shrimp, shelled and deveined
4 sea scallops
4 cups chicken stock (see page 38)
4 cilantro sprigs, for garnish

1. Butterfly fillets by cutting almost through, horizontally. Open fillets out like a book.

2. Divide bok choy among 4 individual heatproof soup bowls. Place a shrimp and scallop over each piece of bok choy.

3. Ladle stock into bowls until three-quarters full. Drape butterflied fillets over bowls.

4. Prepare a wok for steaming (see page 6). Place soup bowls in steamer, cover, and steam until fish turns opaque and broth is heated through, 6 minutes. Garnish with a sprig of cilantro and serve.

Golden Fried Fish Soup

I first tasted this delightful fried fish soup in the Tainan night market. The golden-coated, tender sweet fish creates a great textural contrast in the savory broth. Better eat it quick though, or the fish will get soggy. Put the fish into the broth right before serving so it will stay crispy longer. **SERVES 4**

Broth

4 cups chicken stock (see page 38)

1 tablespoon Chinese rice wine or dry sherry

2 teaspoons fish sauce

1/2 teaspoon sesame oil

1 carrot, roll-cut into 1/2-inch pieces

3 ounces daikon, roll-cut into 1/2-inch pieces

10 ounces firm white fish fillets, such as sea bass or red snapper, each about 1/2 inch thick

1/4 teaspoon salt

1/8 teaspoon white pepper

Batter

1/2 cup all-purpose flour

2 tablespoons cornstarch

1 pinch baking soda (optional)

1 egg yolk

2/3 cup ice water

Vegetable oil, for deep-frying

Watercress sprigs, for garnish

1. To prepare broth, in a medium saucepan combine stock, rice wine, fish sauce, and sesame oil. Bring to a boil over high heat. Add carrot and daikon; decrease heat and simmer until vegetables are tender, about 10 minutes. Keep hot.

2. Cut fish fillets into 2-inch pieces and sprinkle with salt and white pepper.

3. To prepare batter, in a medium bowl combine flour, cornstarch, baking soda, egg yolk, and ice water. Whisk until smooth.

4. In a wok, heat oil for deep-frying to 375°. In small batches, dip fish pieces in batter and add carefully to the oil. Deep-fry, turning once, until golden brown, about 3 minutes. Remove and drain on paper towels.

5. Ladle soup into individual bowls. Add fish to the bowls and garnish with watercress sprigs. Serve immediately.

No Small-fry Fish

Every time I visit Tainan's food markets and outdoor snack stalls, I discover a new specialty that quickly becomes my favorite. The problem is, I now have so many "favorites," that I can't decide where to eat first! If only all my decisions were this difficult. But even with a sea of eating options, I never fail to visit that heavenly spot in the Pao-an Market that's known for its crispy-fried fish soup. Crispy fish served in a flavorful broth may be a bit of a novelty, but after you bite through that light, crispy batter and sink your teeth into the sweet, tender flesh within, you'll quickly get used to this unique sensory experience. Just make sure not to linger too long between bites—no matter how fabulous this fish soup may be, it won't stay crispy for long.

Steamed Minced Meat in a Cup

Hail to the Chef

I still remember how nervous I was the first time I cooked for my mother—she's a tough one to please, and if the meal wasn't up to snuff, it would prove that all those years of watching her in the kitchen didn't teach me a darn thing. But if cooking for Mom is enough to make me cower, I can only imagine the buckets I'd sweat if I had to feed the president every night. I wondered how Chef Hua-jiu Cheung of Taipei's Lai Lai Sheraton Hotel rose to the challenge during his tenure as Taiwan's presidential chef. After seeing him in action, I chalk it up to good-old talent, creativity, and grace under fire. Even the pickiest of presidential palates can't argue with Chef Cheung's skillful interpretations of classic Chinese cuisine. I bet he could even make George Bush, Sr., a broccoli lover.

Although it originally hailed from the Hunan region of China, this soup is now the specialty of Chef Hua-jiu Cheung of the famous Lai Lai Sheraton in Taipei. In Chef Cheung's version, ground meat is mixed with water chestnuts and green onions, then whipped with chicken stock to produce a soft meat mixture that is spooned into the bottom of a cup, covered with more stock, and steamed. **SERVES 4**

Meat Mixture

³/₄ **pound ground chicken or pork**

4 water chestnuts, chopped

1 tablespoon chopped green onion or cilantro

¹/₂ **teaspoon salt**

¹/₈ **teaspoon white pepper**

¹/₂ **cup chicken stock (see page 38)**

3 tablespoons Chinese rice wine or dry sherry

1 tablespoon soy sauce

1 cup chicken stock (see page 38)

8 thin, circular slices carrot

1 teaspoon sesame oil, for garnish

8 cilantro leaves, for garnish

1. To prepare meat mixture, in a medium bowl combine ground meat, water chestnuts, green onion, salt, and white pepper; mix well. Add stock, wine, and soy sauce; whip by hand so that the mixture is aerated, and liquid is evenly incorporated.

2. Divide meat mixture equally between four 6-ounce custard cups; mound mixture slightly in the center. Pour ¹/₄ cup stock into each cup; place 2 slices carrot on top of each.

3. Prepare a wok for steaming (see page 6). Place cups in steamer, cover wok, and steam over high heat until filling is firm and no longer pink, about 20 minutes.

4. To serve, sprinkle each cup with ¹/₄ teaspoon sesame oil and 2 cilantro leaves.

Steamed Vegetable Rolls

A splash of rice wine can intensify the flavors of sauces, soups, and stir-fries, hence wine sauce is the perfect way to add a touch of elegance to steamed vegetable wraps. Serve this and you will be the toast of the town. **MAKES 12 ROLLS, SERVES 4 TO 6**

1 large carrot, peeled
1 small daikon, peeled
3 large fresh shiitake mushrooms, or 1 large portobella mushroom
3 Chinese chives, or 2 green onions
12 asparagus tips, about 3 inches long

Dipping Sauce

1 teaspoon grated ginger
1 tablespoon soy sauce
1 teaspoon rice vinegar
1 tablespoon Chinese rice wine

1. Cut carrot and daikon into 2-inch lengths. Slice lengthwise into paper-thin slices by hand or with mandoline. Cover with wet towels to prevent drying; set aside. Discard mushroom stems and thinly slice caps.

2. Bring a pot of water to a boil. Add chives and blanch for 15 seconds; drain. Place in an ice water bath; drain. Cut into 12 pieces, each about 4 inches long.

3. To make the rolls, layer a slice of carrot over a slice of daikon. Place asparagus tip and a few slices of mushroom over carrot. Roll up into a cylinder. Tie chive around cylinder. Prepare 5 more rolls with daikon as outer layer. Prepare remaining rolls with carrot as outer layer by layering a slice of daikon over carrot and placing filling over daikon.

4. To make the dipping sauce, in a small bowl combine ginger, soy sauce, rice vinegar, and rice wine. Mix well and set aside.

5. Prepare a wok for steaming (see page 6). Place rolls on a heatproof dish and place in steamer. Cover and steam for 3 to 5 minutes.

6. Transfer rolls to a serving plate; serve with dipping sauce on the side.

Garden of Eatin'

On the surface, Taiwan doesn't look like the perfect place to grow a farmers' market full of fruits and vegetables. It's small, and much of its limited space is covered by rocky mountain soils inhospitable to large-scale agriculture. But Mother Nature has tricks up her sleeve, and you can find them, in the form of a wide variety of edible native plants. Just do a little produce hunting in her very own pantry. Cooks in Taiwan know where to hit the jackpot for wildly-growing plants, herbs, and fruit-filled trees, and they know what to do with them back in the kitchen. From wild mushrooms and bitter greens to medicinal herbs and native roots, the homegrown riches of Taiwan's land are worth the search.

Room Full of Mushrooms

Make room for mushrooms. Discover the flavors of rich shiitake, delicate oyster, tender button, earthy crimini, meaty portobella, and velvety straw mushrooms. Which one is your favorite? Take it from me, they are all good. **SERVES 4**

3 (10-inch) wooden skewers, soaked in water

Baked Mushrooms

1 pound fresh mushrooms, such as shiitake, oyster, button, crimini, and portobella

1 tablespoon vegetable oil

1 cup sliced shallots

1 cup drained canned straw mushrooms

2 tablespoons unsalted butter, cubed

1 tablespoon oyster-flavored sauce

1 teaspoon sesame oil

Basting Sauce

2 tablespoons vegetable oil

1 tablespoon dark soy sauce

1 tablespoon Chinese rice wine or dry sherry

1 teaspoon sesame oil

¼ teaspoon sugar

Grilled Mushrooms

9 large fresh shiitake mushrooms, stems removed

Sesame oil, for brushing

1. Preheat oven to 400°. Prepare baked mushrooms: Wipe mushrooms with a clean towel to remove dirt. Place a wide frying pan over medium heat until hot. Add oil, swirling to coat sides. Add shallots and cook, stirring, until golden brown, 4 to 5 minutes. Add all the mushrooms, butter, oyster sauce, and sesame oil; toss well and pour into a foil-lined bowl. Gather the edges of foil; twist to secure. Place on a baking sheet and bake until mushrooms are tender, 18 to 20 minutes.

2. To prepare basting sauce, in a medium bowl combine oil, dark soy sauce, rice wine, sesame oil, and sugar; mix well.

3. To grill mushrooms, leave shiitake caps whole, marking a crisscross pattern on top of cap with a small paring knife. Thread 3 caps horizontally on each wooden skewer. Place a grill pan over high heat until hot. Brush the cooking surface with sesame oil. Decrease heat to medium. Brush both sides of mushrooms with basting sauce. Place mushrooms, cap sides down, in pan and grill until tender, about 2 minutes on each side.

4. To serve, unwrap baked mushrooms and place in center of a serving platter. Surround with grilled mushrooms.

Above: Taiwan's Jilong Beach.
Left: **Martin meeting a stonefaced maiden.**

Like a Rock

Remember when you were little, how you'd lie on the grass and see all sorts of shapes in the clouds? You'd see dog-shaped clouds, house-shaped clouds, and, if you lived near the Los Alamos labs, maybe even mushroom-shaped clouds. Well, on Taiwan's Jilong Beach, you don't need to have your head in the clouds to see nature's artistic side at play. Here, it's the rock formations that inspire the imagination. If you'd rather contemplate mushroom rocks than mushroom clouds, Jilong Beach can fill your bill. There are entire fields of giant mushroom-shaped rocks near the shore, and they always get me thinking about what to make for dinner.

91

Rock and Roll Seafood

I like my soup on the rocks. No, I'm not talking about serving your soup chilled; I mean real river rocks, as in stones. Serve this soup with rocks laid at the bottom of a clay pot. It makes for a unique visual piece at the dinner table—a real icebreaker for any dinner party. **SERVES 4**

Small river rocks, about 2 inches in diameter

Marinade

1 teaspoon sesame oil
1/2 teaspoon salt
1/8 teaspoon white pepper
2 slices ginger, julienned

1/2 pound large raw shrimp, deveined with shells intact
8 small hard-shell clams or mussels, cleaned
1 (1- to 1 1/2-pound) Dungeness or blue crab, cleaned and cut into 4 pieces

1/2 cup Chinese rice wine or dry sherry
1/3 cup chicken stock (see page 38)

1. Place river rocks in a large clay pot with 2 tablespoons water. Heat over medium heat about 10 to 12 minutes, until hot.

2. To prepare marinade, in medium bowl combine sesame oil, salt, white pepper, and ginger. Add seafood and stir to coat; let stand for 10 minutes.

3. Place seafood over hot rocks. Add rice wine and stock. Cover and cook over medium heat until clams open, 8 to 10 minutes. Serve in the clay pot.

Variation

1. Preheat oven to 350°. Place a large frying pan with lid in the oven to heat through, about 20 minutes.

2. Place marinated seafood in pan; add rice wine and stock. Cover pan and return to oven; bake until clams open, 8 to 10 minutes.

3. Transfer seafood to a serving dish. Pour broth over and serve.

Seafood on the Rocks

In the dog days of summer, you've probably bet that it's hot enough to fry an egg on the sidewalk. Well, long before there were any sidewalks, cooks in China took advantage of solar power, turning sun-baked river rocks and stones into the world's first griddle—albeit a lumpy one. You can try a variation of this ancient technique yourself: Heat a clay pot full of *clean* river rocks or stones (gather from the nearest river or a home and garden center—don't just use any rocks as some can explode!) in a 350° oven for about 30 minutes, and you've got a perfect cooking surface for everything from meat and vegetables to seafood. The method is a natural for camping trips, yet it also makes for a dramatic presentation (think steam and smoke) at dinner parties. I've always said that Chinese cooking "rocks," and this technique proves it!

Drunken Shrimp

This is not an AA meeting for shellfish—the two wines in this stir-fry give it a unique flavor. Use a little caution when you add the second wine, especially if you have a gas stove, or you will have the fire department over for dinner. **SERVES 4**

Spirited Alchemy

There's an old Chinese saying that, "In the company of good friends, a thousand cups of wine won't be enough." For winemakers in Taiwan, this is music to the ears. The island has brewed Chinese rice wine of the highest quality for a long time. Today's wine masters still employ many old-fashioned methods from their forefathers, turning out a nectar of the gods that's worthy of the name. Some say that the secret is in the local water, particularly around the village of Puli. That may be true, but you've got to give credit to the winemakers. Their craft combines art, science, and pure magic to produce magical results.

³/₄ **pound medium raw shrimp, deveined with shells intact**
¹/₃ **cup Chinese rice wine or dry sherry**
¹/₂ **teaspoon salt**
2 **tablespoons vegetable oil**
6 **green onions, cut into 3-inch lengths**
1 **tablespoon minced ginger**
¹/₄ **cup chicken stock (see page 38)**
¹/₄ **cup Fen Chiew (distilled spirit) or Vodka**

1. In a medium bowl, combine shrimp, rice wine, and salt; stir to coat. Let stand for 10 minutes; drain.

2. Place a frying pan over high heat until hot. Add oil, swirling to coat sides. Add shrimp and stir-fry for 2 minutes. Add green onions and ginger; stir-fry for 30 seconds. Add stock. Decrease heat to medium-low, cover, and cook for 3 minutes. Remove pan from heat; add wine (be careful; the wine may ignite). Return pan to high heat; let boil for 30 seconds.

3. Transfer to a serving bowl and serve.

Stir–Fried Calamari

Taiwan boasts some of the best seafood dishes anywhere. Dried and fresh squid give a tasty contrast when stir-fried with red bell peppers in a ginger-garlic wine sauce. If you cannot find dried squid at the grocery store, use fresh squid. **SERVES 4**

¼ pound dried squid

¾ teaspoon salt

1 pound fresh squid, cleaned

1 tablespoon cornstarch

Sauce

1 tablespoon Chinese rice wine or dry sherry

½ teaspoon sugar

½ teaspoon salt

⅛ teaspoon white pepper

Vegetable oil, for deep-frying

1 tablespoon minced garlic

1 tablespoon minced ginger

2 green onions, cut into 1½-inch lengths

½ red bell pepper, seeded and cut into ¾-inch diamond shapes

1 teaspoon cornstarch dissolved in 2 teaspoons water

1. Soak dried squid in hot water for 2 hours or overnight; drain. Pat dry with paper towels. Cut squid body in half lengthwise into 2 pieces. Lightly score each piece with crosshatching marks about ½ inch apart. Cut scored pieces into 1 by 2-inch pieces; place in a medium bowl with ¼ teaspoon of the salt; mix well.

2. Cut fresh squid in half lengthwise into 2 pieces. Lightly score each piece with crosshatching marks about ½ inch apart. Cut scored pieces into 1 by 2-inch pieces. Place fresh squid in a bowl and add cornstarch; mix well. Rinse with cold water and drain. Add remaining ½ teaspoon salt; mix well.

3. To prepare sauce, combine rice wine, sugar, salt, and white pepper in a small bowl. Mix and set aside.

4. In a wok, heat oil for deep-frying to 375°. Add dried squid and oil-blanch for 10 seconds. Remove and drain on paper towels.

5. Carefully drain all but 1 tablespoon oil from wok. Heat wok over high heat until hot. Swirl oil to coat sides. Add garlic and ginger; cook, stirring, until fragrant, about 10 seconds. Add fresh squid and stir-fry for 2 minutes. Add dried squid and cook for 2 minutes. Add green onions, bell pepper, and sauce; bring to a boil. Add cornstarch solution and cook, stirring, until sauce boils and thickens. Place onto a serving plate and serve hot.

All Dried Up

Now, don't get me wrong, I love squid. Stuffed, in casseroles, stir-fried, and especially deep-fried—you cook it, I'll eat it. But to put it bluntly, fresh, plain squid is pretty bland. Really, it's much more a textural experience than a flavorful an altogether different breed of cephalopod. It's eaten throughout Asia, both as an ingredient in stews and soups and as a slightly salty, undeniably chewy snack on its own. It's even called "Chinese chewing gum." Quick roasting over charcoal gives it a pungent, toasty and smoky flavor—a striking contrast to the mild flavor of its former self.

Poached Fish over Glass Noodles

The Taipei Food Festival

Where else but Taiwan are people such food fanatics that cooking has taken on the status of an Olympic competition? Every year, stellar chefs from hotel restaurants throughout Taiwan whip themselves into top condition for the Taipei Food Festival, organized by the Taiwan Tourism Bureau. Contestants compete individually and in teams to win championship titles and international recognition for their cutting-edge culinary creations. This is serious stuff, and it's watched with watering mouths and growling stomachs by culinary professionals and amateurs. And while it's fun just being a spectator, I can't help but get into the competitive spirit myself. No matter who takes home the medals, the real winners in these games are those of us who get to do the tasting.

The best part of this Taipei Food Festival dish is the glass noodles, or bean thread noodles, because they soak up all the wonderful flavors of the other ingredients. I can't tell you how many times I have gone right for the glass noodles, bypassing the other goodies. **SERVES 4**

2 ounces dried bean thread noodles

1 dried wood ear

Sauce

³/₄ cup Chinese rice wine or dry sherry

2 tablespoons soy sauce

1 tablespoon dark soy sauce

¹/₂ teaspoon chile garlic sauce

2 cups chicken stock (see page 38)

³/₄ pound firm white fish fillets with skin, such as sea bass or red snapper

1 tablespoon vegetable oil

1 teaspoon minced ginger

2 ounces lean ground pork

1 tablespoon chopped green onion

1¹/₂ teaspoons cornstarch dissolved in 1 tablespoon water

1. Soak bean thread noodles in warm water to cover until softened, about 5 minutes; drain.

2. Soak wood ear in warm water to cover until softened, about 20 minutes; drain. Trim off the hard stem and cut into 1-inch pieces.

3. To prepare sauce, in a medium bowl combine rice wine, soy sauces, and chile garlic sauce. Mix well and set aside.

4. In a medium saucepan bring stock to a boil over medium heat. Add wood ear and cook for 3 minutes. Add bean thread noodles; stir for 1 minute. With a mesh skimmer, transfer wood ear and bean thread noodles to a serving platter.

5. Return stock to a boil. Add fish, decrease heat to medium, and poach for 2 minutes. Remove with a slotted spoon and place over bean thread noodles.

6. Place a wok over high heat until hot. Add oil, swirling to coat sides. Add ginger and cook, stirring, until fragrant, about 10 seconds. Add pork and stir-fry for 2 minutes. Add sauce and bring to a boil. Add green onion and cornstarch solution; cook, stirring, until sauce boils and thickens. Pour sauce over fish and noodles, and serve.

Trout Dressed in Rice Paper

Frying fish in rice paper helps retain its natural moisture and flavor. So whenever I can, I wrap my fish in rice paper before I lower it into hot oil. This trout is served on a bed of Chinese greens with sliced shiitake mushrooms. **SERVES 4**

Sauce

1/4 cup chicken stock (see page 38)

2 tablespoons oyster-flavored sauce

1 tablespoon Chinese black vinegar

1 tablespoon sugar

2 teaspoons cornstarch

1 (8 1/2 -inch) dried rice paper wrapper

1 (1 1/2- to 2-pound) whole trout, cleaned

1/2 teaspoon salt

1/8 teaspoon white pepper

3 cilantro sprigs

1/2 pound Chinese broccoli, cut into 4-inch lengths

1/4 cup vegetable oil

1/2 green jalapeño chile, seeded and minced

1 tablespoon minced ginger

1 cup sliced fresh shiitake mushrooms, stems removed

1/4 cup chicken stock (see page 38)

1. To prepare sauce, in a medium saucepan combine stock, oyster sauce, black vinegar, sugar, and cornstarch; mix well and set aside.

2. Dip rice paper in warm water until pliable, about 10 seconds; drain. Lay rice paper flat on a work surface. Place fish in the center of wrapper, sprinkle with salt and pepper, and lay cilantro sprigs on top. Fold rice paper over fish to enclose.

3. Bring a large pot of water to a boil over high heat. Add Chinese broccoli and cook until slightly tender, 10 to 12 minutes. Remove with a slotted spoon and immediately place in ice water; drain again.

4. Heat oil in a wok over medium-high heat until hot. Shallow-fry fish until the paper is golden brown, 5 to 7 minutes on each side. Remove and drain on paper towels.

5. Remove all but 2 tablespoons oil from the wok. Add chile and ginger; cook, stirring, until fragrant, about 10 seconds. Add Chinese broccoli and mushrooms; stir-fry for 2 minutes. Add stock and bring to a boil. Decrease heat and simmer for 2 to 3 minutes. Transfer to a serving platter.

6. Bring sauce to a boil over medium-high heat. Cook, stirring, until sauce thickens. Place fish over vegetables. Pour sauce over fish and serve.

The Paper Chase

What's your idea of art? Painting? Calligraphy? Well, have you ever stopped to think that the paper itself may be a work of art? Such is the case with the handmade paper from the town of Puli. E-mail and computers may threaten to push paper out of the picture, but this traditional craft is not about to disappear any time soon. The paper makers still choose the proper fiber—bark, rice, wheat, or bamboo, for example—pound it to a pulp in local spring water (nothing else will do), and spread it onto antique wooden frames where it leisurely dries to a smooth, even mat. It may not be as convenient as a 128k Internet connection, but convenience isn't what these artisans are after. Longevity, on the other hand, is, and this ancient art form certainly has it.

Baked Lobster with Green Tea

Chef David Chang of the Hilton Hotel, Taipei, uses green tea powder to add a wonderfully delicate flavor contrast to succulent buttered lobster. This is a relative newcomer to the Taiwanese menu but, given the results, I am sure it won't take long to catch on. **SERVES 4**

1/2 pound dried Chinese wheat noodles

Sauce

1 tablespoon oyster-flavored sauce

2 teaspoons minced garlic

2 teaspoons minced cilantro

1/2 teaspoon green tea powder

2 live lobsters

2 teaspoons minced garlic

1 1/2 teaspoons green tea powder

1/2 teaspoon salt

1/4 cup unsalted butter, at room temperature

2 tablespoons grated Parmesan cheese

1 tablespoon vegetable oil

1. Preheat broiler with rack placed 4 to 5 inches from heating element.

2. Bring a large pot of water to a boil. Add noodles and cook according to package directions. Drain, rinse with cold water, and drain again.

3. To prepare sauce, in a medium bowl combine oyster sauce, garlic, cilantro, and green tea powder. Mix well and set aside.

4. Holding lobsters on their backs, kill instantly by inserting tip of sharp knife between tail section and body shell, cutting to sever spinal cord. Split lobsters lengthwise and remove stomach and intestinal vein. If there is any roe or eggs, remove them and discard. Crack claws. Place lobsters on a baking sheet. Combine garlic, green tea powder, and salt in a medium bowl and sprinkle over the flesh side. Spread butter on top and sprinkle with cheese.

5. Place lobsters under broiler and cook until golden brown, 15 to 20 minutes. Remove from oven.

6. Place a wok over high heat until hot. Add oil, swirling to coat sides. Add noodles and sauce. Cook for 1 minute; toss to coat. Transfer to a platter. Place lobsters over noodles and serve.

Above: **Tengren tea shop in Taipei.** *Opposite:* **Tea plantation in Sun Moon Lake area.**

The Green Tea Revolution

Worried about the oxidative damage that free radicals may do to your cells? Relax! Sit down with a healthy cup of green tea and you'll feel much better. And this is not a revolutionary claim: Studies have consistently shown that consuming green tea, which is packed with healthful antioxidants called polyphenols, can help boost the antioxidant concentration in your body. These antioxidants form a sort of defense system that protects the body from damage caused by harmful compounds known as free radicals, from sunlight and from pollution. Research has found that they play an active role in the prevention of heart disease and some cancers. As always, scientists need to do further research to learn how and to what extent green tea's polyphenols work their magic, but in the meantime, their being there is a good reason to pour yourself one more cup—and another, and another ...

All the Tea in Taiwan

Rich soil, a mild climate, and plenty of sunlight: these are the key ingredients to growing some of the world's best tea. And guess what—Taiwan's got all three in ample supply. In fact, conditions in parts of the island are so ripe for tea growing that plantations can produce up to six harvests per year! Expert tea pickers get up while the dew still drips off the tea leaves to scope out the youngest, most tender buds (you've got to pick them before they get too big) and pluck them by hand. Such tricky picking requires a sharp eye and nimble fingers, but pros can harvest pound upon pound of tea leaves each day. After picking, processors sort, clean, dry, and roast the leaves. If they're destined for black tea, they go through a final fermentation step; if green tea is the goal, the leaves are ready for the teapot.

101

Wok–Sautéed Chicken with Green Tea

At a tea banquet in the Chu Lung Recreation Resort, I was served many interesting dishes, all containing tea. That's where I got the idea for this chicken stir-fried with green tea leaves. The delicate tea definitely "leafs" its mark. **SERVES 4**

Marinade

2 tablespoons boiling water

¼ teaspoon green tea leaves

1 tablespoon soy sauce

1 teaspoon cornstarch

½ pound boneless, skinless chicken, cut into ½-inch pieces

Sauce

2 tablespoons soy sauce

2 teaspoons Chinese rice wine or dry sherry

1 teaspoon sesame oil

½ teaspoon sugar

2 tablespoons vegetable oil

1 teaspoon minced garlic

1 teaspoon minced ginger

½ cup diced English cucumber

½ cup diced onion

1 red bell pepper, seeded and cut into ½-inch diamond shapes

2 tablespoons chicken stock (see page 38)

1 teaspoon cornstarch dissolved in 2 teaspoons water

1. To prepare marinade, pour boiling water in a cup; add tea leaves and let stand for 5 minutes. Transfer 2 teaspoons of the green tea to a bowl (reserve remaining green tea and leaves) and add soy sauce and cornstarch. Add chicken and stir to coat. Let stand for 30 minutes.

2. To prepare sauce, in a small bowl combine soy sauce, rice wine, sesame oil, and sugar; mix well and set aside.

3. Place a wok over high heat until hot. Add oil, swirling to coat sides. Add garlic and ginger; cook, stirring, until fragrant, about 10 seconds. Add chicken and stir-fry for 1½ minutes. Remove chicken and set aside.

4. Return wok to high heat. Add cucumber, onion, and bell pepper; stir-fry for 1 minute. Add stock, reserved green tea and leaves; cover and cook for 1 minute. Return chicken to wok and add the sauce; bring to a boil. Add cornstarch solution and cook, stirring, until sauce boils and thickens.

5. Transfer to a serving plate and serve.

Smoked Chicken

At any Chinese banquet, you'll likely find a dish of smoked chicken gracing every table. Wok smoking adds a distinctive flavor to foods. The smoking ingredients for this dish— raw rice, tea leaves, brown sugar, and five-spice powder—are as easy to find as they are to use. **SERVES 4**

Poaching Liquid

3 cups water

1/4 cup Chinese rice wine or dry sherry

3 tablespoons dark soy sauce

2 tablespoons soy sauce

1 tablespoon sugar

2 teaspoons minced ginger

4 chicken legs

Smoking Mixture

2/3 cup oolong or black tea leaves

1/2 cup packed brown sugar

1/3 cup long-grain rice

1 teaspoon Chinese five-spice powder

Basting Sauce

1 tablespoon dark soy sauce

1 teaspoon sesame oil

1. To prepare poaching liquid, combine water, rice wine, soy sauces, sugar, and ginger in a pot. Bring to a boil over high heat. Add chicken; decrease heat and simmer for 15 minutes. Remove chicken; let cool and pat dry with paper towels.

2. Line the inside of a wok and its lid with aluminum foil.

3. To prepare the smoking mixture, in a small bowl combine tea leaves, brown sugar, rice, and five-spice. Spread evenly in the foil-lined wok. Set a round cake rack over smoking mixture. Place chicken on the rack.

4. To make basting sauce, in a small bowl combine dark soy sauce and sesame oil; mix well.

5. Heat wok, uncovered, over high heat until mixture begins to smoke. Cover wok with lid; decrease heat to medium-low and smoke for 7 to 10 minutes. Turn off heat and let stand for 3 minutes before removing lid.

6. Brush chicken with basting sauce. Transfer chicken to a platter and serve.

That's Smoking!

Smoking may not be such a good way to treat your lungs, but it's a great way to treat poultry and seafood. And in Chinese cuisine, where there's smoke, there's a delicious meal, thanks to the aromatic ingredients that infuse the food with their smoky flavors. When you plan to turn your kitchen into a Chinese smokehouse, bear in mind a few useful hints: open your windows and turn on your stove's exhaust fan; use an old wok if you have one; make sure to carefully line your wok with aluminum foil to protect it from the high heat of smoking; and leave a little extra foil hanging over the wok's edge with which to create a smoke-tight seal with the wok's lid. After all, you want to smoke the food, not your house!

Steamed Chicken and Fish Taiwan–Style

What a gem! This dish proves that not all of Taiwan's treasures are found in museums, some are in its kitchens too—like the Grand Hotel's kitchen. Chef Xiao-Hua Liu inspired this variation on his classic Steamed Fish Fillet with Mushroom and Ham. In this version, we lay noodles at the bottom of the bowl to soak up all the wonderful flavors from the other ingredients. **SERVES 4**

1/4 **pound dried rice noodles, about** 1/4 **inch wide**

2 **dried black mushrooms**

1 **(1-pound) package soft tofu, drained**

1/4 **pound firm white fish fillets, such as sea bass or red snapper**

1 **cup shredded napa cabbage**

1/3 **cup sliced bamboo shoots**

2 **green onions, cut into 2-inch pieces**

1/4 **cup julienned Chinese ham**

1 **carrot, thinly sliced and blanched, for garnish**

Soup

4 **cups chicken stock (see page 38)**

1 **tablespoon Chinese rice wine or dry sherry**

1 1/2 **teaspoons salt**

1/8 **teaspoon white pepper**

4 **chicken thighs**

1. Soak rice noodles in warm water to cover for 30 minutes; drain. Soak mushrooms in warm water to cover until softened, about 20 minutes; drain. Discard stems and slice caps.

2. Cut tofu in half horizontally to make 2 pieces, each about 3/4 inch thick. Cut each piece into quarters to make eight pieces. Cut fish fillet into 1-inch pieces.

3. To prepare soup, in a large pot combine stock, rice wine, salt, and white pepper. Bring to a boil. Add chicken; poach over medium-low heat until chicken is no longer pink, 25 to 30 minutes. Remove chicken and set aside.

4. Prepare a wok for steaming (see page 6). Arrange tofu in a 2-quart heatproof casserole dish. Lay rice noodles over tofu, and place napa cabbage on top. Arrange chicken in center of napa cabbage. Place mushrooms, bamboo shoots, green onions, fish, and ham around chicken. Pour soup into the dish, cover, and steam over high heat for 10 minutes.

5. Remove casserole from wok and garnish with sliced carrot.

Twice-Cooked Quail

I like cooking quails so much, I decided to cook these twice. They are marinated with soy sauce and shallow-fried until golden brown. Then I cook them again in a steam bath of chicken stock with ginger slices. When something is worth doing, it's worth doing twice. **SERVES 4 TO 6**

Marinade

1 tablespoon soy sauce
1 tablespoon dark soy sauce

6 quails, cleaned
Cornstarch, for dusting
5 napa cabbage leaves, trimmed
2 tablespoons salt
About 1/4 cup vegetable oil
6 cups chicken stock (see page 38)
10 slices ginger
2 tablespoons Chinese rice wine or dry sherry

1. To make marinade, in a medium bowl, mix soy sauce and dark soy sauce.

2. Cut quails in half lengthwise; add to the marinade and turn to coat. Let stand for 30 minutes; drain.

3. Dust quails with cornstarch; shake to remove excess. Let stand for 5 minutes.

4. Rinse cabbage with cold water. Sprinkle salt over cabbage leaves and let stand for 2 minutes. Rinse with cold water; squeeze to remove excess liquid. Cut cabbage into 1-inch pieces and set aside.

5. Place a wide frying pan over medium heat until hot. Add oil; when oil is hot, add quails. Pan-fry quails until golden brown, 3 to 4 minutes on each side. Remove and drain on paper towels.

6. Prepare a wok for steaming (see page 6). Place quails in a heatproof casserole. Add cabbage, stock, and ginger. Place casserole in steamer; cover and steam for 30 minutes. Add rice wine and steam for another 20 minutes.

You can't get away from the presence of water in Taiwan. After all, it is an island. No wonder the Taiwanese have a certain reverence for it as a giver and sustainer of life. It sustains life in the seas, in the soil, and atop the earth; it cleanses us outside and in; it's a medium for cooking foods; and without it the island would lose a profound source of natural beauty. When in Taiwan, I experienced firsthand that natural beauty, as well as water's rejuvenating effects, when I visited the island's natural mineral hot springs. Bathing in these waters was once a part of everyday rural life, but the springs are now international destinations with spas and hotels to accommodate health-seekers from all over the world. They may not be fountains of youth, but they sure made me feel like a kid in a play-pool again.

Taiwan–Style Hot Pot

This recipe is for a basic hot pot, but you can add your choice of fresh vegetables, meat, or seafood into the mix, and the choices are limitless. Nowadays, some Asian supermarkets have entire sections devoted solely to hot pot ingredients: pork meatballs, fish cakes, and seafood ready-prepared for immediate hot pot dipping, as well as chopsticks and baskets for helping to hold the cooked food. The more things you add to your pot, the better the broth—to be drunk at the end—will taste. **SERVES 4**

$1/4$ **pound lean boneless beef, thinly sliced**

$1/4$ **pound medium raw shrimp, shelled and deveined**

$1/4$ **pound fresh baby squid, cleaned, with hoods and tentacles separated**

$1/4$ **pound fresh mushrooms, such as white button, sliced**

$1/4$ **pound baby bok choy, cut into quarters**

Broth

2 cups chicken stock (see page 38)

2 cups water

$1/2$ **cup sweet cooking rice wine (mirin)**

$1/4$ **cup soy sauce**

Brown bean sauce, chile garlic sauce, oyster-flavored
    sauce, *sa cha* sauce, or sweet chile sauce, for dipping

1. Arrange beef, shrimp, squid, mushrooms, and bok choy separately on serving plates.

2. To prepare broth, in a medium saucepan, combine stock, water, rice wine, and soy sauce. Bring to a boil over high heat.

3. Place a set of dipping sauces in separate bowls in front of each diner.

4. Set a hot pot or electric wok in center of dining table. Arrange meat and vegetable plates around pot. Pour hot broth into hot pot and adjust heat so broth simmers gently.

5. Each diner selects his or her choice of ingredients from the meat and vegetable plates, and cooks them in hot broth to the desired doneness. Ingredients can then be dipped in the desired sauce before eating.

Moonlighting in Taiwan

Do you want to find out what life in Taiwan is really like? Do you want to blend in like a local? Well, for a taste of the real Taiwan, and a great night out to boot, visit one of the island's night markets. These gathering places are the ultimate hangouts for young and old; there's no better place to catch up on local gossip or find out the new flavor-of-the-month video game. And speaking of flavor, you can eat your way through China at these nightly food festivals. Feasting is the focus, but who can ignore the social fringe benefits of the whole scene? Strike up a conversation about stock prices while standing in line for noodle soup—the *real* "liquid asset" in any food-fan's portfolio. Or join a family as it huddles around a bubbling hot pot to do some domestic dunking. I promise you'll feel right at home.

Stir–Fried Beef and Mushrooms

This is a simple dish—cubes of tender flank steak stir-fried with portobella and oyster mushrooms—but certainly not a boring one. When you use two kinds of earthy mushrooms, there is no room for boredom. **SERVES 4**

6 ounces beef flank steak
1 portobella mushroom
3 large oyster mushrooms
2 tablespoons vegetable oil
$1/4$ cup chicken stock (see page 38)
$1/4$ cup diced red bell pepper
$1/4$ cup diced green bell pepper
$1/2$ cup sliced bamboo shoots
1 tablespoon *chu hou* paste

1. Cut flank steak into $3/4$-inch cubes. Remove stems from mushrooms and cut the caps into 1-inch pieces.

2. Place a wok over high heat until hot. Add oil, swirling to coat sides. Add beef and stir-fry for 1 to 2 minutes. Remove beef from wok.

3. Return wok to high heat. Add both kinds of mushrooms and stock; cover and cook until mushrooms are tender, 2 to 3 minutes. Add bell peppers and bamboo shoots; cook, stirring, for 30 seconds. Return beef to the wok and add *chu hou* paste; toss and cook until heated through.

4. Transfer to a platter and serve.

Flankly, My Dear ...

Whenever I prepare beef stir-fries, I always aim straight for the flank—the flank steak, that is. This cut of meat is finally getting the respect it deserves. Thanks to consumers' concerns about cooking with leaner cuts of beef, fit-and-trim flank steak has become the beef of choice for health-conscious meat eaters. And as for those naysayers who claim that flank is fibrous and tasteless, I just can't see—or taste—what their "beef" is all about. When thinly sliced across the grain—in other words, perpendicular to the direction the meat's fibers run—it's deliciously tender and conveniently quick-cooking, making it perfect for stir-fries. As for the flavor, it's all there. It's just the fat that isn't.

Northern–Style Braised Lamb

This wonderful dish is well worth a trip to the market to gather all the ingredients. The lamb shank is browned in a wok and braised in aromatic liquid until the meat is meltingly tender. Better make plenty of rice to soak up all the scrumptious sauce. **SERVES 4**

Marinade

2 tablespoons dark soy sauce

1 tablespoon Chinese rice wine or dry sherry

1 teaspoon Chinese five-spice powder

2 pounds lamb belly or shoulder

Braising Sauce

2$^1/_2$ cups chicken stock (see page 38)

$^1/_4$ cup rice vinegar

2 tablespoons sugar

1 tablespoon soy sauce

1 tablespoon dark soy sauce

1 tablespoon sweet chile sauce

2 star anise pods

1 dried tangerine peel, about 1$^1/_2$ inches square

3 tablespoons vegetable oil

6 cloves garlic

2 slices ginger

2 green onions, chopped

$^1/_4$ cup Chinese rice wine or dry sherry

Chopped fresh mint leaves, for garnish

1. To prepare marinade, in a large bowl, combine dark soy sauce, rice wine, and five-spice. Cut lamb into 2-inch pieces; add to marinade and stir to coat. Cover and refrigerate for 1 hour.

2. To prepare braising sauce, in a medium bowl, combine stock, vinegar, sugar, soy sauces, sweet chile sauce, star anise, and tangerine peel. Mix well and set aside.

3. Place a wok over high heat until hot. Add oil, swirling to coat sides. Add garlic, ginger, and green onions; cook, stirring, until fragrant, about 1 minute. Add lamb and cook until browned on all sides, about 2 minutes. Add rice wine and deglaze pan. Add braising sauce and bring to a boil. Decrease heat to low, cover, and cook for 1 hour.

4. Remove star anise. Transfer lamb to a platter; pour sauce over. Garnish with chopped mint.

The Collagen Connection

Do you ever wonder how tough old chunks of meat like shoulder, belly, and shank become so meltingly tender when cooked with a little liquid over low heat for hours? The answer lies in the connective tissue collagen, a protein that anchors muscle to bone, to other muscles, and to anything else that connects with it. These cuts are high in collagen (any cut near a joint is), and while collagen itself is tough and elastic, slow, steady heating in liquid turns it into gelatin—the same stuff that's in the dessert. And just like the dessert, the gelatin in meat has a smooth, tender texture that gives a voluptuous feel to the whole dish. So toss an old joint of meat into the pot with some flavorful liquid, let mild heat work its leisurely magic, and soon enough, what would've once given your jaw a real workout will have fallen off the bone with tenderness.

Braised Pigs' Feet with Mushrooms

Because they symbolize good fortune, it is traditional to eat pigs' feet for birthday celebrations. But who needs a birthday, this dish is reason enough to celebrate. **SERVES 4**

8 dried black mushrooms

Sauce

3 cups water

1½ tablespoons dark soy sauce

1 tablespoon Chinese rice wine or dry sherry

2 star anise pods

1 tablespoon sugar

½ teaspoon salt

⅛ teaspoon white pepper

2 pounds pigs' feet, cleaned

3 tablespoons dark soy sauce

Vegetable oil, for deep-frying

4 cloves garlic

4 slices ginger

Fried Rice

2 tablespoons vegetable oil

2 cups cooked long-grain rice

¼ cup diced carrot

¼ cup frozen sweet corn, thawed

¼ cup frozen peas, thawed

Salt

White pepper

1. Soak mushrooms in warm water to cover until softened, about 20 minutes; drain. Remove stems; cut caps in half and set aside.

2. To prepare sauce, in a medium bowl combine water, soy sauce, rice wine, star anise, sugar, salt, and pepper. Mix and set aside.

3. Bring a large pot of water to the boil. Add pigs' feet and blanch for 3 minutes; drain and place in a large bowl. Add the soy sauce and stir to coat. Let stand for 20 minutes; remove and pat dry with paper towels.

4. In a wok, heat oil for deep-frying to 375°. Add pigs' feet and deep-fry, turning occasionally, for 3 minutes. Remove and drain on paper towels.

5. Carefully drain all but 2 tablespoons oil from wok. Add garlic and ginger; cook, stirring until fragrant, about 1 minute. Add pigs' feet, mushrooms, and sauce; bring to a boil. Decrease heat to low, cover, and simmer until pigs' feet are tender, about 50 minutes. Continue to simmer, uncovered, 10 minutes more, until sauce is reduced by one-third. Discard star anise. Transfer to a serving platter.

6. To make fried rice, place clean wok over high heat until hot. Add oil, swirling to coat sides. Add rice, carrot, corn, and peas; stir-fry for 2½ minutes. Season with salt and white pepper to taste. Serve with pigs' feet.

Spicy Noodles with Vegetables

Noodles are a popular sidewalk food-stall treat. Rice noodles, clear noodles, fat noodles; in sweet, sour, or spicy sauce; stir-fried, deep-fried, steamed, or served in soup. The possibilities are endless. This dish of rice noodles stir-fried with baby bok choy in chile garlic sauce is one of my favorites. Now you can have the flavor of the street without leaving your own kitchen. **SERVES 4**

1/4 pound dried rice vermicelli

Sauce
1/3 cup chicken stock (see page 38)
1 tablespoon dark soy sauce
1 tablespoon sesame oil
1 1/2 teaspoons chile garlic sauce

2 tablespoons vegetable oil
1 tablespoon minced garlic
1 green onion, thinly sliced
2 cups julienned baby bok choy
1/2 cup julienned Virginia ham
1/4 cup Sichuan preserved vegetables (see page 58; optional), rinsed

1. Soak rice vermicelli in warm water to cover until softened, about 30 minutes; drain.

2. To prepare sauce, in a small bowl combine stock, soy sauce, sesame oil, and chile garlic sauce. Mix well and set aside.

3. Place a wok over high heat until hot. Add oil, swirling to coat sides. Add garlic and cook, stirring, until fragrant, about 10 seconds. Add green onion, bok choy, ham, and preserved vegetables; stir-fry for 2 minutes. Add rice vermicelli and sauce; stir to coat well and cook for 1 minute.

4. Place noodles on a platter and serve hot.

Long Live Noodles!

No Chinese birthday, wedding, anniversary, or New Year's celebration meal would be complete without one particular dish, and I'm not talking about cake. It's noodles. Why? Noodles in Chinese culture carry symbolic weight, and it's easy to figure out just what they symbolize. After all, what are noodles, if not long? And that length symbolizes length in one's life, marriage, job, and general prosperity. This makes noodles auspicious additions to any Chinese celebration. To take full advantage of noodles' symbolic connotations, be careful not to cut or break the noodles while preparing or eating them. To stay on the safe side, put manners aside and slurp each strand into your mouth in one piece. It's not only fun, it's good luck, too.

The Original Taiwan

Before mainland Chinese arrived on the scene about one thousand years ago, Taiwan was home to around ten major indigenous tribes, themselves migrants from the Malay Peninsula, Indonesia, and other parts of the South Pacific. They were the first to name the island *Taiwan,* which means "terraced bay." There are around three hundred thousand indigenous Taiwanese living on the island, and their culture adds an exciting dimension to Taiwan's ethnic mix. I got a taste of this mix when I visited a tribal village. Even though some people have assimilated into modern society, many of the original Taiwanese proudly maintain their traditions, customs, cuisines, languages, and ways of life as farmers and fishermen. Their close relationship to the earth and their heritage can teach us all a little something about the true meaning of conservation.

Above: Taiwan's traditions live on: Martin celebrates with local tribesmen.
Left: Local women weave traditional patterns into their cloth.

115

Sweet Wraps

Instead of thanking your favorite Mr. Postman, thank your favorite chef. These sweet packages are made with spring roll wrappers filled with sweet red bean paste, candied ginger, and dried fruit, then deep-fried for a crispy golden treat.

MAKES 20 WRAPS, SERVES 10 TO 12

Filling

$2/3$ **cup sweetened red bean paste**

$1/2$ **cup chopped mixed dried fruits, such as apricots, pears, peaches, and raisins**

$1/2$ **cup chopped toasted walnuts**

$1/4$ **cup finely chopped candied ginger**

2 teaspoons grated orange zest

2 teaspoons toasted sesame seeds

20 (6-inch) spring roll wrappers or dried rice paper wrappers

Vegetable oil, for deep-frying

Candied citrus peels or powdered sugar, for garnish

1. To prepare filling, in a medium bowl, combine red bean paste, dried fruit, walnuts, candied ginger, orange zest, and sesame seeds. Mix well and set aside.

2. Cut spring roll wrappers into 4- to 5-inch squares. If using rice paper, dip rice paper in warm water until pliable, about 10 seconds. Drain on a clean towel.

3. To make the wraps: Lay wrapper flat on a work surface. Place 1 tablespoon filling in center of wrapper. Roll up wrapper, turning in the sides so the filling is completely enclosed.

4. In a wok, heat oil for deep-frying to 375°. Deep-fry wraps in small batches and cook, turning occasionally, until golden brown, about 3 minutes total. Remove and drain on paper towels.

5. Arrange sweet wraps on a dessert platter. Garnish with candied citrus peels or dust with powdered sugar, and serve.

Sweets on the Side

What better garnish to serve with these delicate little bundles of sweet fruits and nuts than . . . more sweet fruits and nuts? Make glistening candied citrus peel by cooking short strips of orange, lemon, and lime peel (wash the fruit first) in a simple syrup of $1/4$ cup sugar melted in $1/2$ cup water. Cook until the peel is tender and translucent. Let the peel sit for a few minutes, and then remove it to dry on a cooling rack. For candied walnuts, over low heat dissolve 2 tablespoons of sugar in an equal amount of water and cook to a golden caramel, and then stir in $1/2$ cup of walnuts, coating them with the caramelized sugar. Immediately spread them on an oiled cookie sheet to cool, separating them with a fork. Alternatively, you can buy candied walnut halves at your grocery store. They are so delicious, they rarely last until I'm finished with a recipe.

Jasmine–Flavored Ice Cream

Instead of serving tea with your dessert, how about serving tea in your dessert? The delicate flavor of jasmine tea and the exotic taste of lychee fruit make this ice cream a great reason to skip tea time altogether! **SERVES 4**

4 cups heavy whipping cream
12 egg yolks
1 cup sugar
1 cup jasmine tea leaves
Chilled lychee, for garnish

1. Place cream in a saucepan; bring to a boil over medium heat. Remove from heat and set aside.

2. To make the custard, in a large bowl, whisk together egg yolks and sugar until thickened. Gradually add warm cream, whisking to combine. Transfer mixture to a saucepan and cook over medium-low heat, stirring, until custard has thickened enough to lightly coat a metal spoon. (Be careful not to boil custard or it will curdle.)

3. Pour custard into a medium bowl; add tea leaves and let stand for 30 minutes. Pour mixture through a fine sieve into a medium, clean bowl. Cover with plastic wrap and refrigerate until chilled.

4. In an electric or manual ice cream maker, freeze custard according to manufacturer's directions.

5. Serve ice cream garnished with lychee, or freeze in an airtight container for up to one month.

More Than Just a Cuppa

How do you take your tea? With sugar? Milk? A squirt of lemon? How about taking it in a big bowl with a spoon and sprinkles on top? Tea adds such a fabulous flavor to dishes and snacks that if you think of it as just a drink, you're putting a lid on its creative potential. Throughout Asia, tea's true talents flourish in such treats as Japanese-inspired green tea mochi candies, tea-flavored preserved plums, green tea pumpkin seeds, and tea oil. There are also New Year's cakes made with tea, tea-flavored lollipops, tea crackers, and tea-flavored ice cream—my idea of the perfect iced tea.

Tapioca Iced Tea

You can find this popular iced tea drink in coffee and tea bars all over Taiwan. Pearls of chewy tapioca are added to iced tea and milk to create a refreshing sweet treat. Serve this drink in a clear glass so you can get the visual experience of seeing tapioca pearls dancing around at the bottom of your cup. **SERVES 6**

About 4 cups water
3/4 cup large (1/4-inch) pearl tapioca
1/3 cup sugar

Milk Tea

4 cups water
4 jasmine or black tea bags
1/3 cup sugar
1/3 cup evaporated milk

Ice cubes

1. In a 2-quart pan combine 3 cups water, tapioca, and sugar. Place over medium heat and cook, stirring until sugar dissolves. Decrease heat to medium-low; cook, stirring occasionally, until tapioca becomes translucent, about 30 minutes. During cooking, add remaining 1 cup water, if needed, to maintain the same level of liquid in pan.

2. Drain tapioca through a sieve, rinse under cold water, and drain again.

3. While tapioca is cooking, prepare milk tea: In a nonreactive pan, heat water to boiling. Turn off heat, add tea bags, and let steep for 10 minutes. Remove tea bags. Add sugar; stir to dissolve. Stir in milk. Let mixture cool, then refrigerate until chilled.

4. To serve, place 2 or 3 ice cubes in each glass; add 1/3 cup tapioca and 1 cup milk tea.

Iced Tea You Can Really Sink Your Teeth Into

If you think iced tea is solely for sipping, chew on this: In Asia, iced tea just wouldn't be the same if it didn't require a little chewing, too. That's because Asian iced tea gets a lively textural boost from the addition of chewy tapioca pearls. They don't do much for the flavor, but boy do they make the iced-tea experience more "interactive." If you'd like to try this multisensory drink at home, follow these tips to maximize the masticating: Use the larger, chewier tapioca pearls—the ones that are roughly pea sized. If you can find them, go for the black tapioca pearls—they're chewier, too, which makes them a lot more fun. (And here's a secret: black "tapioca" pearls get their chew from a healthy dose of potato starch.) Finally, if you want to slurp your tapioca tea, find a big straw and slurp carefully, or you'll wind up swallowing a mouthful of these slippery spheres all at once.

Fermented Rice Pudding

On cold winter nights, curl up with a good book and a bowl of fermented rice pudding. This sticky rice dessert tastes sweet and slightly sour, just like the plum wine it is made with. You can find fermented rice, with its liquid, in most Asian markets.

SERVES 5

3 eggs, lightly beaten
1 1/2 cups whole milk
1/2 cup sugar
1 tablespoon liquid from fermented rice
1/3 cup cooked long-grain rice
Butter, at room temperature, for cups
1/2 cup raisins

Sauce

1 cup plum wine
3 tablespoons fermented rice
3 tablespoons plum sauce

1. Preheat oven to 325°. In a large bowl, whisk together eggs, milk, sugar, and liquid from fermented rice. Add cooked rice and mix well.

2. Butter five 6-ounce custard cups. Divide raisins among the cups and fill cups with rice mixture.

3. Place custard cups in a roasting pan; add boiling water until the water level reaches halfway up the sides of the cups. Carefully place pan in the oven. Bake until a knife inserted in center comes out clean, about 1 hour and 15 minutes. Add boiling water to pan as needed to maintain water level.

4. To make the sauce, in a small saucepan combine plum wine, fermented rice, and plum sauce. Bring to a boil over medium-high heat; stir and cook for 1 minute. Let cool.

5. Serve custard in cups or run a knife around edges and invert onto dessert plates; drizzle sauce on the side.

Scraping the Bottom of the Barrel

Sometimes, when you scrape the bottom of the barrel, you end up with unexpected buried treasures. Such is the case with fermented rice liquid, or rice wine lees. This is the flavorful, yeasty "juice" that's left at the bottom of a vat of fermenting rice after the finished wine is removed, and winemakers in China save it, along with some of the leftover fermented rice, to sell as another ingredient in the Chinese cooking arsenal. It turns up in Shanghai-style dishes and in Northern Chinese cooking, where it adds an eye-opening aroma to seafood. Desserts get an unforgettable flavor from rice wine lees, too. And for new mothers, tradition has it that there's no better way to restore energy after childbirth than with a little rice wine lees judiciously sprinkled throughout the meal.

THAILAND

THAILAND

Land of Color

WHEN I THINK OF THAILAND, I think of color: the saffron robes of Buddhist monks, the delicate pinks, blues, and golds in the costumes of traditional Thai folk dancers, the wildly colored flowers that make you wonder whether they're real or painted. And more than anything else, I see Thailand's vibrant produce markets, filled with a rainbow's spectrum of fruits, vegetables, and spices. From scorching red Thai chiles to deep indigo eggplants, the cuisine of Thailand is as colorful as an artist's canvas.

The two months I spent on my last visit to Thailand gave me ample time to absorb all the local color. But as my flight back to the States lifted off the runway and I waved my last good-bye, I knew I carried home a deep appreciation for the country's culture and its cuisine. I also learned that two months of exploration could barely scratch the surface of the mystery and beauty of this ancient kingdom.

When it comes to the people of Thailand, the veil of mystery is easy to lift. One of the first things that struck me soon after my landing in Bangkok was the natural graciousness of the Thai people. No matter where you go or whom you meet, someone is sure to greet you with a *"Sawadsee"* and a smile, and you don't need to be a VIP to get this kind of star treatment; just make eye contact with the people passing you on the street and you'll see a virtual sea of smiles. No wonder Thailand's resorts and hotels have gained an international reputation for top-notch hospitality.

The graciousness of the Thai people goes beyond friendliness and generosity. I call it a contagious sense of calm. In the midst of Bangkok's hustle and bustle, blaring horns and rushing crowds, and even when putting up with nosey culinary adventurers like me, my Thai friends have an uncanny ability to look inward—into their soul and into their culture—and find peace there. It wasn't long before I found that I, too, was able to grab onto some of that inner peace—a godsend when you're spending twenty-hour days filming a television show, traveling from town to town in sometimes pretty rustic conditions.

Seven Centuries of Unity and Diversity

Throughout its seven hundred–year history, Thailand has remained safely, peacefully independent. As the rest of Southeast Asia suffered the various indignities of foreign colonialism, Thailand continued to do its own bidding. Thailand has since created its own cultural amalgam out of the many different peoples who have settled there.

With Burma to the northwest, Laos and Cambodia to the east, and Malaysia to the south, the free exchange of ideas, costumes, languages, religions, crafts, and ways of life all added to the flavorful mix of Thai culture. Influence has come from beyond Thailand's immediate borders, too. Visitors from China, Vietnam, India, Indonesia, the Middle East, and, eventually, Europe also tossed their own herbs and spices into the developing Thai cultural curry.

Thai Regional Cuisines

Traveling from region to region in Thailand can feel like moving across continents and centuries. Languages change from village to village even though they are barely a few hundred miles apart. But nowhere do you notice that regional diversity more than in the country's kitchens, restaurants, and street vendors' stalls. And even though drawing regional lines is an arbitrary game at best, it helps the interested cook get a better handle on such a rich cuisine.

The North

Northern Thailand, with its green river valleys and remote villages hidden between craggy mountains, has existed in relative seclusion until recent years. The rail line didn't connect northern Thailand to the rest of the country until the 1920s. Due to its geographical isolation, the region hasn't lost its native language or culture to the temptations of the modern age.

Northern-style Thai cuisine naturally bears this air of the old-fashioned and familiar. Neighboring Laos and Burma also add distinctive flavors and colors to the North's culinary landscape. You can taste the cultural exchange in fragrant, souplike, Burmese-inspired curries, which are milder than typical Thai curries and are often studded with noodles and meats. The tangy flavors and bright colors of tamarind, turmeric, and ginger also carry a little of Burma's spirit into this part of Thailand. Laos tosses in its two cents with spicy red curries and surprisingly explosive yet addictive spice sauces and pastes spiked with chiles and tart lime.

Aside from these dishes, count on a Northern preference for sticky, glutinous rice, often rolled into balls and dipped in sauces, over long-grain rice; thinner, soupier curries without coconut milk; and homemade pork sausages that pop up in everything from stir-fries to steamed rice. And just as in the rest of Thailand, Northerners enjoy fresh, raw vegetables and salads. But like the region's curries, these salads are a bit more on the mild side—just like the natives, themselves!

Golden Temple, Chiang Mai.

The Northeast

Northeastern Thailand, which lies along the Laotian and Cambodian borders, makes a striking contrast to the lushness of the river-sliced, mountainous North. One could easily argue that of all Thailand's regions, the Northeast wound up with the shortest straw in the draw. It's a land of desert plains where extreme temperatures, unpredictable floods, and endless droughts sustain meager agriculture even in the best of times.

But a people as determined and clever as the northeastern Thais haven't for a minute let necessity keep them from inventing some show-stopping culinary delicacies. With meager gardens, pastures, and livestock, and without much access to the seas, simplicity wasn't so much

James Bond Island Rock, Phuket.

an option as a fact of life. Ingenious cooks turned the simple ingredients they did have into what are now some of the country's best-loved specialties.

Fiery chile is something of a mascot of the region's cooking, as well as a lifesaver for its cooks—when you need to add quick, inexpensive flavor to a dish, a little bit of chile goes a long way. Northeastern Thai cuisine is neck-in-neck with the South in the race for the spiciest fare in the land.

River fish curries, pungent dried and fermented freshwater fish specialties (an acquired taste, but it sure keeps well), and spicy green papaya salads called yam, all prove that the area's chefs don't need a wealth of culinary riches to get cooking. These regional treats have impressed many of Bangkok's internationally trained chefs—and this internationally traveled cook—enough to see this cuisine not as peasant food, but rather as another shining example of Thailand's culinary resourcefulness and creativity.

The South

Southern Thailand is the neck of land squeezed between the Gulf of Thailand in the east and the Indian Ocean in the west, stretching down to a narrow border with Malaysia. Even if you haven't been there, if you've seen a movie, a poster, or a postcard showing a palm-studded, sunny-skied heaven-on-earth in Technicolor shades of green and blue, you've seen southern Thailand.

During my stay there, I found my own little nugget of southern Thai paradise in the region's kitchens and on its dinner tables. The food of the South is as rich, tropical, and unique as the region. Many dishes show off the tropical fruits abundant in the region: pineapples, mangoes, papayas, tiny sweet bananas, and the local favorites, durians, pomelos, and jackfruits.

Coconut in its many guises stars here, proving as versatile an ingredient to Thai cooks as the soybean is to those in China. Coconut milk, grated and shredded coconut meat, and coconut oil are key players in innumerable dishes, and the sugar from the coconut palm adds that balance of sweetness that keeps Thai cuisine's heat and salt in check.

Since southern Thailand has long been a stopping point for sailors and traders from as far as India and England, it's turned the mixed bag of foreign delicacies into dishes all its own. Mussaman curry, an edible gift from Muslim visitors, is a rich coconut curry flavored with cardamom, cloves, cinnamon, and peanuts, a milder departure from many chile-laced Thai curries.

I indulged in seafood as much as I could when in the South. Truthfully, it isn't hard to go overboard—both at the table and on the fishing boat! Every creature of the sea is fair game here, from pomfret, grouper, and other marine fish to massive Phuket lobsters and prawns the size of my forearm. Whether steamed whole on banana leaves, barbecued with a marinade of chile and fish sauce, simmered in clay pots, or stirred into a smooth coconut curry, these swimming treasures—and those of us who love eating them—are in good hands with skillful southern chefs.

The Central Plains

The Central Plains of Thailand—a fertile region watered by the Chao Phraya River—are truly the heart of the country. The nation's rice bowl as well as its fruit orchard, the Central Plains feed not only Thailand, but also much of Southeast Asia. Here is where we find Bangkok, the ancestral home to the first Thai kingdom at Sukhothai. The Thai monarchy was born in this region, and the Buddhist faith first flourished here. Today, Bangkok is still the quintessential

Thai city with all the modern trappings of an international urban center, but one that blends ancient cultures with modern complexity.

The cuisine of Bangkok and the Central Plains is, in many ways, just as down to earth as the rest of the country's. The public markets are gathering places for people, produce, and wandering street vendors, whose offerings can really get your appetite going. Thai street food is a world apart, with snacks to grab on the run of a variety most unfamiliar to most Westerners. Choose from crispy crab cakes, Thai-style barbecued pork and chicken, steamed stuffed baby squid, sticky rice and sausages wrapped in banana leaves, and dozens of desserts that are bound to feature fresh fruit or coconut in one way or another. And that's just on the first block!

I can sum up my favorite street eats in three words: noodles, noodles, noodles! Rice, wheat, egg, or bean thread, stir-fried, in soups, or with curry—Bangkok's street vendors and cafes have just the noodle you're looking for. In fact, Thailand's national dish, *phad thai*, traces its humble beginnings back to Bangkok's markets and food stalls. This simple stir-fry of rice noodles, eggs, meats, and tofu, with a standard array of toppings combines all the elements of that uniquely appealing flavor blend that may just be the edible incarnation of Thailand itself.

Thailand Flavors

Thai food is a little like an orchestral performance, and the whole trick to conducting that perfect symphony of flavors lies, literally, in the balance. Thai cuisine incorporates ingredients and techniques from all over the map in such a way that the whole is greater than the sum of its parts. The cuisine may share regional ingredients with its neighbors; lemongrass, fish sauce, limes, palm sugar, coconut, and chiles are all Southeast Asian staples. But it combines the hot with the sweet and the sour with the salty so magically that the overall effect is just like the careful mingling of colored silk threads that become Thailand's jewel-toned silks—another one of this country's treasures.

Even if your closest contact with Thai culture is the *phad thai* you always order at your favorite Thai restaurant, you've already had a little taste of the basics you need to know to conjure up the tastes of Old Siam in your own kitchen. My advice: Just break it down to a simple four-part harmony. Do you remember learning about the "four basic tastes" when you were younger—sweet, sour, salty, and bitter? Well, just replace bitter with spicy, and you've got the tools for authentic Thai taste.

Martin helps local farmers maintain their rice paddies.

Of course, spicy heat is the poster child of Thai cooking, but no respectable Thai cook would think about making a meal that's nothing but spicy; they balance it with bright sour notes, mellow sweetness, and just enough saltiness to accentuate the other players.

The Building Blocks

How do Thai cooks do it? All mystical instincts aside, it's a mindful approach to ingredients that does the trick. For the spicy heat, every chile imaginable is right under your nose. Accentuating the heat with warmly spiced depth are coriander and cumin seeds, cinnamon, and cloves. Fresh ginger and galangal lend an icy spiciness that's tempered with a slight sweetness. Peppercorns—black, white, and green—also help heat things up.

For sweetness, there is palm sugar, with its rough, dark-brown crystals and slightly caramelized flavor. All sorts of fruits and fruit juices help hold up the sweet end of the scale, like tamarind pods, which yield a rich pulp that's both sweet and sour.

For tasty tartness, Thai cooks call upon regular and kaffir limes (the latter, most often used for their leaves). Hardly a dish makes it to the table without a squirt of refreshing lime juice. And one of my favorite herbs, lemongrass, has such an incomparable aroma and flavor that I can't find another ingredient that's a really acceptable substitute for it.

When it comes to salty flavor, the king in Thai kitchens is *nam pla,* Thai fish sauce. The way that this pungent liquid's flavor blends and mellows in combination with other members of the "supporting cast" proves that the balancing principles of Thai cuisine can work wonders. *Kapee,* a thick paste made from salted, fermented fish is another sea-based source of saltiness. Like fish sauce, it has the power to bowl you over on its own, but when cooked with other ingredients, it adds amazing depth and pleasing saltiness.

Even if you can't pigeonhole them into a sweet/sour/salty/spicy category, plenty of other herbs help make Thai dishes as stimulating and satisfying as they are. Fresh mint, plump bulbs of young garlic and shallots, cilantro (roots, stems, leaves, and all), countless varieties of basil, and the fragrant sword-shaped pandanus leaves all deserve applause in my book.

Putting It All Together

Two words take individual ingredients one step higher on the climb toward a truly balanced Thai meal: make paste! Spicy paste, that is. At the heart of almost every curry, dip, or sauce in the Thai repertoire, you'll find a simple paste that combines representative ingredients from each of the four categories (and then some) into a concentrated bullet of flavor.

You can buy spice pastes in cans and jars, but there's just nothing like a homemade spice paste that's bright and bursting with fresh flavors. Thai cooks pulverize their pastes into a homogenous blend using a mortar and pestle, adding water, coconut milk, or oil to really make it pasty. But if you prefer, you needn't work your elbows to the creaking point, thanks to blenders and food processors. I have to admit, though, that the rhythmic scraping and mixing in an old stone mortar somehow make the paste taste a bit more...truly Thai.

So now that you've got your paste made, choose the direction you'd like to take it. How about a walk down Curry Road? Obviously, curries are one of the most popular destinations for spice pastes. No Thai meal is complete without a curry (which is actually more a style of cooking than a specific dish in itself). And while you may be familiar with Indian curries based primarily on dry spices, the combination of herbs and fresh spices in Thai spice pastes lead to moister, soupier affairs—great for pouring over heaping mounds of jasmine rice.

Each of the four most familiar Thai curries seems particularly well-suited to certain suggested accompaniments. For example, red curries pair really well with beef, and you'll often find green curry—which, despite its refreshing color, is often hotter than red—with chicken. On the other hand, yellow curry and Mussaman curry wind up paired with beef and chicken almost equally. But truthfully, just let your tastebuds be your guide as to what to do with the curries you choose to make.

Suit Yourself

Before you plunge headlong into the book, let me say a word about recipes: I don't know of any Thai home cooks who religiously follow them to the eighth of a teaspoon when making their own special spice pastes. And don't forget about personal preferences either—sure, a properly prepared Thai meal will be both spicy and sour, but you may not like tongue-scorching heat as much as the next guy. If you'd rather shunt the paste more toward the sour end of the spectrum, go ahead and add more lemongrass or lime juice until it tastes balanced to you.

The recipes in this book are amalgams of what I've learned from "spice experts" in Thailand, and they're guaranteed to please when prepared as-is, but don't hesitate to make changes here and there when the fancy strikes. I bet the results will impress you just as much. Remember, it's time to explore!

Red Curry Paste

MAKES ⅓ CUP

13 small dried red chiles, seeds removed

1 tablespoon coriander seeds

1 teaspoon cumin seeds

2 tablespoons thinly sliced lemongrass (bottom 5 to 6 inches only)

¼ cup chopped shallots

1 tablespoon chopped galangal

1 tablespoon chopped garlic

1 tablespoon water

1 tablespoon vegetable oil

2 teaspoons chopped kaffir lime leaves

1 teaspoon shrimp paste

1. Soak chiles in warm water to cover until softened, about 20 minutes. Drain.

2. Place coriander and cumin seeds in a small frying pan over low heat; cook, shaking pan frequently, until fragrant, about 4 minutes. Place seeds in a spice grinder and grind into a powder.

3. In a blender, process chiles, ground seeds, lemongrass, shallots, galangal, garlic, water, oil, lime leaves, and shrimp paste until well blended.

4. Store airtight in the refrigerator for up to 3 weeks, or freeze for up to 4 months.

Green Curry Paste

MAKES ⅓ CUP

1 tablespoon coriander seeds

1 teaspoon cumin seeds

5 green or black peppercorns

2 tablespoons thinly sliced lemongrass (bottom 5 to 6 inches only)

10 fresh green Thai chiles, thinly sliced

¼ cup chopped shallots

1 tablespoon chopped garlic

1 tablespoon chopped galangal

1 teaspoon chopped kaffir lime leaves

1 teaspoon chopped cilantro roots or stems

2 tablespoons vegetable oil

2 tablespoons water

1 teaspoon shrimp paste

1. In a small frying pan over low heat, cook coriander seeds, cumin seeds, and peppercorns, shaking pan frequently, until fragrant, about 4 minutes. Place seeds in a spice grinder and grind into a powder.

2. In a blender, process ground seeds, lemongrass, chiles, shallots, garlic, galangal, lime leaves, cilantro, oil, water, and shrimp paste until smooth.

3. Store in the refrigerator for up to 3 weeks, or freeze for up to 4 months.

Prawns with Red Curry

Place 1 cup unsweetened coconut milk in a wok over medium heat for 30 seconds. Add 1 tablespoon red curry paste and slowly bring to a boil, stirring constantly, about 1 minute. Add 6 ounces shelled and deveined raw shrimp, and cook until they turn pink, 2 to 3 minutes. Add 2 tablespoons fish sauce and 3 tablespoons sugar; cook for 1 minute. Transfer to a serving bowl and serve.

Duck with Green Curry

Place ½ cup unsweetened coconut milk in a wok over medium heat for 30 seconds. Add 1 tablespoon green curry paste and bring slowly to a boil, stirring constantly, about 1 minute. Add another ½ cup coconut milk; bring to a boil. Add ¼ pound Thai or Asian eggplants cut into bite-size pieces and cook until slightly softened, about 3 minutes. Add 1 cup cooked duck meat, cut into bite-size pieces, 1 tablespoon fish sauce, and 1 tablespoon sugar; cook for 2 minutes. Transfer to a serving bowl and serve.

Chicken with Yellow Curry

Place 2/3 cup unsweetened coconut milk in a wok or saucepan over medium heat for 30 seconds. Add 1 tablespoon yellow curry paste and slowly bring to a boil, stirring constantly, about 1 minute. Add 6 ounces thinly sliced boneless, skinless chicken and cook until it is no longer pink, 3 to 5 minutes. Add 1 tablespoon fish sauce and 1 tablespoon sugar; cook for 1 minute more.

Beef with Massaman Curry

Place 3/4 cup unsweetened coconut milk in a wok or saucepan over medium heat for 30 seconds. Add 2 tablespoons Massaman curry paste and slowly bring to a boil, stirring constantly, about 1 minute. Add 1/2 cup thinly sliced red onion, stirring until slightly softened, about 1 minute. Add 6 ounces thinly sliced beef flank steak and cook, stirring until no longer pink, about 2 minutes. Add 3 tablespoons tamarind water, 1 tablespoon fish sauce, and 1 tablespoon sugar; cook for 2 minutes. Garnish with 1/4 cup pine nuts and serve.

Yellow Curry Paste

MAKES 1/3 CUP

2 small dried red chiles, seeds removed

1 teaspoon coriander seeds

1 teaspoon cumin seeds

2 tablespoons thinly sliced lemongrass (bottom 5 to 6 inches only)

1/4 cup chopped shallots

1 tablespoon chopped garlic

1 teaspoon chopped ginger

2 teaspoons curry powder

1 teaspoon shrimp paste

1. Soak chiles in warm water to cover until softened, about 20 minutes; drain.

2. Place coriander and cumin seeds in a small frying pan over low heat; cook, shaking pan frequently, until fragrant, about 4 minutes. Place seeds in a spice grinder and grind into a powder.

3. In a blender, process chiles, ground seeds, lemongrass, shallots, garlic, ginger, curry powder, and shrimp paste until smooth.

4. Store in the refrigerator for up to 3 weeks, or freeze for up to 4 months.

Massaman Curry Paste

MAKES 1/4 CUP

3 small dried red chiles, seeds removed

1 tablespoon coriander seeds

1 teaspoon cumin seeds

2 cloves

5 black peppercorns

2 tablespoons thinly sliced lemongrass (bottom 5 to 6 inches only)

2 tablespoons sliced shallot

2 cloves garlic

2 slices galangal, each the size of a quarter

1 teaspoon water

1 teaspoon shrimp paste

1. Soak chiles in warm water to cover until softened, about 20 minutes; drain.

2. Place coriander, cumin, cloves, and peppercorns in a small frying pan over low heat; cook, shaking pan frequently, until fragrant, 3 to 4 minutes. Place mixture in a spice grinder and grind into a powder.

3. In a blender, process chiles, ground spices, lemongrass, shallot, garlic, galangal, water, and shrimp paste until smooth.

4. Store in the refrigerator for up to 3 weeks, or freeze for up to 4 months.

Shrimp-Flavored Dip

A traditional accompaniment to this dipping sauce is banana blossom, an 8- to 10-inch pod with brownish red overlapping leaves. The exotic blossoms can be found in some Thai markets. Don't worry if you can't locate them; the dip is also delicious with raw or blanched vegetables—celery, bell peppers, cucumbers, and Chinese long beans would all work well. **MAKES 1/2 CUP**

Dipping Sauce

1 tablespoon dried shrimp
3 cloves garlic
5 fresh red Thai chiles
1 teaspoon shrimp paste
1/2 cup fresh lime juice
1 tablespoon sugar
Raw or blanched vegetable pieces, for dipping

Banana Blossom Accompaniment (optional)

1/2 cup unsweetened coconut milk
1 banana blossom, cut in half, blanched

1. To make dipping sauce, soak dried shrimp in warm water to cover until softened, about 20 minutes; drain.

2. In a blender or mortar and pestle, combine dried shrimp, garlic, chiles, and shrimp paste; process or pound until slightly smooth.

3. Add lime juice and sugar; mix well.

4. Serve as a dip with vegetables.

5. To make banana blossom accompaniment: In a small saucepan, heat coconut milk to simmering. Remove from heat and pour on top of banana blossom. Serve with dipping sauce.

Golden Siam

Thais take great pride in their seven centuries of self-rule. That rule began in the mid–thirteenth century when they built the capital city of Sukhothai. Sukhothai means "the dawn of happiness," and for over two hundred years of peace and prosperity, that dawn blossomed into a bright, sunny day. The art of this period that remains in the country's heartland is proof that, indeed, this was a time of great happiness. The Buddha icons, both here, in what remains of the old capital, and in the National Museum in Bangkok, carved in the unmistakably elegant Sukhothai style, beam with delicate smiles so blissful and tranquil, that you can almost imagine what it must have been like to live in that time of relative safety and freedom.

Sukhothai: Thailand's first capital, near Chiang Mai.

137

Grilled Fish Dip

Serve this piquant mixture with raw or blanched vegetables for dipping. Try pieces of jicama, celery, bell pepper, cucumber, and Chinese long beans—whatever looks fresh and inviting at the market. **MAKES ABOUT 1¹/₂ CUPS**

¹/₂ **pound catfish fillets**

Vegetable oil

4 fresh red Thai chiles, chopped

3 cloves garlic, grilled or dry-fried in a pan

2 shallots, grilled or dry-fried in a pan

2 tablespoons fresh lime juice

1 tablespoon fish sauce

¹/₂ **teaspoon shrimp paste**

1 teaspoon sugar

¹/₄ **teaspoon salt**

Raw or blanched vegetables pieces, for dipping

1. Heat a grill pan over medium-high heat until hot; brush lightly with oil. Place fish in pan and cook, turning once, until it turns opaque, 3 minutes on each side.

2. Flake fish into a bowl; set aside.

3. In a blender, process chiles, garlic, shallots, lime juice, fish sauce, shrimp paste, sugar, and salt until smooth.

4. In a bowl, combine blended mixture with flaked fish and mix well.

5. Serve as a dipping sauce for vegetables.

Spicy Peanut Dip

This dip, with its coconut milk, red curry, and peanut flavor accents, is a great foil for meat or chicken satays or for raw, blanched, or grilled vegetables, such as jicama, green beans, bell pepper, and cucumber. **MAKES ABOUT 1 CUP**

1/2 **cup coconut cream**
2 tablespoons red curry paste (see page 133)
1/2 **cup unsweetened coconut milk**
1 1/2 **tablespoons sugar**
1/2 **teaspoon fresh lime juice**
1 tablespoon peanut butter
1/4 **cup roasted peanuts, chopped**
Raw, blanched, or grilled vegetable pieces, or chicken or meat satay

1. For coconut cream: Open a can of unsweetened coconut milk (do not shake it first) and spoon the thick cream off the top.

2. Place coconut cream in a saucepan over medium heat until the oil surfaces, about 1 minute. Add curry paste and cook, stirring until fragrant, about 1 minute. Add coconut milk and cook for 1 minute. Decrease heat to medium-low; add sugar, lime juice, peanut butter, and peanuts. Simmer for 1 to 2 minutes.

3. Serve as a dipping sauce for vegetables or satay.

Minced Pork and Tomato Dip

You probably wouldn't think of including pork in a dip recipe—unless, of course, it's the pork that's doing the dipping. But Thai cooks are experts at harmonizing ingredients both standard and surprising, and this rich dip is one such example. Use it as you would any other dip and you'll wonder why you don't put pork in your dips more often. **SERVES 4**

3 medium tomatoes
1 tablespoon vegetable oil
$1/2$ cup finely chopped onion
2 tablespoons minced cilantro stems
1 tablespoon minced garlic
2 teaspoons minced fresh Thai chile
$1/2$ pound ground pork
$1/2$ cup unsweetened coconut milk
3 tablespoons fish sauce
2 tablespoons sugar
2 tablespoons chopped Thai or sweet basil leaves
$1/2$ teaspoon crushed green peppercorns
Raw, blanched, or grilled vegetables, for dipping

1. Core tomatoes. Cut into slices $1/4$ inch thick. Stack slices, a few at a time, and cut into strips $1/4$ inch wide. Cut across strips to make $1/4$-inch cubes. You should have $1^{1}/2$ cups. Set aside.

2. Place a wok over high heat until hot. Add oil, swirling to coat sides. Add onion, cilantro stems, garlic, and chile. Cook, stirring, for 1 minute. Add pork and cook until browned and crumbly, about 2 minutes.

3. Add coconut milk, fish sauce, sugar, basil, and peppercorns. Decrease heat and simmer for 5 minutes or until mixture thickens to the consistency of a dip.

4. Serve warm or at room temperature as a dipping sauce for vegetables.

Thai Fish Cakes with Cucumber Condiment

These curry-flavored fish cakes are made in the traditional Thai style, with chunks of white fish and chopped long beans. I am adding a contemporary touch with fresh cucumber salsa. To shape patties more easily, oil your hands first. This will prevent the fish cake mixture from sticking to them. **MAKES 12 CAKES, SERVES 4 TO 6**

Fish Cakes

1 pound firm white fish fillet, such as sea bass or halibut, minced

6 Chinese long beans, or 24 green beans, cut into 1/8-inch lengths

1/4 cup chopped cilantro leaves

3 kaffir lime leaves, finely minced

1 tablespoon red curry paste (see page 133)

1 egg, lightly beaten

1 teaspoon cornstarch

1 teaspoon sugar

1/4 teaspoon salt

Cucumber Condiment

1/4 cup thinly sliced English cucumber

1/4 cup rice vinegar

2 tablespoons sliced shallots

1 tablespoon cilantro leaves

1 1/2 teaspoons sugar

1/8 teaspoon salt

1/4 cup chopped roasted peanuts

Vegetable oil, for frying

1. To make fish cakes, in a bowl combine fish, beans, cilantro, lime leaves, curry paste, egg, cornstarch, granulated sugar, and salt; mix well with fingers. For each cake, roll 2 tablespoons of fish cake mixture into a ball. Flatten the balls to make 2-inch patties. Set aside.

2. To make cucumber condiment, in a bowl combine cucumber, vinegar, shallots, cilantro, sugar, and salt. Mix and set aside.

3. Place a wok or wide frying pan over medium-high heat. Add oil to a depth of 1/4 inch. When oil is hot, add fish patties, a few at a time. Pan-fry, turning once, until golden brown, 2 to 3 minutes. Lift out with a slotted spoon and drain on paper towels.

4. Just before serving, sprinkle chopped peanuts over cucumber condiment. Serve with fish cakes.

Khmer Master Builders

Wandering around the ancient Khmer ruins at Phimai gave me a true appreciation for the history of this magnificent civilization. For six hundred years, the Khmer kingdom, while firmly "anchored" in Angkor in present-day Cambodia, also built imposing stone temples *(wat)* throughout Southeast Asia. Skeletons of these architectural and symbolic marvels pepper the countryside (it's said that each temple aims to replicate the form of heaven on earth). Some are recently restored to near-former glory, but many more still await rediscovery under shrouds of moss and leaves. The ruins at Phimai are by far the best preserved, and many have compared them to the original Angkor Wat, one of the man-made wonders of Southeast Asia.

Diced Chicken and Shrimp in Egg Net

As an alternative to using bamboo skewers to make the egg net, use a tin can with many little holes punched into the bottom. Or if you just want the taste without the hassle, make a thin pancake out of the batter to wrap around the filling. How's that for elegance with ease? **MAKES 10 TO 12 NETS, SERVES 4 TO 6**

Egg Net

1 package 8- to 12-inch-long bamboo
   skewers (about 100 per packet)

Vegetable oil, for coating pan

6 eggs, lightly beaten

Filling

1 tablespoon coriander seeds

1 tablespoon green peppercorns

2 cloves garlic

2 tablespoons vegetable oil

$1/2$ pound ground or minced chicken

$1/4$ cup chopped onion

$1/4$ pound medium raw shrimp, shelled,
   deveined, and finely chopped

2 tablespoons sugar

1 tablespoon fish sauce

$1/3$ cup chopped roasted peanuts

2 fresh red Thai chiles, thinly sliced

$1/3$ cup chopped cilantro leaves

1. To make the egg net: Secure all the bamboo skewers with rubber bands to make a skewer brush. Place a 9-inch frying pan over low heat. Dip a paper towel in oil, then wipe towel over pan to lightly coat with oil. Working close to the pan, dip bamboo brush in beaten eggs. Quickly drizzle eggs over pan, crisscrossing to make a net. Cook until eggs are set, about 1 minute; transfer carefully to a plate. Repeat to make 9 to 11 more egg nets.

2. To make the filling: With a mortar and pestle, pound coriander seeds, green peppercorns, and garlic into a fine paste.

3. Place a wok over high heat until hot. Add oil, swirling to coat sides. Add garlic-spice paste and stir-fry until fragrant, about 30 seconds. Add chicken and onion; stir-fry for 2 minutes.

4. Add shrimp, sugar, and fish sauce; stir-fry for 1 minute. Add peanuts, chiles, and cilantro; stir-fry for 30 seconds.

5. To serve, place 2 tablespoons of filling in the center of each egg net and wrap net around filling like an envelope.

Smelling Fishy

Every time I open a bottle of *nam pla*, the fish sauce that's as important to Thai cuisine as soy sauce is to Chinese cuisine, my eyes go wide and my nose goes *whoa!* This stuff doesn't smell like roses. But what do you expect from the sun-ripened liquid extract of small, fermented fish? If that description scares you, it needn't. Believe me, Thai cooking wouldn't be half as exciting without pungent *nam pla*. Let's just say that you'll notice fish sauce less by its presence than by its absence: Combined with other ingredients, it blends into the background to lend its flavor to the sweet-sour-salty-spicy taste balance that characterizes Thai cuisine.

Meatballs on Skewers

More than a shopper's haven, the night markets of Thailand are also a food lover's paradise. There is so much to see and so much to eat. The perfect food is something that allows you to walk around and eat at the same time. I have the ultimate suggestion—meatballs on skewers. These Thai-style beef meatballs are so good they might stop you dead in your tracks! **SERVES 6**

6 (8-inch) bamboo skewers

Glazing Sauce

2 tablespoons *char siu* sauce

2 tablespoons water

1 teaspoon chile garlic sauce

Meatballs

²/₃ pound ground beef

¹/₂ cup finely chopped cilantro leaves

2 tablespoons finely chopped shallots

1 teaspoon minced garlic

1 teaspoon minced ginger

¹/₂ teaspoon minced fresh Thai chile

1 tablespoon oyster-flavored sauce

2 teaspoons soy sauce

2 teaspoons fish sauce

2 teaspoons sesame oil

2 teaspoons palm sugar or brown sugar

2 teaspoons cornstarch

1 teaspoon coarsely ground green or black peppercorns

1 small green bell pepper, seeded and cut into 1-inch squares

1 small red bell pepper, seeded and cut into 1-inch squares

1. Soak skewers in water for at least 15 minutes.

2. To make glazing sauce, in a bowl combine *char siu* sauce, water, and chile garlic sauce. Mix and set aside.

3. To make meatballs, in a large bowl combine ground beef, cilantro, shallots, garlic, ginger, chile, oyster sauce, soy sauce, fish sauce, sesame oil, palm sugar, cornstarch, and peppercorns. Knead with your hands to mix thoroughly. Roll into 18 meatballs, using a rounded tablespoon of meat mixture for each.

4. Preheat oven to 350°. Thread 3 meatballs on each skewer, threading squares of green and red bell pepper between each meatball. Place skewers in a shallow baking pan.

5. Bake meatballs for 10 minutes. Reset oven to broil. Brush meatballs with glazing sauce. Set pan about 3 inches from heat source. Broil for about 2 minutes on each side. Serve.

Pick a Pack of Peppercorns

Mention pepper and Thailand in the same sentence, and most people would conjure up images of great balls of fire: Thai chiles. But did you know that today Thailand is the world's foremost producer of black and white peppercorns, the dried, unripe fruit of the tropical *Piper nigrum* tree? (Green peppercorns, also popular in Thailand and Southeast Asia, are unripe seeds of *P. nigrum* pickled in brine.) In fact, common peppercorns took the credit for most of Thai cuisine's bite long before Western traders brought chiles to Thailand. In exchange for those chiles, the Thais contributed their native peppercorns to the world's growing spice trade, so it turned out to be a fair exchange—and a hot one.

Cucumbers Stuffed with Beef and Shrimp

I can't claim anything close to the talent of the world-famous professional Thai vegetable and fruit carvers, but when preparing the cucumbers for this dish, I feel like an accomplished amateur—and so can you! **MAKES 10 CUCUMBER CUPS, SERVES 4 TO 6**

Filling

2 ounces ground beef

2 ounces raw shrimp, shelled, deveined, and finely chopped

1 tablespoon green onion, chopped

1 tablespoon fish sauce

1/2 fresh Thai chile, minced

1/2 teaspoon sugar

1/8 teaspoon white pepper

2 cucumbers, cut crosswise into 1 1/2-inch lengths

2 tablespoons cornstarch

1/4 cup sweet chile sauce

1. Preheat oven to 350°.

2. To make filling, in a bowl combine ground beef, shrimp, green onion, fish sauce, chile, sugar, and white pepper.

3. Hollow out seeds from cucumber, leaving a cylinder. Dust the inside of each cucumber piece with cornstarch, and stuff with 1 tablespoon of the filling. Place upright, in a shallow baking pan. Bake, uncovered, until filling is firm, 18 to 20 minutes.

4. Serve with sweet chile sauce.

Visual Culinary Arts

If you are invited to an elaborate Thai banquet and come upon a stunning flower arrangement in intricately carved vases on the table, inform your eyes that they are actually feasting on the handiwork of a different kind of culinary artist: a Thai vegetable and fruit carver. They have been perfecting their awesome sculpting skills since the days when Palace Cuisine was the height of Thai dining. With a little knife and a lot of dexterity, aesthetic sense, and patience, the artists improve upon Mother Nature's handiwork, turning mangoes, melons, chiles, and ginger into sculptures that look far too good to eat.

Savory Cups

Assembling your own appetizer is great fun. Pick and choose from the various condiments in each cup. Spoon them onto a lettuce leaf, drizzle with sweet seafood sauce—and munch away! **SERVES 4**

Sauce

1 tablespoon dried shrimp
2 tablespoons vegetable oil
3 tablespoons minced shallots
1 tablespoon shrimp paste
2 teaspoons fish sauce
1 cup palm sugar or brown sugar
¹/₂ cup water

2 Belgian endives, or 1 head butter lettuce

Condiments

¹/₄ cup shredded coconut flakes, toasted
¹/₄ cup diced whole lime (¹/₄-inch cubes)
¹/₃ cup chopped roasted peanuts
1 tablespoon minced ginger

1. To make sauce, soak dried shrimp in warm water to cover until softened, about 20 minutes. Drain and coarsely chop. Place a saucepan over high heat until hot. Add oil, swirling to coat sides. Add shallots and stir-fry until slightly softened, about 1 minute. Decrease heat to medium; add shrimp, shrimp paste, fish sauce, palm sugar, and water; cook for about 2 minutes. Remove from heat and let cool to room temperature.

2. Separate endive leaves; wash, drain, and chill.

3. Place condiments in separate dishes.

4. To serve, spoon a little of each condiment in an endive leaf. Drizzle a little sauce over each serving.

Crispy Seafood Parcels

My favorite part of eating these little parcels is the sound they make when I bite down—crunch. The parcels are made of bean curd sheets deep-fried to a delightful crisp. Their interiors are studded with emerald green garlic chives and cilantro.

MAKES 12 ROLLS, SERVES 4 TO 6

4 (5 by 15-inch) dried bean curd sheets

Filling

3 cloves garlic, chopped

1 tablespoon chopped cilantro leaves

1 cup cooked shelled crabmeat, flaked

1/2 cup cooked shelled shrimp, chopped

1 tablespoon chopped garlic chives

1 tablespoon cornstarch

1/2 teaspoon sugar

1/2 teaspoon salt

1/8 teaspoon white pepper

1 tablespoon vegetable oil

2 tablespoons flour mixed with 1 tablespoon water

24 garlic chives or green onion tops, blanched (optional)

Vegetable oil, for deep-frying

1/4 cup sweet chile sauce

1. Soak bean curd sheets in warm water to cover until softened, about 15 minutes; drain and cut each sheet into three 5-inch squares.

2. To make filling, with a mortar and pestle, pound garlic and cilantro into a paste. Place in a bowl and add crabmeat, shrimp, garlic chives, cornstarch, sugar, salt, white pepper, and oil; mix well and set aside.

3. To make each roll: Place a bean curd square on work surface with 1 corner facing you. Place 2 rounded tablespoons of filling across wrapper slightly above the corner. Fold corner over the filling, then roll over once. Fold in left and right sides, brush sides and top of triangle with flour paste, then roll up completely to enclose filling. Tie each roll with 2 blanched chives.

4. In a wok, heat oil for deep-frying to 350°. Deep-fry rolls, a few at a time, turning once, until golden brown, about 1 1/2 minutes on each side; drain on paper towels. Serve warm with sweet chile sauce.

Haute Couture of the Higher Order

Thailand's national treasure, the Emerald Buddha, resides in the Phra Kaew Temple within the walls of the Grand Palace in Bangkok. Not just any religious relic, this Buddha image has a wardrobe befitting its stature: at the turn of the nineteenth century, King Rama I began the fashion trend by outfitting the icon in duds appropriate to each season. During the hot, dry months, it wears a diamond-studded gold tunic, while another golden robe, this time flecked with blue, is *à la mode* for the rainy season. And when King Rama III came to power, he added a third garment to the collection, specifically for the cool months, made of enamel-covered solid gold. To this day, Thailand's king still sees that the Emerald Buddha is decked out in the right finery at the beginning of each new season.

Son-in-Law Eggs

While in Thailand, I attended a Thai wedding full of wonderful traditions and, of course, delicious food. One of the dishes served during the banquet was son-in-law eggs. Now that I have the recipe, I can serve this to my mother-in-law at our next family get-together. **SERVES 6**

2 fresh red Thai chiles
6 large eggs
2 tablespoons vegetable oil
1/2 medium onion, thinly sliced tip to tip
1/4 cup water
2 tablespoons tamarind water (see page 189)
1 tablespoon fish sauce
2 teaspoons palm sugar or brown sugar
1 teaspoon cornstarch dissolved in 2 teaspoons water
2 tablespoons crispy fried onion (see page 164), for garnish

1. Julienne 1 chile; thinly slice the other. Set aside.

2. Place eggs in a large pan and cover with cold water. Bring to a simmer over medium heat, then cook for 12 minutes; drain. Rinse eggs with cold water until cool enough to handle; remove shells.

2. Place a wok over high heat until hot. Add oil, swirling to coat sides. Add eggs and decrease heat to medium. Cook, turning occasionally, until eggs are blistered and golden brown, about 3 minutes. Remove eggs and drain on paper towels.

3. Return wok to medium-high heat; add sliced onion and stir-fry until soft, 1 to 2 minutes. Add julienned chile and stir-fry for 30 seconds. Decrease heat to medium; add water, tamarind water, fish sauce, and palm sugar. Bring to a boil. Add the eggs; cover and braise for 2 minutes. Add cornstarch solution and cook until sauce is slightly thickened.

4. Place eggs on a serving plate and pour sauce over. Garnish with crispy fried onion and sliced chile.

Egg on Your Face

Listen up, all you misbehaving husbands! A plate of son-in-law eggs is *not* what you want your mother-in-law to serve the next time she has you and your wife over for dinner. One story behind this cautionary recipe says that if you regularly come home from a "late night at the office" smelling like a combination of beer hall and French perfume, your mother-in-law will make you these unwelcome treats to let you know that she's on your tail. The lesson: Shape up, or have your own "son-in-law eggs" similarly handed to you on a platter. Do you need any more convincing?

Seafood in Golden Cups

Stairway to the Heavens

Sitting loftily three thousand feet up the face of Suthep Mountain is Wat Prathat Doi Suthep, Chiang Mai's most famous temple. And even though I had to climb three hundred-plus steps, following the gilt-encrusted *naga,* or "serpentine," staircase, to get to the top, it was well worth the hike. Legend says that an elephant carrying a Buddha relic was charged with finding the most auspicious site on which to build the relic's temple; wherever the beast stopped, the monks would break ground. Not content to stay in the lowlands, the elephant kept climbing—and climbing—and the monks made good on their word. As a result, visitors not only get a bird's-eye view from the temple, but they get quite a workout as well.

After visiting the golden temple Wat Prathat Doi Suthep in Chiang Mai, I feasted on seafood-filled golden cups back at the Regent Hotel. This adapted recipe uses egg roll wrappers shaped in a muffin pan and baked until golden for the cups. **SERVES 6**

Vegetable oil spray
6 egg roll wrappers

Filling

2 tablespoons vegetable oil
2 tablespoons minced garlic
¹/₄ pound medium raw shrimp, shelled, deveined, and diced
2 ounces bay scallops, diced
2 tablespoons finely chopped lemongrass (bottom 5 to 6 inches only)
2 tablespoons finely chopped green onion
1 tablespoon deep-fried garlic (see page 164)
1 teaspoon minced cilantro stems
2 tablespoons chicken stock (see page 38)
1 tablespoon fish sauce
2 teaspoons tamarind water (see page 189)
¹/₂ teaspoon sugar
4 teaspoons coarsely ground green peppercorns
Pinch of white pepper

1. Lightly coat each cup of a standard-sized muffin pan with vegetable oil spray. Loosely fit an egg roll wrapper into each cup; wrapper edges will extend beyond top of cup. Lightly coat each wrapper with vegetable oil spray.

2. Preheat oven to 375°. Bake wrapper cases until edges of shells are golden brown, 6 to 7 minutes. Let shells cool.

3. To make filling, place a wok over high heat until hot. Add oil, swirling to coat sides. Add minced garlic and stir-fry until golden, about 30 seconds. Add shrimp and scallops; stir-fry for 1 minute. Add lemongrass, green onion, deep-fried garlic, cilantro, stock, fish sauce, tamarind water, sugar, peppercorns, and white pepper; cook for 2 minutes. Filling should be juicy but not wet. Let mixture cool.

4. Spoon filling into pastry cups just before serving.

Meatballs Wrapped in Noodles

Innovative Thai chefs are always creating new dishes. Meatballs are traditional and familiar to everyone, but use them to encase quail eggs, and wrap them with strands of noodles, and you've got a new twist on an old dish. The balls are deep-fried, creating a crunchy noodle shell. Quail eggs can be found in most Asian grocery stores and in some specialty food stores. **MAKES 16 MEATBALLS, SERVES 4 TO 6**

1 pound thin fresh Chinese egg noodles
3 cloves garlic, minced
1/4 cup chopped cilantro stems
3/4 pound ground pork
1 egg, lightly beaten
3/4 teaspoon salt
1/8 teaspoon white pepper
16 hard-cooked and shelled quail eggs
Vegetable oil, for deep-frying
Sweet chile sauce, for dipping

1. Rinse noodles under cold water 3 times. Drain thoroughly and set aside in long strands.

2. With a mortar and pestle, pound garlic and cilantro stems into a fine paste.

3. Place paste in a bowl with pork, egg, salt, and white pepper; mix well. Wrap meat mixture around quail eggs. Divide noodles into 16 equal portions. Wind 1 portion of noodles around each egg-filled meatball, until it is completely covered; press noodles to form a tight wrap.

4. In a wok, heat oil for deep-frying to 350°. Deep-fry wrapped eggs, a few at a time, turning occasionally, until golden brown, about 5 minutes. Remove with a slotted spoon and drain on paper towels.

5. Serve with sweet chile sauce for dipping.

Land of Abundance

"In the water there are fish; in the fields there is rice. The faces of the people shine bright." So said King Ramkhamhaeng the Great, the first king of Sukhothai, in A.D. 1292. And so say the Thai people today. If there's anything that characterizes Thai life, it's abundance: abundance of peace; of natural resources; of the goodwill and courtesy of the ever-smiling Thais; of fresh, flavorful, ingredients; and of the culinary ingenuity that turns those earthly treasures into Thailand's mouthwatering foods. Over its long, independent history, Thailand has turned back all foreign invaders. Meanwhile, its cuisine is quickly conquering the world.

Golden Corn Cakes

When they give you lemons, you make lemonade; when they give you corn, you make golden corn cakes; it's that simple. The natural sweetness from the kernels of corn makes these cakes simply delicious. **MAKES 6 CAKES, SERVES 3 TO 6**

3 ears corn on the cob, or 2 cups drained canned,
    or thawed, frozen, corn kernels

3 eggs

3 tablespoons cornstarch

1/2 teaspoon salt

1/8 teaspoon white pepper

2 tablespoons chopped green onions

2 teaspoons minced garlic

Vegetable oil, for frying

1. With a sharp knife or cleaver, remove kernels from the cobs to make 2 cups.

2. In a bowl, beat eggs lightly. Whisk in cornstarch, salt, and white pepper. Add corn, onions, and garlic; mix well.

3. Place a wok or wide frying pan over medium-high heat. Add oil to a depth of 1/4 inch. When oil is hot, drop batter into pan in 1/4-cup portions. Cook uncovered, turning once, until golden brown, about 2 minutes per side. Lift out with a slotted spoon and drain on paper towels. Serve hot.

The Kernel of Ingenuity

Rice is the staple grain in most of Thailand, but in the northern hills where growing conditions aren't exactly optimal for rice, local tribal villagers, like the Ahka, Yao, Meo, and Lahu peoples, grow anything they can. Thanks to trade with the West, Thailand's northern hills now sustain plentiful crops of sweet, bright yellow corn. From the corn, northern Thai cooks make corn cakes—and curries with golden corn, and kernel-studded soups, and even surprising desserts such as corn custards and puddings. They're all so good! But don't get me wrong: I still miss rice, but barely.

Thai Hot and Sour Chicken Soup

Mention hot and sour soup, and you're likely reminded of your neighborhood Chinese restaurant. Well, the Chinese are not the only ones who mix hot and sour flavors in a soup. The Thais have their own version, using lemongrass, lime, and seasonings. They typically serve the soup with the seasonings left in, but if you prefer, strain it before serving. **SERVES 4**

A Cultural Retreat

Visiting The Rose Garden Country Resort and Cultural Center in Nakorn Pathom is like taking a crash course—a very concentrated crash course—in Thailand's colorful culture. The resort stages demonstrations of traditional arts ranging from silk-weaving, fruit-carving, and floral arrangement to regional dancing, elephant training, and even kickboxing, and guests are encouraged to join in. I soaked up some culinary culture with Chef Wanwipa, who shared his recipe for traditional Thai hot and sour soup. As a bonus, some of the beautiful local dancers glided through the resort's gardens, in a creative sort of dance, to bring us the freshest ingredients available. It's Thai hospitality at its best.

³/₄ **pound boneless, skinless chicken breast**

4 cups chicken stock (see page 38)

2 stalks lemongrass (bottom 5 to 6 inches only),
  cut into thirds and lightly crushed

1 or 2 small fresh chiles, lightly crushed

3 kaffir lime leaves, torn into pieces

3 slices galangal, lightly crushed

¹/₂ **teaspoon crushed dried red chiles**

1 small tomato, cut into ¹/₂**-inch cubes**

3 tablespoons fish sauce

1 teaspoon sugar

¹/₂ **cup drained canned straw mushrooms**

4¹/₂ **tablespoons fresh lime juice**

¹/₄ **cup lightly packed Thai or sweet basil leaves**

¹/₄ **cup lightly packed cilantro leaves, for garnish**

1. Cut chicken into ¹/₂-inch cubes.

2. In a 3-quart pan, combine stock with lemongrass, chiles, lime leaves, galangal, and crushed red chiles. Bring to a boil; decrease heat, cover, and simmer for 20 minutes. Strain stock, if desired, and discard seasonings (Thai style is not to strain broth). Return to pan. Add chicken, tomato, fish sauce, and sugar; simmer for 10 minutes. Add mushrooms and cook for 3 minutes. Add lime juice and basil; cook for 1 minute.

3. To serve, ladle soup into bowls and sprinkle with cilantro.

Northern Thai Beef Noodle Soup

I'd bet that most of you were brought up on chicken noodle soup. Well, let me introduce you to its Thai beef noodle cousin. Tender pieces of flank steak and chewy egg noodles are added to a spicy stock with coconut milk. **SERVES 4**

Spice Paste

4 fresh Thai chiles, coarsely chopped

1 tablespoon chopped shallots

2 slices ginger, each the size of a quarter

1 teaspoon coriander seeds

1/2 teaspoon turmeric powder

Vegetable oil, for deep-frying

2 ounces plus 10 ounces dried Chinese egg noodles

2 cups unsweetened coconut milk

2 cups water

1/2 pound beef flank steak, thinly sliced across the grain

2 1/2 tablespoons fish sauce

2 tablespoons soy sauce

2 tablespoons thinly sliced shallots

1/4 cup sliced pickled mustard greens

1 tablespoon crushed dried red chiles

2 baby bok choy, blanched, cut in half lengthwise

1. To make spice paste, in a small pan, combine chiles, shallots, ginger, coriander seeds, and turmeric powder; cook over low heat, stirring constantly, until fragrant, 8 to 10 minutes. With a mortar and pestle, pound into a fine paste.

2. In a wok, heat oil for deep-frying to 320°. Deep-fry 2 ounces of the noodles until lightly browned and crisp, about 2 minutes; drain on paper towels and set aside.

3. In a large pot of boiling water, cook the remaining 10 ounces of noodles according to package directions. Drain, rinse, and drain again.

4. Combine 1 cup of the coconut milk with 1 cup of the water in a 3-quart pot; bring to a boil over high heat. Add spice paste and cook for 1 minute. Add beef, fish sauce, and soy sauce; cook for 2 minutes. Add the remaining 1 cup coconut milk and 1 cup water; bring to a boil. Decrease heat and simmer for 2 minutes.

5. To serve, place boiled noodles in 4 large soup bowls. Ladle soup over noodles. Top with shallots, pickled mustard greens, dried chiles, and bok choy. Garnish with deep-fried noodles.

Old Chiang Mai

To get to the center of Old Chiang Mai, I swam sixty feet of moats and scaled the ancient stone walls that surround this seven-hundred-year-old city. Nah, I did it the sensible way, walked across a bridge and through one of its gates, and saved myself a few hundred calories in the process. Strolling around Chiang Mai, I could feel a great sense of connection to the Old City—a living museum of the Lanna Kingdom. Maybe that's because its planners oriented each of its walls to line up cosmologically with the cardinal points of the compass, and to symbolize the celestial mountains and seas. At the city's center, the Wat Sadoe Muang (Temple of the Navel of the City) used to stand with a pillar that linked Old Chiang Mai to heaven. And even though neither structure has survived, I could still feel the spirit that they bequeathed to the Old City.

Rice and Ginger Soup

Rice and ginger are common crops grown by the native hill tribes in Thailand, so it's easy to see how a combination of the two could make a delicious soup. This soup is often eaten at breakfast accompanied by fresh fruit such as papaya. **SERVES 2 TO 4**

Local Rice Makes Good

Thailand and jasmine rice: They're now as linked as Silicon Valley and computer chips. But it wasn't always that way. Not too long ago, jasmine rice only grew in the central Thai village of Bang Klar. It didn't find too many fans in other parts of the country because prevailing tastes preferred a firmer grain than the relatively soft jasmine. But in the early '70s, when Thailand searched for a variety of rice to export, it found that jasmine rice flourished in the country's rice-growing regions. As production of fragrant, enticingly floral jasmine rice increased, so did the Thai people's fondness for it. Now, just the aroma of the long white grains will carry my mind back to the rice harvest of Thailand.

Garlic in Oil

$1/4$ cup vegetable oil

7 cloves garlic, minced

$1/3$ cup julienned young ginger

2 to 3 ribs Chinese celery, cut into $3/4$-inch lengths

4 fresh Thai chiles, thinly sliced

$1/2$ cup chopped cilantro leaves

4 cups chicken stock (see page 38)

$3/4$ pound boneless, skinless chicken breast, thinly sliced

1 tablespoon fish sauce

1 tablespoon soy sauce

$1/8$ teaspoon white pepper

2 cups cooked rice

1 green onion, thinly sliced, for garnish

1. To make garlic in oil: Place oil in a small pan over medium-high heat. Add garlic, stirring frequently until golden brown, about 2 minutes. Immediately remove from heat and pour oil and garlic into a heatproof bowl.

2. Place a 2-quart pan over high heat until hot. Add 2 tablespoons of the garlic oil, swirling to coat sides. Add ginger, celery, chiles, and cilantro; stir-fry until fragrant, about 30 seconds.

3. Add stock and bring to a boil. Add chicken and cook, stirring until no longer pink, about 2 minutes. Season with fish sauce, soy sauce, and white pepper.

4. Add cooked rice; decrease heat to medium and cook for 2 minutes.

5. Ladle rice soup into individual bowls. Serve with 1 teaspoon garlic oil on each serving as a condiment (save remaining garlic oil for other uses). Garnish with green onion.

Thai Rice Soup

Breakfast in Thailand wouldn't be breakfast without rice soup. The soup is already seasoned with wonderful spices, but if you would like, accompany the soup with crispy fried shallots (see page 164), store-bought sesame fish snacks, or anything crunchy.
SERVES 2 TO 4

Sauce

¹/₄ **cup distilled white vinegar**
2 fresh Thai chiles, thinly sliced

4 cups water
2 tablespoons shredded ginger
1 tablespoon thinly sliced lemongrass (bottom 5 to 6 inches only)
1¹/₂ teaspoons salt
1 teaspoon sugar
1¹/₂ cups cooked rice
³/₄ **pound firm white fish fillets, such as sea bass or halibut, sliced into thin strips**
2 green onions, thinly sliced

1. To make sauce, in a bowl combine vinegar and chiles. Set aside.

2. Place water in a 3-quart saucepan; bring to a boil. Add ginger, lemongrass, salt, and sugar; cook for 1 minute. Add rice; cook for 1 minute.

3. Add fish; decrease heat to medium-low and simmer for 2 minutes. Stir in green onions. Serve with sauce.

Rice and Shine

Wheaties may be the "Breakfast of Champions" on this side of the pond, but the Thais wake up each morning to a big steaming bowl of rice soup. It is one of the most popular ways to break the fast all over Asia, and the Thai version has a texture and list of condiments that ensure no one will ever mistake it for the Chinese *jook* of my childhood (see recipe on page 62). Lemongrass and vinegar will make you pucker first thing in the morning, a pinch of sugar for sweetness, maybe a splash of fish sauce for saltiness, and—of course—fresh spicy chiles to make its Thai pedigree official. How's that for a balanced meal?

Green Papaya Salad with Shrimp

Here, the union of succulent shrimp and crunchy green papaya fruit creates salad bliss. The lime chunks prevent the papaya from browning. If you find them to be too sour, I suggest serving lime wedges on the side. You can squeeze your own juice to taste. Green papaya can be found in most Asian grocery stores. Yellow papaya is not a good substitute, because the texture is too soft. **SERVES 4 TO 6**

¹/₄ cup dried shrimp

2 small dried red chiles

6 cloves garlic

1 firm green papaya (about 2 pounds)

Dressing

¹/₄ cup fish sauce

3 tablespoons tamarind water (see page 189)

3 tablespoons palm sugar or brown sugar

2 tablespoons fresh lime juice

1 cup shredded napa cabbage

³/₄ pound shelled cooked shrimp

¹/₂ cup diced lime with peel

1. In separate bowls, soak dried shrimp and chiles in warm water to cover until softened, about 20 minutes; drain. With a mortar and pestle, pound dried shrimp into a rough paste; remove and set aside. Place garlic and chiles in mortar and pound until finely crushed; set aside.

2. Peel papaya. With a Japanese-style or regular shredder, cut into long, thin shreds. Place in mortar and crush slightly.

3. To make dressing, in a small pan, combine fish sauce, tamarind water, and palm sugar. Bring dressing to a boil over high heat. Remove from heat to cool. Stir in lime juice.

4. In a bowl, combine dried shrimp, chile-garlic mixture, and papaya; mix well.

5. Place papaya mixture over cabbage in a serving bowl. Arrange shrimp on top and drizzle dressing over. Serve with diced lime.

Lean, Green Papaya Machine

On a hot summer day, nothing beats digging a spoon into a soft, juicy, golden yellow papaya. But the larger, firm, green variety sold in Asian grocery stores, and increasingly in Western markets, has its charms, too. Don't expect dessert-intensity sweetness out of these pear-shaped members of the melon family. Thai and other Southeast Asian cooks treat green papayas like a vegetable for a reason. They're crunchier and blander in flavor, but still have a refreshing moistness that makes them salad superstars.

Lemongrass Salad

On hot and humid Thai afternoons, I love to sit down to a refreshing light meal. For the health conscious, here is a tip to cut down on the fat in this dish. Rinse the chicken under cold water the minute it emerges from the hot water. This method removes most of the oils from the chicken so that no congealed fat is present.

SERVES 8

Dressing

1/4 cup minced lemongrass (bottom 5 to 6 inches only)

1/2 cup fresh lime juice

1/3 cup Thai roasted chile paste

1/4 cup fish sauce

1/4 cup sugar

2 teaspoons crushed dried red chiles

1 1/2 cups water

1 cup minced raw boneless chicken

2 teaspoons vegetable oil

3/4 pound large raw shrimp, shelled and deveined

1 cup shredded sweetened coconut

2 cups shredded cabbage

5 Chinese long beans, or 20 green beans, cut into 1-inch lengths and blanched

1 cup roasted peanuts or macadamia nuts, coarsely chopped

1 cup chopped cilantro leaves

1 cup thinly sliced red onion

1 cup mint leaves

1/4 cup kaffir lime leaves, minced

1. To make dressing, in a bowl combine lemongrass, lime juice, chile paste, fish sauce, sugar, and chiles. Mix and set aside.

2. In a 1-quart saucepan, bring water to a boil. Add chicken and cook, stirring once or twice, until chicken is no longer pink, about 2 minutes. Drain, rinse with cold water, and drain again.

3. Heat a grill pan over medium-high heat until hot. Brush pan with 1 teaspoon oil. Grill shrimp until the flesh turns pink, about 2 minutes on each side. Brush shrimp with a little oil during grilling to prevent sticking. Remove and set aside.

4. Spread coconut in a small pan; toast over medium heat, shaking pan frequently, until lightly browned, 4 to 5 minutes.

5. In a large salad bowl, combine cabbage and beans with coconut, peanuts, cilantro, onion, mint, and lime leaves. Add chicken and dressing; toss well.

6. Transfer to a serving platter; top with grilled shrimp and serve.

No Grass Greener

I hate to be the bearer of bad news, but there is simply no substitute for lemongrass. None. These long, pale, green-yellow stalks—the bottom 5 to 6 inches of which is used in recipes—bring a tart note to the balance of flavors that's one of Thai cooking's unique calling cards. Its flavor is lemony, but not quite in the same way as a regular lemon, and you just can't get that flavor from any other ingredient. Luckily, nowadays you can get lemongrass in the fresh herbs section of your supermarket, thanks to increased interest in Southeast Asian cuisines. Peel off the dry outer leaves around the root, and then prepare according to the recipe. Keep lemongrass in your refrigerator, loosely wrapped, for no more than a couple weeks. And— all right, I admit it—in a real pinch, 1 teaspoon grated lemon zest can stand in for 1 stalk of lemongrass.

Pomelo Salad

In Thai culture, the pomelo is a "golden" fruit that has connotations of good luck. The chefs at the Dusit Island Resort and Hotel in Chiang Rai serve their guests this special pomelo fruit salad with pork and shrimp in sweet coconut cream dressing. Lucky for us, they also shared this wonderful recipe. SERVES 4

Dressing

1/4 cup coconut cream

2 tablespoons fresh lime juice

2 tablespoons fish sauce

2 tablespoons sweet chile sauce

2 tablespoons palm sugar or brown sugar

2 tablespoons chopped green onion

1 pomelo, grapefruit, or orange

1 tablespoon vegetable oil

1 tablespoon minced garlic

1/4 pound ground pork

1/2 pound medium raw shrimp, shelled and deveined

1/2 teaspoon salt

1/8 teaspoon white pepper

8 to 10 butter lettuce cups

2 tablespoons toasted shredded coconut, for garnish

8 to 10 Thai or sweet basil leaves, for garnish

1. Make dressing: For coconut cream, open a can of unsweetened coconut milk (do not shake it first) and spoon the thick cream off the top. Place 1/4 cup cream in a bowl with lime juice, fish sauce, chile sauce, and palm sugar; whisk to blend. Stir in green onion and set aside.

2. With a sharp knife, cut peel off citrus, cutting deeply enough to remove the white pith; cut out each segment from the membrane.

3. Place a wok over high heat until hot. Add oil, swirling to coat sides. Add garlic and cook, stirring, until fragrant, about 10 seconds. Add pork and cook until browned and crumbly, 1 to 2 minutes. Add shrimp and cook for 2 minutes. Add salt and white pepper; cook for 30 seconds. Remove from heat and let mixture cool to room temperature.

4. To assemble salad, stir citrus segments into dressing. Add pork mixture and mix well. Spoon salad into lettuce cups. Garnish each with shredded coconut and a basil leaf.

Northern Thai Scallop Salad

After a hard day of spice hunting at Bangkok's famous Central Market, I was treated to dinner at the Spice Market restaurant in the Regent Hotel, and, true to the restaurant's name, the food there—including this scallop salad—had a wonderful balance of sweet, sour, and spicy flavors. **SERVES 4**

Dressing

3 tablespoons fresh lime juice
2 tablespoons sweet chile sauce
1¹/₂ tablespoons fish sauce
2 walnut-size shallots, finely chopped
3 tablespoons finely chopped lemongrass (bottom 5 to 6 inches only)
2 tablespoons finely chopped cilantro leaves
2 teaspoons minced kaffir lime leaf
2 teaspoons minced fresh Thai chile

³/₄ pound sea scallops
1 teaspoon cornstarch
¹/₂ teaspoon salt
1 small head romaine lettuce, shredded

1. To make dressing, in a large bowl, combine lime juice, chile sauce, fish sauce, shallots, lemongrass, cilantro, lime leaf, and chile; set aside.

2. Cut scallops in half horizontally. Place in a bowl with cornstarch and salt; stir to coat. Let stand for 10 minutes.

3. Bring a pan of water to a boil. Add scallops, decrease heat, and simmer until scallops turn opaque, 3 to 4 minutes; drain.

4. Add warm scallops to dressing and gently mix.

5. To serve, arrange lettuce on a platter and place scallops on top.

Thailand's Favorite Limey

Thais believe that the fragrance of the kaffir lime leaf wards off evil spirits. I believe that it attracts fans of delicious food—like me! This fragrant, green, bumpy-textured citrus fruit is a mainstay in Thai soups, curries, and dressings. And while the limes themselves aren't very juicy, their magic lies in their leaves. Fresh kaffir lime leaves are aromatic, waxy, and a vibrant green; their double-lobed shape makes them look like a figure eight. Use them as you would bay leaves, adding them to slow-simmering dishes that could use an infusion of their citrus flavor. And if you can't find them fresh, use frozen, dried, or powdered leaves; ¹/₂ teaspoon of the powdered leaves equals about 2 teaspoons minced fresh leaves. In a pinch, 1 teaspoon grated lime zest for each kaffir lime leaf will do.

Crispy Catfish Salad

Crispy Creations

Give your salads, soups, and curries crisp texture and a burst of flavor with a sprinkling of deep-fried garlic, onions, or shallots. That's what Thai cooks do, and they work wonders for waking up a dish. Thinly slice garlic cloves, or peeled shallots or onions, separating the slices into rings. Gently deep-fry at 325° until golden brown (*not* burnt) and crispy, 3 to 5 minutes. Drain on paper towels, and store in a sealed container in the refrigerator, or buy ready-made fried garlic, shallots, and onions in Asian specialty stores.

Another unusual salad I sampled at the Regent Hotel in Bangkok was this spicy fish salad. Its trademark is the flaked, deep-fried catfish. **SERVES 4**

Marinade

1/4 cup fresh lime juice

2 tablespoons fish sauce

1 teaspoon soy sauce

2 1/2 tablespoons sugar

1 tablespoon minced garlic

2 teaspoons minced fresh chile

1 1/2 pounds whole catfish or catfish fillets

Dressing

1 tablespoon fresh lime juice

1 tablespoon fish sauce

1 tablespoon palm sugar or brown sugar

1 teaspoon chile paste

1 teaspoon minced fresh chile

1 tablespoon flour

Vegetable oil, for deep-frying

1 head romaine lettuce, cut into bite-size pieces

2 tablespoons minced lemongrass (bottom 5 to 6 inches only)

1 tablespoon thinly sliced shallot

1 tablespoon chopped cilantro stems

1/4 cup chopped roasted peanuts

1 tablespoon crispy fried garlic (see sidebar)

1 tablespoon dried shrimp, soaked in warm water 20 minutes, drained, finely chopped

1. Prepare a fire in a charcoal grill or preheat a gas grill. To make marinade, in a bowl combine lime juice, fish sauce, soy sauce, sugar, garlic, and chile. Add fish and turn to coat. Let stand for 10 minutes. To make dressing, in a bowl combine lime juice, fish sauce, palm sugar, chile paste, and chile; stir to dissolve sugar. Lift fish from marinade and drain briefly.

2. Place fish on a lightly oiled grill. Grill for 5 to 7 minutes per side.

3. Transfer fish to a clean cutting board, and butterfly it by cutting along the spine. Carefully remove spine from fish; discard head and tail. Press fillet firmly with a fork to compress it; dust with flour and shake lightly to remove excess. In a wok, heat oil for deep-frying to 375°. Deep-fry fish, turning once, until golden brown, 3 to 4 minutes. Remove with a slotted spoon and drain on paper towels.

4. Place lettuce, lemongrass, shallot, and cilantro in a large bowl. Add dressing and toss; arrange on a platter. With a fork, flake fish into pieces and place on top of salad. To serve, sprinkle with peanuts, garlic, and dried shrimp.

Chicken Glass Noodle Salad

Salads are popular treats in northern Thailand, and so is chicken. Combine the two, and you have a local classic. This recipe was inspired by my visit to Huen Phen (Full Moon) restaurant in Chiang Mai. **SERVES 4**

4 ounces dried bean thread noodles

3 dried black mushrooms

2 tablespoons dried shrimp

1 tablespoon vegetable oil

6 ounces boneless, skinless chicken breast, cut into 1/4-inch dice

1/4 cup drained canned straw mushrooms, sliced

1/2 cup diced cucumber

1/2 cup diced red bell pepper

1/4 cup thinly sliced shallots

4 green onions, thinly sliced

Sauce

3 tablespoons fish sauce

2 1/2 tablespoons fresh lime juice

1 1/2 tablespoons sugar

1/2 teaspoon crushed dried red chiles

Garnish

1/4 cup chopped roasted peanuts

1 teaspoon thinly sliced fresh Thai chile

8 mint leaves, shredded

1. Soak noodles in warm water to cover until softened, about 5 minutes; drain. In a large pot of boiling water, cook noodles for 1 minute; drain, rinse with cold water, and drain again. Cut into 4-inch lengths.

2. In separate bowls, soak dried mushrooms and dried shrimp in warm water to cover until softened, about 20 minutes; drain. Discard mushrooms stems and dice caps. Finely chop shrimp.

3. To make sauce, in a bowl combine fish sauce, lime juice, sugar, and dried chiles.

4. Place a wok over high heat until hot. Add oil, swirling to coat sides. Add black mushrooms and dried shrimp; cook, stirring, for 1 minute. Add chicken and straw mushrooms; stir-fry for 2 minutes. Add sauce, decrease heat, and simmer for 2 minutes. Remove from wok and let cool.

5. Place noodles in a salad bowl. Add chicken mixture, cucumber, bell pepper, shallots, and green onions; toss to coat. Garnish with peanuts, chile, and mint.

Heir Transparent

Whether you call them glass noodles, cellophane noodles, bean threads, or Chinese vermicelli, the translucent noodles made from mung bean starch are a common ingredient in Thai salads, soups, and noodle dishes. Little wonder they're becoming easier to spot in Western grocery stores. Just look in the Asian food aisle for plastic packages that appear to be filled with white bunches of stiff nylon fishing line—that's the catch you're after. Soak these thirsty noodles in plenty of warm water to soften before using in a recipe—5 to 10 minutes should do it. Or, for a light garnish, deep-fry handfuls of the dry noodles until they puff into a crispy nest.

Beef Salad

The secret to getting the right texture in this salad dressing is finely ground roasted rice. The rice also adds a very aromatic flavor. Thai chefs use it in many of their salad dressings and soups. For soup, sprinkle the ground rice on top right before serving.

SERVES 4 TO 6

1 pound beef flank steak

$^1/_4$ teaspoon salt

$^1/_8$ teaspoon black pepper

Dressing

1 tablespoon rice

$^1/_2$ cup thinly sliced shallots

$^1/_2$ cup coarsely chopped mint leaves

$^1/_2$ cup coarsely chopped cilantro leaves

$^1/_3$ cup fresh lime juice

3 tablespoons fish sauce

1 tablespoon chopped green onion

1$^1/_2$ teaspoons finely chopped lemongrass (bottom 5 to 6 inches only)

1$^1/_2$ teaspoons crushed dried red chiles

1$^1/_2$ teaspoons sugar

3 cups shredded iceberg lettuce

Mint sprigs, for garnish

1. Season beef with salt and pepper.

2. Place beef in a lightly oiled grill pan over high heat. Cook, turning once, until medium-rare to medium (depending on preference), 3 to 4 minutes on each side. Remove and cover with aluminum foil; let stand for 15 minutes. Cut beef into thin slices across the grain.

3. To prepare dressing: Place rice in a small frying pan over medium heat; cook, shaking pan frequently, until lightly browned, 3 to 4 minutes. Immediately remove from pan to cool. Grind rice finely in a spice grinder. In a bowl, combine rice, shallots, mint, cilantro, lime juice, fish sauce, green onion, lemongrass, chiles, and sugar; mix well.

4. Arrange lettuce on a platter. Just before serving, toss meat with dressing; place on lettuce. Garnish with mint sprigs.

Salad Smarts

In Thailand, it gets hot. Really hot. So hot that the idea of firing up a wok makes a body want to wilt. While I was there, I learned that one good way to break the heat is to dive into a cool Thai salad. So it's no surprise at the popularity of simple chilled salads brimming with the refreshing flavors and textures from mint, lime, basil, and cilantro. Add any sampling of local Thai produce—the choices are endless. It doesn't get any simpler: a little slicing or chopping is often all the prep work the ingredients need. Thai salads are the perfect prescription for beating the Thai heat, and a great start for a delicious, healthful meal.

Spicy Roasted Eggplants with Tofu

Now this dish is a real catch—Thai and Asian eggplants on one plate! The texture and sweet flavor of the eggplant are unbeatable. If you can't find Thai eggplant at the market, substituting with Asian eggplant will still make this dish a winner. **SERVES 2**

1 tablespoon dried shrimp
1 pound mixed Thai and Asian eggplants, roll-cut
4 tablespoons vegetable oil
¹/₂ cup pine nuts
8 ounces regular-firm tofu, drained
¹/₄ cup sliced onion
4 cloves garlic, chopped
3 tablespoons water
2 tablespoons oyster-flavored sauce
1 tablespoon Thai roasted chile paste
4 fresh red Thai chiles
¹/₂ cup Thai or sweet basil leaves

1. Soak dried shrimp in warm water to cover until softened, about 20 minutes; drain and coarsely chop.

2. Preheat oven to 350°. Combine eggplants and 2 tablespoons of the oil in a shallow baking pan. Toss to coat. Bake until eggplants are tender, about 15 minutes.

3. Spread pine nuts in a small pan. Place over medium heat, shaking pan frequently until nuts are golden brown, about 4 minutes.

4. Cut tofu into 1¹/₂-inch squares.

5. Place a wok over high heat until hot. Add the remaining 2 tablespoons oil, swirling to coat sides. Add onion and garlic; stir-fry for 1 minute. Add dried shrimp, water, oyster sauce, chile paste, chiles, and eggplant; cook for 1 minute.

6. Stir in tofu and basil leaves; toss for 30 seconds. Garnish with pine nuts, and serve.

I'd heard of singing for your supper, but never catching it—until I visited the night market at Phitsanoluk, where the folks at a fun-loving food stall gladly play games with your food. Say you order a dish of stir-fried greens. The cook whips it up, but instead of pouring it neatly from the wok to the plate, he hands you the plate, directs you to stand in a truck bed about forty feet from him, turns his back to you, and hoists your greens out of the wok and over his head, right in your direction. Quick! Hold up that plate like a baseball mitt and pretend it's the deciding game of the World Series. Your meal may depend on it. Of course, it's all just a game, and if your catching skills have gotten a little rusty in the off-season, don't worry; you'll still get to eat. There are enough greens to go around, even for the rookies.

Garden-Fresh Vegetables in Coconut Milk

A Season for Reflection

During Thailand's annual rainy season, from July to October, disciples of Buddha traditionally took a break from spreading the Enlightened One's teachings across the countryside, not because the rain was messy and inconvenient, but because they wanted to avoid trampling on young, delicate plants made even more delicate by the rains. Devout Buddhists continue to practice this "Rains Retreat," also known as Khaupansa, or Buddhist Lent, today. Some serious devotees remain indoors for the entire period. They keep themselves busy by attending to the needs of the monks and novices, practicing charity, making devotional candles, and most importantly, reflecting on the doctrines of Buddhism.

Thailand's bountiful soil produces top-grade produce, and this dish showcases some of the finest offerings. Here fresh vegetables are sautéed in a traditional coconut milk and basil sauce. **SERVES 4**

¹/₄ pound sweet potato

1¹/₂ cups unsweetened coconut milk

2 tablespoons red curry paste (see page 133)

2 Asian eggplants, roll-cut

4 Chinese long beans, or 16 green beans, cut into 1¹/₂-inch lengths

3 tablespoons fish sauce

2 tablespoons sugar

¹/₂ cup Thai or sweet basil leaves

1. Peel sweet potato and cut into ¹/₂-inch cubes. Place in a small pan with enough water to cover. Bring to a boil, decrease heat, and simmer until barely soft, about 5 minutes. Drain.

2. Place ³/₄ cup of the coconut milk in a wok or pan over medium heat for 30 seconds. Add curry paste and slowly bring to a boil, stirring constantly, about 2 minutes. Add the remaining coconut milk; bring to a boil. Decrease heat to medium-low; add sweet potato, eggplants, and beans; simmer for about 3 minutes.

3. Add fish sauce and sugar; cover and cook until beans are tender-crisp, about 4 minutes more. Stir in basil leaves, cook for 30 seconds, and serve.

Fish Soufflé with Coconut Milk

Chef Sirilak of the Grand Hyatt Erawan, Bangkok, made me the best fish soufflé I have ever tasted. I loved the flavor balance of red curry, lemongrass, and coconut milk with the chunks of tender sweet fish. This is my new favorite Thai dish. **SERVES 4**

Spice Paste

2 tablespoons minced lemongrass (bottom 5 to 6 inches only)

1 walnut-size shallot, finely chopped

2 teaspoons minced garlic

2 teaspoons minced Thai or sweet basil leaves

1 teaspoon red curry paste (see page 133)

1 teaspoon minced cilantro stems

1/2 teaspoon minced fresh Thai chile

1/4 teaspoon minced kaffir lime leaf

1/2 pound firm white fish fillet, such as sea bass or halibut, coarsely chopped

1 egg, lightly beaten

1/3 cup plus 1/4 cup unsweetened coconut milk

2 tablespoons fish sauce

1 tablespoon cilantro leaves, for garnish

1 small fresh Thai chile, slivered, for garnish

1. To prepare spice paste, with a mortar and pestle, pound lemongrass, shallot, garlic, basil, curry paste, cilantro stems, chile, and lime leaf into a juicy paste.

2. Scrape paste into a bowl. Add fish, egg, the 1/3 cup coconut milk, and fish sauce; mix well. Spoon mixture equally into four oiled 6-ounce custard cups.

3. Prepare a wok for steaming (see page 6). Place cups in steamer and steam over medium heat until filling is firm, 8 to 10 minutes. Spoon the 1/4 cup coconut milk equally over each soufflé. Sprinkle with a few cilantro leaves and slivers of chile, and serve.

Steamed Fish in Banana Leaf

Usually when I steam fish, I steam the whole fish or use fish fillets. This time I cut the fish into chunks and season them with Thai spices and coconut milk. I made little cups out of banana leaves and spooned the fish into each cup to steam. The banana leaf cup lends a light aroma to the fish. **SERVES 4**

Fish Mixture

1¼ cups unsweetened coconut milk

1½ tablespoons red curry paste (see page 133)

2½ teaspoons sugar

1 egg, lightly beaten

½ pound firm white fish fillets, such as sea bass or red snapper, cut into ½-inch cubes

½ cup chopped water chestnuts

2 tablespoons fish sauce

2 tablespoons shredded Thai or sweet basil leaves

2 banana leaves, cut into four 5½-inch circles

12 whole Thai or sweet basil leaves, plus 4 basil sprigs, for garnish

1 small fresh red chile, thinly sliced, for garnish

1. To prepare fish mixture, in a bowl, whisk together coconut milk, curry paste, sugar, and egg until evenly blended. Stir in fish, water chestnuts, fish sauce, and shredded basil.

2. Line the bottom of four banana cups (see diagram) with 3 basil leaves. (If banana leaves are unavailable, use four 1-cup ramekins.) Spoon fish mixture into banana cups, dividing equally.

3. Prepare a wok for steaming (see page 6). Place banana cups in steamer, cover, and steam over high heat until cooked, about 10 minutes.

4. Garnish each serving with a basil sprig and a few slices of chile. Serve warm.

Banana Leaf Cups

The beauty of this traditional Thai dish lies in its elegant, tropical presentation—making it great for a party! So start by cutting a 5½-inch circle out of a banana leaf and proceed from there. . . .

1. Fold circle into thirds and crease.

2. Fold in left and right sides, about 2 inches. The flaps will overlap each other and form a rectangular shape.

3. Re-open the leaf. Pinch a "crease" inward, as shown, so that points A and B meet and form a small flap.

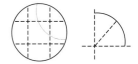

4. Staple the flap to an adjacent wall of the cup. Repeat with the remaining sections to create a rectangular cup.

Fish with Spicy Basil Sauce

Southern Thailand is world famous for its rich renderings of fresh seafood, like fish cutlets in spicy sauce. In this version, steaks of white fish are pan-fried until golden and served with a spicy tomato and basil sauce. **SERVES 4**

3 tablespoons vegetable oil

1¼ pounds firm white fish steaks or fillets, such as halibut or sea bass

1 tablespoon minced garlic

½ cup diced onion

2 teaspoons Thai chile sauce

1 cup diced tomato

3 tablespoons water

2 tablespoons rice vinegar

1½ tablespoons fish sauce

1 tablespoon sugar

1 teaspoon cornstarch dissolved in 2 teaspoons water

¼ cup Thai or sweet basil leaves

¼ cup coarsely chopped cilantro leaves

6 asparagus spears, blanched

1. Heat a wok over medium heat until hot. Add 2 tablespoons oil, swirling to coat sides. Place fish in pan and cook, turning once, until golden brown, about 3 minutes on each side. Remove fish from wok.

2. Increase heat to high. Heat the remaining 1 tablespoon oil in wok. Add garlic, onion, and chile sauce; cook, stirring, for 1 minute. Add tomato, water, vinegar, fish sauce, and sugar; cook for 1 minute. Add cornstarch solution and cook, stirring, until sauce boils and thickens.

3. Return fish to wok. Stir in basil and cilantro; heat through.

4. To serve, place asparagus on a serving plate, arrange fish on asparagus, and pour sauce over the top.

Steamed Sea Bass with Pickled Garlic

Pickled garlic can be purchased at Asian or gourmet grocery stores. The brine-packed cloves of garlic come in glass jars. It has a pungent taste that adds a lot of flavor to the steamed fish. **SERVES 4**

1 (1½- to 2-pound) whole fish, such as sea bass or red snapper, cleaned
2 tablespoons vegetable oil
6 fresh Thai chiles, thinly sliced
3 cloves pickled garlic, chopped
1 green onion, thinly sliced
3 tablespoons chicken stock (see page 38)
3 tablespoons brine from pickled garlic
1 tablespoon soy sauce
2½ teaspoons palm sugar or brown sugar
1 teaspoon chopped cilantro leaves
3 tablespoons fresh lime juice
Mint leaves, for garnish

1. Cut 3 diagonal slits, each ½ inch deep, across each side of fish. Place fish in a heatproof dish.

2. Prepare a wok for steaming (see page 6). Place fish in steamer. Cover and steam fish over high heat until it turns opaque, 8 to 10 minutes.

3. Place a wok over high heat until hot. Add oil, swirling to coat sides. Add chiles, pickled garlic, and green onion; cook, stirring, until fragrant, about 30 seconds. Add stock, garlic brine, soy sauce, palm sugar, and cilantro; cook for 2 to 3 minutes.

4. Pour sauce over fish and drizzle lime juice over the top. Garnish with mint leaves.

The Khantoke Way

In a Northern Thai *khantoke* dinner (*khan* means "bowl"; *toke* indicates a low, round table), diners sit on the floor around a bamboo or lacquered pedestal holding many dishes. My old knees groaned at the seating arrangements, but my growling stomach overruled them the moment I set eyes on the glutinous rice, curries, steamed fish, stir-fried meats, salads, raw and cooked vegetables, noodles, and condiments that commonly appear at *khantoke* meals. All the dishes are set out, and diners politely serve themselves whatever they like, family style. True, the variety may seem indulgent, but restraint is the game plan: Thai dining philosophy tends toward eating smaller portions more frequently. I believe Western experts call this healthful practice "grazing," but I call it one satisfying *khantoke*. . . . *Mooooooo!*

Shop with the Fishes

Necessity is the mother of invention, and back in the olden days, when Thai farmers needed to bring their harvest to market—and when they realized they needed a better way to get it there than by the country's scanty land routes—they "invented" the floating market. Thailand may not have had an I-80, but it did have plenty of canals, or *klongs,* and farmers took advantage of these as shipping routes. Naturally, as enough of their harvest-heavy boats collected in the canal en route, the confluence turned into an ad hoc trading center, and the floating market was born. This was the way things went for years. But as progress marches on, leaving landlubbing grocery stores in its wake, the floating market is fading for all but the tourists and those who refuse to give up this part of Thai's cultural heritage.

Floating Market.

Crispy Fish with Chile Sauce

Chef Sayun Sugkaw of Tong Kao (Triple Nine) restaurant in Chiang Rai served us his specialty—deep-fried fish with spicy chile dip. One bite and you will be shouting triple bravos! **SERVES 4**

Spice Paste

2 walnut-size shallots, finely chopped

1 tablespoon minced garlic

1 teaspoon minced fresh Thai chile

1 teaspoon minced cilantro stems

$1/4$ teaspoon white peppercorns

1 tablespoon water

Sauce

$1/4$ cup unsweetened coconut milk

$1/4$ cup tamarind water (see page 189)

$1/4$ cup water

$1^1/2$ tablespoons fish sauce

1 (1- to $1^1/2$-pound) whole fish, such as sea bass or red snapper, cleaned

$1/4$ cup cornstarch

Vegetable oil, for deep-frying

6 slices ginger, each the size of a quarter, julienned, for garnish

Basil sprigs, for garnish

1. To make spice paste, with a mortar and pestle, pound shallots, garlic, chile, cilantro, and white peppercorns into a juicy paste. Scrape into a bowl and stir in water.

2. To make sauce, in a bowl combine coconut milk, tamarind water, water, and fish sauce.

3. Across each side of fish, cut diagonal slits $3/4$ inch deep. Dust fish with cornstarch.

4. In a wok, heat oil for deep-frying to 350°. Add ginger and deep-fry until golden, about 2 minutes. Remove with a slotted spoon and drain on paper towels.

5. Increase heat to 375°. Deep-fry fish, turning once, until golden brown and flesh is opaque, 6 to 8 minutes total. Remove fish and drain on paper towels. Spoon 2 tablespoons of the deep-frying oil into a small pan and heat over medium heat. Add spice paste and cook, stirring, for 2 minutes. Add sauce, decrease heat, and simmer for 5 minutes.

6. To serve, place fish on a serving plate and pour sauce on top. Garnish with ginger and basil sprigs.

Stuffed Squid with Spicy Sauce

The Chinese have inspired many Thai creations. This stuffed squid stir-fry contains black mushrooms and oyster sauce, popular Chinese ingredients. Remember to stuff the squid loosely with pork filling; too tight, and the filling will fall out as the meat absorbs liquid and expands. **SERVES 4**

Filling

6 ounces ground pork

1/4 cup finely diced onion

1 tablespoon chopped cilantro leaves

2 cloves garlic, minced

1 tablespoon fish sauce

1 tablespoon soy sauce

1 teaspoon sugar

1/8 teaspoon white pepper

1 egg, lightly beaten

6 to 8 medium squid, cleaned, tentacles removed and reserved for other use

2 tablespoons vegetable oil

1/4 cup sliced onion

1 tablespoon minced garlic

1/2 pound fresh shiitake mushrooms, stems removed, thinly sliced

1/4 cup water

1 tablespoon Thai roasted chile paste

1 tablespoon oyster-flavored sauce

1 green onion, thinly sliced

1. To make filling, in a bowl combine ground pork, onion, cilantro, garlic, fish sauce, soy sauce, sugar, white pepper, and egg; mix well. Stuff each squid loosely with filling to within 1 inch of top. Weave a wooden toothpick across each top to secure. Place squid in a single layer in a heatproof dish.

2. Prepare a wok for steaming (see page 6). Cover and steam squid over high heat for 6 minutes. Remove squid and set aside.

3. Drain and reserve water from wok and place wok over high heat until hot. Add oil, swirling to coat sides. Add onion and garlic; stir-fry until garlic is fragrant and onion is slightly soft, about 1 minute. Add mushrooms, water, chile paste, and oyster sauce; stir-fry for 1 minute. Add squid and reserved steaming water. Stir in green onion; cook for 1 minute.

4. Place squid on a serving plate; pour sauce over and serve.

Prawn Cocoons

Just because I call this dish Prawn Cocoons doesn't mean that you have to hide them. I make my cocoons by skewering prawns on stalks of lemongrass and wrapping them in Chinese angel hair noodles. I prefer Chinese angel hair to the Italian variety because it has a softer texture. If you do decide to use Italian angel hair, you must boil the noodles first. **SERVES 4**

8 extra-large raw prawns
$1/4$ teaspoon salt
$1/8$ teaspoon white pepper
6 ounces fresh Chinese angel hair noodles
4 stalks lemongrass

Dipping Sauce

$1/3$ cup sweet and sour sauce
3 tablespoons chile garlic sauce

Vegetable oil, for deep-frying

1. Shell and devein prawns, leaving tails intact. Butterfly prawns and rinse out veins; pat dry with paper towels. Sprinkle prawns with salt and white pepper.

2. Untangle noodles and rinse with cold water; drain.

3. Cut off bottom 5 to 6 inches of lemongrass and save for future use. Cut the remaining woody stalks in half horizontally, to make 8 skewers. Thread each prawn lengthwise on a skewer. Divide noodles into 8 equal portions. Wind 1 portion of the noodles around each prawn so it is completely covered; press noodles to form a tight wrap.

4. To make dipping sauce, in a small bowl combine sweet and sour sauce and chile garlic sauce.

5. In a wok or saucepan, heat oil for deep-frying to 350°. Deep-fry prawns, a few at a time, turning once, until golden brown, about 7 minutes. Remove and drain on paper towels.

6. Serve with dipping sauce.

Cocoon Tycoon

Jim Thompson came to Thailand as a United States intelligence officer after World War II. An educated, charming personality with a love of art, culture, and the good life, Thompson warmed up to his new home and stayed after leaving the service. He was soon enchanted by the traditional handwoven silks, which at the time was a cottage industry in rural Thailand and one in total disrepair. Thompson turned his commercial instincts—he was also a shrewd businessman—to reviving and expanding the country's silk industry while maintaining authenticity and traditional production methods. The rest is, as they say, history. In the spring of 1967, Jim Thompson mysteriously disappeared while vacationing in Malaysia's Cameron Highlands. More than thirty years later, we still aren't sure what happened to him, although theories abound. Luckily for fans of elegant silk, Thai silks go on, just like the legend of their benefactor.

Curried Shrimp

Where there is water there are shrimp, and for Chef Vichit Mukura of the Oriental Hotel, Bangkok, where there are shrimp there is delicious curried shrimp. **SERVES 4**

16 large (³/₄ pound) raw shrimp, heads and shells attached
³/₄ cup unsweetened coconut milk
1 tablespoon yellow curry paste (see page 134)
¹/₂ cup diced tomato
1 to 2 teaspoons slivered fresh Thai chile
2 tablespoons fish sauce
1 tablespoon sugar
¹/₂ teaspoon salt

1. To split shrimp: Hold each shrimp shell down, and with a heavy knife, split along back from head to tail, leaving head attached. Remove shell; butterfly body and remove veins. Pat dry with paper towels.

2. In a wok over medium heat, bring coconut milk and curry paste to a boil. Decrease heat and add tomato, chile, fish sauce, sugar, and salt; cook for 3 minutes.

3. Add shrimp; cook until flesh is opaque and shrimp turn pink, 5 to 7 minutes. Transfer to a serving bowl.

Don't Ask Wai, Ask Wai Not?

Raise your hands to anywhere between your chest and forehead. With fingertips pointing up, press your palms together. Now bow your head. Congratulations. You've just performed the *wai* (pronounced "why"), Thailand's graceful sign of greeting and farewell that reinforces social structure, expresses respect, and serves as a religious acknowledgment. Thais have been *wai*-ing for years, and they have a complex set of rules specifying when, where, how, why, and whom to *wai*. Here are the basics: Social status and then age (not gender) determine who *wais* first, with the lower-ranking and younger person initiating the *wai*. (If an older person *wais* first, it supposedly takes seven years off the younger person's life, so be careful!) The lower the head and the higher the hands, the greater the respect expressed. Finally, monks never *wai* a layman, not even the king, indicating how respected Buddhist disciples are in Thai society.

Steamed Shrimp in Coconut Cream

Chef Narin at Bangkok's Lemongrass Restaurant creates this culinary masterpiece with shrimp steamed in coconut cream sauce. The intensity of hot chiles is very high, so if you would prefer, tone down the spiciness by using fewer chiles. **SERVES 4**

10 to 12 (¹/₂ pound) large raw shrimp
2 to 3 teaspoons slivered fresh Thai chiles
¹/₃ cup thinly sliced shallots
¹/₂ cup coconut cream
¹/₄ cup unsweetened coconut milk
¹/₄ cup fresh lime juice
1¹/₂ tablespoons sugar
1 tablespoon fish sauce

1. Shell, devein, and butterfly shrimp, leaving tails intact. Place shrimp in a single layer in a heatproof dish. Sprinkle with chiles and shallots.

2. For coconut cream, open a can of unsweetened coconut milk (do not shake it first), and spoon the thick cream off the top. Stir remaining coconut milk in can to blend. In a bowl, whisk together coconut cream, coconut milk, lime juice, sugar, and fish sauce. Pour over shrimp.

3. Prepare a wok for steaming (see page 6). Place shrimp in steamer, cover, and steam over medium heat until shrimp turn pink, 4 to 5 minutes. Serve.

The Secret Password: Lemongrass

When looking for the best places to eat in an unfamiliar city, it helps to have advice from folks in the know. That's especially true when one of the hottest eateries sits on a quiet little street in what could pass for a local's house. When my crew and I got tipped off to the Lemongrass Restaurant, we wondered whether we'd gotten the address right. Outside, it's just an unassuming building with a barely noticeable sign. Inside, it's one of Bangkok's most popular dining spots, a converted house, with several rooms of intimately spaced tables and an outdoor garden to boost the romance factor. But coming from the Bay Area with its stratospheric real estate prices, what strikes me about the restaurant is how rising property values in this trendy Bangkok district are turning it and its neighbors' owners into paper millionaires. Increasingly, locals are cashing in on the boom, selling their houses to restaurant developers, too. So when you're sitting at a table at the Lemongrass, you might be occupying a few square feet that are worth thousands of times the price of your meal.

Creamy Prawn Curry with Young Coconut

Tender young coconut and freshwater prawns make this dish a standout. During my visit to the Royal Cliff Beach Hotel in Pattaya, Chef Mana Seksantakul showed me how to make this wonderful dish, and I even got to handpick my own young coconut!

SERVES 4

1¹/₂ cups unsweetened coconut milk

3 tablespoons yellow curry paste (see page 134)

¹/₂ pound extra-large freshwater prawns, heads and tails left on

3 tablespoons sugar

1¹/₂ tablespoons fish sauce

¹/₂ cup diced red bell pepper

¹/₂ cup diced green bell pepper

2 kaffir lime leaves, torn into pieces

¹/₂ cup Thai or sweet basil leaves

¹/₂ cup freshly grated young coconut flesh (see sidebar)

¹/₄ cup macadamia nuts, for garnish

1. Place ³/₄ cup of the coconut milk in a wok or saucepan over medium heat for 30 seconds. Add curry paste and slowly bring to a boil, stirring constantly, about 2 minutes. Add prawns and cook for 3 minutes. Add remaining ³/₄ cup coconut milk; bring to a boil. Add sugar and fish sauce; bring to a boil. Add bell peppers and lime leaves; cook for 1 minute.

2. Stir in basil leaves and coconut; cook for 30 seconds.

3. Transfer to a serving bowl and garnish with nuts.

No Nut Like a Coconut!

If you haven't already noticed, coconut winds up in all sorts of Thai dishes. Toasted shreds, chips, or flakes top salads, soups, and desserts; the milk or cream flavors curries, soups, and sauces, as well as desserts; sweet coconut water (what's sloshing around when you shake a coconut) makes a refreshing drink; and the tender white flesh is a delicious addition to stews and desserts—if you can keep from eating it as is. Finding canned coconut milk is a snap these days. If the recipe calls for the milk, shake the can before opening; for cream, open an unshaken can and scoop off the thick layer that's risen to the top. Locating fresh coconut flesh is a little trickier. If you can't find it at stores, buy a whole coconut, pierce the "eyes" to drain the water, then hold the coconut eyes up and pound it with a hammer about an inch below the eyes around its circumference until it cracks. Break it into smaller chunks, separating the fresh meat from the shells. It takes some work, but the rewards of fresh coconut flesh are worth it.

Curried Shrimp with Pineapple

No Vein, No Pain

You can do a lot of things with fresh shrimp, but before you do anything, I'd suggest you devein them: Remove the legs if they're still attached and peel off the shell (leave the tail on if you plan to butterfly the shrimp). Run a sharp knife lightly along the shrimp's back to expose the dark digestive tube, gently lift the tube out with the knife's tip, and rinse the shrimp under cool water to wash away any leftover grit. If the recipe calls for butterflied shrimp, make an even deeper cut along the back than you made for deveining, and extend the cut along the whole length of the shrimp. Separate both sides along the cut to open the shrimp, then flatten it, and it's ready to go.

Pineapple is often added to curried shrimp for an invigorating punch of sweetness. In this dish, the intense flavor of red curry balances perfectly with the taste of fresh pineapple. **SERVES 4**

16 large (about ³/₄ pound) medium raw shrimp
2 teaspoons cornstarch
2 cups unsweetened coconut milk
2 tablespoons red curry paste (see page 133)
2 cups diced pineapple (1-inch cubes)
3 kaffir lime leaves, torn into small pieces
3 tablespoons fish sauce
3 tablespoons sugar
1 tablespoon fresh lime juice
¹/₄ cup chopped peanuts, for garnish

1. Shell and devein shrimp, leaving tails intact. Dust shrimp with cornstarch.

2. Place coconut milk in a wok or pan over medium heat for 30 seconds. Add curry paste and slowly bring to a boil, stirring constantly, about 2 minutes. Add shrimp and pineapple; cook for 3 minutes. Add lime leaves, fish sauce, and sugar; cook for 1 minute. Stir in lime juice and cook for 30 seconds more.

3. To serve, transfer to a serving bowl and sprinkle with nuts.

Stir–Fried Crab in Curry Sauce

Phuket is the seafood capital of Thailand. And there, at the Baan Rim Pa restaurant, you can sample fabulous seafood creations, like this crab in curry sauce from Chef Paiwan Klongklaw. **SERVES 4**

1 (1¹/₂- to 2-pound) live Dungeness or blue crab
2 tablespoons vegetable oil
2 tablespoons red curry paste (see page 133)
¹/₂ cup diced yellow onion
¹/₃ cup unsweetened coconut milk
3 fresh Thai chiles, seeded and thinly sliced
2 ribs Chinese celery, cut into 1¹/₂-inch lengths
1 tablespoon fish sauce
1 tablespoon oyster-flavored sauce
1 teaspoon sugar
¹/₄ teaspoon turmeric powder
¹/₄ teaspoon black pepper
1 egg, lightly beaten (optional: to thicken sauce)
2 green onions, cut into 1¹/₂-inch lengths
¹/₄ cup Thai basil or sweet basil leaves

1. Pull top shell off crab and reserve; discard gills. Twist off the claws and legs; crack them with a cleaver or mallet. Cut the body into 4 to 6 pieces.

2. Place a wok or frying pan over high heat until hot. Add oil, swirling to coat sides. Add curry paste and stir-fry until fragrant, about 1 minute. Add onion and stir-fry until soft, about 1 minute. Add crab; stir-fry for 5 minutes. Add coconut milk and bring to a boil. Decrease heat to medium-low; add chiles, Chinese celery, fish sauce, oyster sauce, sugar, turmeric, and pepper. Cover and cook for 2 minutes.

3. Add egg and cook, stirring, just until it begins to set, about 1 minute. Stir in green onions and basil leaves; cook for 1 minute.

4. Arrange crab and top shell on a serving plate; pour sauce over.

River of Light

Have you ever seen a river on fire? That's what Chiang Mai's River Ping looks like each November during *Loy Krathong*, an annual nighttime celebration dating back seven hundred years to the Sukhothai era. During Loy Krathong, participants *loy*, or set adrift, small lotus-shaped floats *(krathong)* decorated with orchids, leaves, and flowers. In the heart of each *krathong*, an orange candle glows, surrounded by incense, to thank the goddess of water, Mae Khong Kha, for generously watering the rice fields. For Buddhists, casting afloat the shimmering *krathong* with a brief preliminary prayer serves as a sort of spiritual cleansing. The combination of candles, fireworks, the stars reflected in the river, and the radiant faces of the revelers makes Loy Krathong a megawatt festival.

Curried Crab on Noodle Pancake

The Chinese Connection

For more than two hundred years, Chinese immigrants have been making their way to Thailand, where they have settled and built thriving Chinese communities that blend smoothly with mainstream Thai society. The daily buzz in Bangkok's Chinatown—its festivals, its businesses, its lingua franca, and its food—is so unmistakably Chinese that it sometimes makes me forget I'm in Thailand. That Chinese connection extends beyond Bangkok, too. While in Phuket in southern Thailand, I had the pleasure of dining with Chef Prasang of Lai-an Chinese Restaurant, Phuket's first to specialize in Chinese cuisine. Although Chinese by birth, Chef Prasang soaked up some local color by adopting a more Thai-sounding name when he came here. By the same token, his dishes—like this curried crab served over a classic Hong Kong–style noodle pancake—reflect a similar blending of cultures, and with tasty results.

One of my favorite foods when I was growing up was noodles pan-fried into a golden brown pancake. In Thailand, noodle pancakes are served with stir-fry or any type of saucy dish (like this curry crab) poured on top. SERVES 4

1 (1¹/₂-pound) live Dungeness or blue crab

¹/₄ cup cornstarch

8 ounces fresh Chinese egg noodles

4 tablespoons vegetable oil

2 cloves garlic, minced

1 walnut-size shallot, sliced

2 tablespoons yellow curry paste (see page 134)

³/₄ cup unsweetened coconut milk

1 tablespoon fish sauce

1 teaspoon sugar

¹/₈ teaspoon white pepper

1 to 2 teaspoons minced fresh Thai chile

¹/₃ cup Thai or sweet basil leaves

¹/₄ cup coarsely chopped cilantro leaves

2 green onions, cut into 1-inch lengths

1. Pull off top shell of crab; discard gills. Twist off the claws and legs; crack them with a cleaver or mallet. Cut the body into 4 to 6 pieces. Dust crab with cornstarch; shake off excess.

2. In a large pot of boiling water, cook noodles according to package directions. Drain, rinse with cold water, and drain again.

3. Place a wide nonstick frying pan over medium-high heat until hot. Add 1 tablespoon oil, swirling to coat sides. Spread noodles over bottom of pan. Cook until bottom is golden brown, 4 to 5 minutes. With a wide spatula, carefully turn pancake over. Add 1 tablespoon oil and cook until second side is golden brown, 3 to 4 minutes. Transfer to a serving platter and keep warm.

4. Place a wok over high heat until hot. Add the remaining 2 tablespoons oil, swirling to coat sides. Add garlic, shallot, and curry paste; cook, stirring, until fragrant, about 30 seconds. Add crab and stir-fry for 3 minutes.

5. Add coconut milk, fish sauce, sugar, and white pepper; bring to a boil. Decrease heat to low; cover and simmer, stirring once or twice, until crab is cooked, 6 to 8 minutes. Stir in chile, basil, cilantro, and green onions; heat through.

6. To serve, arrange crab alongside noodle pancake on a serving platter and pour sauce over.

Broiled Lobsters in Tamarind Sauce

In Phuket, lobster is a specialty. Most local restaurants feature lobster on their main menu, and many of them set up huge lobster displays right out front. **SERVES 2**

1 (1¹/₂-pound) live lobster
2 teaspoons sesame oil

Sauce

2 tablespoons vegetable oil
¹/₃ cup chopped shallots
2 cloves garlic, minced
1 to 2 teaspoons thinly sliced fresh chile
1 green onion, chopped
¹/₄ cup water
¹/₄ cup tamarind water (see page 189)
2 tablespoons palm sugar or brown sugar
2 tablespoons fish sauce

Cilantro sprigs, for garnish

1. Preheat broiler. Hold lobster on its back; kill instantly by inserting tip of a sharp knife between tail section and body shell, cutting to sever spinal cord. Split lobster lengthwise and remove stomach and intestinal vein. If there is any roe or eggs, remove them and set aside. Crack claws.

2. Place split lobster on broiler pan, split side up. Brush with sesame oil.

3. Place lobster 4 to 6 inches from heat; broil until meat is lightly browned, about 8 minutes.

4. To prepare sauce, place a small saucepan over high heat until hot. Add oil, swirling to coat sides. Add shallots, garlic, chile, and green onion; cook, stirring, until shallots begin to soften, about 1 minute. Add water, tamarind water, palm sugar, and fish sauce. Decrease heat and simmer for 3 minutes. Add roe (if any) and cook for 30 seconds. Place a lobster half on each of 2 dinner plates. Pour sauce over, garnish with cilantro sprigs, and serve.

Tempt Me with Tamarind

Tamarind pods don't look too inviting—dusty brown with a fibrous brown pulp sticking to its several seeds. But when that pulp is processed into a thick, purple-brown paste with an irresistible sweet-tart flavor reminiscent of sour plums, it's proof that beauty is only pod-deep. Tamarind—whether in the form of paste, powder, or liquid concentrate—gives a fruity sour flavor to dishes throughout Southeast Asia, including Thailand. (Some say it's the secret to a perfect *phad thai*.) To make tamarind liquid, combine ¹/₂ cup hot water with 2¹/₂ tablespoons tamarind pulp (scraped from the pod) or packaged paste and soak until softened, 10 to 15 minutes. Squeeze this pulp to extract the juices, and then strain to remove any seeds. When making tamarind liquid from concentrate or powder, follow the package directions. Since tamarind isn't always easy to find, some lime or lemon juice mixed with brown sugar to taste can substitute if necessary.

Poached Clams

When I cooked this recipe on my television show, I used razor clams, but since razor clams are difficult to find I suggest using whatever clams are available at your fish market. Littleneck clams, butter clams, or cherrystone clams will do just fine.

SERVES 4 TO 6

2 dozen medium clams
1 tablespoon thinly sliced lemongrass (bottom 5 to 6 inches only)
3 kaffir lime leaves, torn into pieces

Sauce

1 tablespoon vegetable oil
3 cloves garlic, minced
1 to 2 teaspoons thinly sliced fresh Thai chile
2 tablespoons fresh lime juice
1 tablespoon water
2¹/₂ teaspoons sugar
1 teaspoon salt

1. Scrub clams; discard any with open shells that don't close when tapped.

2. In a wide frying pan, place clams in water to cover. Add lemongrass and lime leaves. Cover and simmer over medium heat until shells open, 6 to 8 minutes.

3. Remove clams with a slotted spoon, discarding any unopened shells, and place in a serving bowl.

4. To make sauce, place a 1-quart pan over high heat until hot. Add oil, swirling to coat sides. Add garlic and cook, stirring, until fragrant, about 10 seconds. Add chile, lime juice, water, sugar, and salt. Cook for 30 seconds.

5. Pour sauce over clams and serve immediately.

Fried Oysters in Roasted Chile Paste

All of Southeast Asia likes fried oysters—Malaysia, Thailand, and Hong Kong. In Thailand, fried oysters are served with a roasted chile sauce. In this recipe, the oysters are first blanched to plump them up. This makes them bigger and moister. **SERVES 2**

1 (10-ounce) jar oysters

1/4 cup cornstarch

3 tablespoons water

1 tablespoon oyster-flavored sauce

2 teaspoons Thai roasted chile paste

1 tablespoon sugar

2 tablespoons vegetable oil

1 tablespoon chopped garlic

2 fresh red Thai chiles, thinly sliced

1/4 cup Thai or sweet basil leaves

1/4 cup walnut halves

1. Drain oysters; cut in half if large. Place oysters in a small pan of simmering water to barely cover. Simmer for 1 minute; lift out with a slotted spoon and transfer to paper towels to drain. Dust oysters with cornstarch.

2. In a small bowl, combine water, oyster sauce, chile paste, and sugar.

3. Place a wok over high heat until hot. Add oil, swirling to coat sides. Add garlic and cook, stirring, until fragrant, about 10 seconds. Add oyster sauce mixture. Decrease heat to medium-low and cook for 30 seconds.

4. Add oysters; cover and cook for 2 minutes. Stir in chiles, basil, and walnuts; cook for 30 seconds.

Trial by Fire

First impressions last. And my first impression of Thai cuisine involved its sinus-scorching heat, courtesy of the country's national spice, the chile pepper. Actually, Thai cooks rely on a market's worth of chiles (which aren't native to Thailand, but came from the New World with the spice trade) to give their foods bite. Just strolling through Bangkok's markets and looking at the baskets of peppers, each a different color, shape, and size, made my eyes water. Finger-sized green, red, and yellow ones—added fresh or as dried flakes or powders—give a moderate punch to curries and stews. For five-alarm flavor, Thais turn to *prik kee noo,* the tiny red, green, and yellow bird's-eye chiles. Generally, the smaller the chile, the bigger the heat, and these guys prove it. Whenever handling chiles, wear gloves to protect your hands from the irritating oils. If you rub those oils into your eyes or mouth, you're in for a fiery surprise.

Simmered Mussels in a Clay Pot

James Bond used plenty of muscle to put Cold War villains in their place, but Chef Khun Praset, from the Kamala Bay Terrace Resort in Phuket—just a stone's throw from "James Bond Island"—knocked me out with his own "mussel power" when he prepared this aromatic dish of mussels infused with distinctly Thai flavors. It just goes to show that the pan (or the clay pot) is mightier than the sword! **SERVES 4**

Sauce

1 tablespoon minced garlic
1 teaspoon minced fresh Thai chile
1¹/₂ tablespoons sugar
¹/₄ cup fresh lime juice
¹/₄ cup fish sauce

16 large New Zealand mussels, or 3 dozen medium-size mussels
10 slices galangal, each the size of a quarter
5 kaffir lime leaves, torn into pieces
4 walnut-size shallots, thinly sliced
2 stalks lemongrass (bottom 5 to 6 inches only),
  split in half lengthwise, lightly crushed
¹/₄ cup Thai or sweet basil leaves
²/₃ cup boiling water

1. To make sauce, with a mortar and pestle, pound garlic, chile, and sugar into a juicy paste. Scrape into a bowl. Add lime juice and fish sauce; mix well.

2. Scrub mussels; discard any with open shells that don't close when tapped.

3. Place mussels in a clay pot or wide frying pan. Scatter galangal, lime leaves, shallots, lemongrass, and basil over the top. Add boiling water. Cover and simmer over medium heat until shells open, 5 to 7 minutes for large mussels, 3 to 5 minutes for smaller ones. Remove from pan and discard any unopened shells.

4. Pour mussels and cooking liquid into a large bowl and serve. Pass sauce at the table for dipping.

Go Galangal

By now, the spicy-sweet bite of ginger is on the tip of most everyone's tongue, but the taste of its decidedly Southeast Asian cousin, galangal, isn't quite as familiar. You'd be wise to get to know this rhizome, with its thin, pale yellow skin and woody pink shoots. It's part of Thailand's indispensable curry arsenal—the curry recipes in this book call for it—and it lends its pungent flavor and aroma to many Thai soups and stews, where raw slices of it simmer until you remove them before you serve the soup. (You don't want to eat the galangal slices, which have a medicinal flavor on their own.) If you can't find raw galangal, you may have better luck looking for galangal powder, also called laos powder, 1 teaspoon of which equals about a ¹/₂-inch piece of fresh galangal. And although galangal and ginger are cousins, you can't substitute one for the other and get the same results.

Frog's Legs with Spicy Basil Sauce

Temple Etiquette

Temples are sacred to the Thai people, and when visiting the country's temples, do as Thais do—behave with respect. For starters, dress properly. That means no shorts or short skirts. Because facing a Buddha image while wearing shoes is considered taboo, worshipers always remove their footwear before entering the temple. And since Thai temples have no pews or seats, go ahead and sit on the floor, but make sure that your legs and feet are tucked under your body and out of sight; it's important not to have your feet pointing at anyone. Finally, keep your head bowed lower than any Buddha icon and monks present. It's all about respect.

Life along the water's edge is colorful to say the least, and certainly a side of Thailand that is seldom seen from the road. At many restaurants by the river edge, frogs are a specialty. Yes, these tasty amphibians can be roasted, stir-fried, steamed, or added to soup. Here I sauté them in a spicy basil sauce. **SERVES 4 TO 6**

¹/₄ cup flour
¹/₄ cup cornstarch
6 pairs frog's legs
3 tablespoons vegetable oil
2 tablespoons julienned galangal
1 tablespoon whole green or black peppercorns
1 tablespoon oyster-flavored sauce
1 teaspoon sugar
2 teaspoons dark soy sauce
¹/₄ cup water
¹/₂ cup Thai or sweet basil leaves
4 fresh red Thai chiles, chopped

1. In a bowl, combine flour and cornstarch. Dredge frog's legs in flour mixture; shake to remove excess.

2. Place a wok or frying pan over high heat until hot. Add 2 tablespoons oil, swirling to coat sides. Place frog's legs in pan and cook, turning once, until golden brown and tender, 2 to 3 minutes on each side. Remove and drain on paper towels.

3. Add remaining 1 tablespoon oil to hot wok. Add galangal and peppercorns; stir-fry until fragrant, about 30 seconds. Add oyster sauce, sugar, soy sauce, and water; cook for 1 minute. Return frog's legs to wok, stir in basil and chiles, and cook for 30 seconds.

Thai–Style Chicken Sandwich

Even though the sandwich wasn't invented in Thailand, a sandwich with a Thai twist is something that we can all invent. For this one, ground meat is stir-fried with eggs and chiles, and wrapped in a hot dog bun. Just squeeze tightly or the filling might end up falling onto your plate. (Sliced sandwich bread may be riskier still.) **SERVES 4**

2 tablespoons vegetable oil

$1/4$ cup diced onion

$1/4$ pound ground or minced chicken

1 tablespoon fish sauce

2 teaspoons Thai chile sauce

2 teaspoons sugar

2 eggs, lightly beaten

$1/4$ cup Thai or sweet basil leaves, chopped

2 teaspoons chopped green onion

4 hot dog buns, or 8 slices sandwich bread

Iceberg lettuce leaves

$1/4$ red onion, sliced into rings

1 large tomato, sliced

1. Place a wok or frying pan over high heat until hot. Add oil, swirling to coat sides. Add diced onion and stir-fry for 1 minute. Add chicken and stir-fry for 1 minute.

2. Stir in fish sauce, chile sauce, and sugar. Add eggs and stir-fry for 1 minute.

3. Add basil leaves and green onion; cook for 30 seconds.

4. To serve, spoon chicken mixture into buns. Tuck a lettuce leaf, a few red onion rings, and a tomato slice into each sandwich and serve.

Tuk Tuk of the Road

It's the three-wheeled offspring of a motor scooter and a golf cart, and it's the fastest land-based way to negotiate Bangkok's traffic—other than running for your life. And it may also be heading down the same path into history as the ox-cart. It's the *tuk tuk,* Thailand's slightly souped-up pedicab, adopted from Japan in the 1950s after it was banned in the Land of the Rising Sun. For a thrill ride, hop into its padded bed (usually about the size of a small sandbox) and hope that your driver's eyesight and reflexes are as sharp as his daredevil maneuvers require. The *tuk tuk* goes where taxis, buses, and even some motorcyclists fear to tread. But they may soon turn off their engines for good as riders are flocking to taxis and other more modern modes of transport, and environmentalists bemoan their belching exhaust while the government simply worries about riders' safety. The *tuk tuk's* next stop may be the history museum.

Grilled Chicken in Pandan Leaves

Pandan Pandemonium

The fragrant, green pandan—or screw pine—leaf pops up in all sorts of Southeast Asian dishes, where its color and pungent aroma graces everything from savory rice and tofu dishes to sweet desserts. Thai cooks are particularly fond of wrapping these long, tapered leaves around chunks of chicken or pork, as well as extracting their essence in the form of a formidably flavored liquid called *toey,* which is sold in bottles. You may be able to find fresh pandan leaves at Southeast Asian groceries or produce markets, but small packages of dried and frozen leaves may be easier to find. They don't quite measure up to the real McCoy, though, so don't feel bad about omitting them from recipes.

These packets remind me of Chinese foil-wrapped chicken. Chicken is marinated in sesame oil, fish sauce, and garlic, then wrapped in a pandan leaf to grill. Serve this dish with glazed walnuts. They add a wonderful sweet and crunchy contrast to the chicken. **MAKES 8 PACKAGES, SERVES 4**

Marinade

1 tablespoon sesame oil

1 teaspoon fish sauce

$1/2$ teaspoon cornstarch

$1/8$ teaspoon white pepper

1 clove garlic, minced

**$1/2$ pound boneless, skinless chicken breast,
    cut into $1/2$-inch cubes**

**8 (2 by 8-inch) pieces pandan leaves,
    or 8 (6-inch) squares aluminum foil**

Glazed walnuts (see page 117)

1. To make marinade, in a bowl combine sesame oil, fish sauce, cornstarch, pepper, and garlic. Add chicken and stir to coat. Cover and refrigerate for 1 hour.

2. Prepare a fire in a charcoal grill or preheat a gas grill.

3. Roll each pandan leaf into a cone; fill each cone with 2 tablespoons chicken mixture. Wrap remaining leaf ends over tops to enclose. Fasten each cone with a toothpick. (If using foil, fold over filling to enclose in a packet.)

4. Grill packets over medium-hot fire for 5 minutes on each side.

5. Serve hot or warm, with tops cut open to reveal the chicken. Garnish with glazed walnuts.

Chicken with Chiles and Basil

Tell It Like the Thais

Traveling all over Asia, I can't help picking up some of the local lingo. But for some reason, my vocabulary doesn't extend too far beyond the edible! Here are some common Thai food terms I've learned that will help on your next culinary journey: *Kaeng* means "liquid," although it's generally applied to curry. Three of the most popular *kaeng* dishes are *kaeng khieo wan* (green curry), *kaeng ped* (red curry), and *kaeng Mussaman* (Muslim-style curry). *Yam* is the general word for salad, although the popular green papaya salad is referred to as *som tam*. Meat salads are considered different from *yam,* and go by *larb.* As for noodles, they're called *sen* or *mee* when made from rice, wheat, or mung bean starch, but *kway tiow* is the name for large, fresh rice noodles. And don't forget dessert! Thai sweets, some of which have a surprising savory edge, are called *khanom.*

A peek into the dining room of a Thai family would reveal casual yet tasty dishes such as chicken with spicy chiles and sweet basil. The simplicity and flavor harmony of Thai cuisine beckon you to cook Thai food tonight. **SERVES 4**

3/4 **pound boneless, skinless chicken breast**
1/8 **teaspoon salt**
1/8 **teaspoon white pepper**
2 **tablespoons vegetable oil**
3 **cloves garlic, thinly sliced**
2 **walnut-size shallots, thinly sliced**
4 **fresh Thai chiles, seeded and thinly sliced**
5 **Chinese long beans, or 20 green beans, cut into 1**1/2**-inch lengths**
1/4 **cup chicken stock (see page 38)**
1 **cup Thai or sweet basil leaves**
1 **tablespoon fish sauce**
1 **tablespoon dark soy sauce**
2 **teaspoons palm sugar or brown sugar**

1. Thinly slice chicken at an angle across the grain. Season with salt and white pepper.

2. Place a wok or wide frying pan over high heat until hot. Add oil, swirling to coat sides. Add garlic and shallots; stir-fry until fragrant, about 30 seconds.

3. Add chicken and stir-fry until no longer pink, about 3 minutes. Add chiles, beans, and stock; cook for 2 minutes. Add basil, fish sauce, soy sauce, and palm sugar. Cook for 1 minute and serve.

Chicken and Eggplant in Green Curry

"Hot! Hot!" That's what I shout when I eat green curry. Then I shout, "Good! Good!" when I've finished the meal because I'm ready for more. Even though green curry is very spicy, I still like to eat it, especially stir-fried with chicken and eggplant. **SERVES 4**

1 cup unsweetened coconut milk

3 tablespoons green curry paste (see page 133)

³/₄ pound boneless, skinless chicken, thinly sliced

1¹/₂ tablespoons palm sugar or brown sugar

1 tablespoon fish sauce

¹/₄ pound Thai or Asian eggplants, cut into bite-size pieces

4 asparagus spears, cut into 1¹/₂-inch lengths

¹/₄ cup sliced bamboo shoots

2 kaffir lime leaves, julienned

¹/₄ cup Thai or sweet basil leaves

1 fresh Thai chile, seeded and thinly sliced, for garnish

1. Place ¹/₂ cup of the coconut milk in a wok or saucepan over medium heat for 30 seconds. Add curry paste and slowly bring to a boil, stirring constantly, about 2 minutes. Add remaining ¹/₂ cup coconut milk; bring to a boil.

2. Add chicken and cook, stirring, until it is no longer pink, about 3 minutes. Add palm sugar, fish sauce, eggplants, asparagus, bamboo shoots, and lime leaves; cook for 2 minutes. Add basil leaves and cook for 1 minute. Transfer to a serving dish and garnish with sliced chile.

Eggplant Extravaganza

A wise man once said that an eggplant shopping spree in Thailand is like a box of chocolates—you never know what you're going to get. If all you know of eggplants is the bulky dark purple globe, take a peek into Thailand's eggplant treasure trove to find long, slender varieties ranging in color from pale amethyst to obsidian; round, ivory ones that look better suited to a pool table than a kitchen table; and clusters of tart, green pea-sized eggplants that get added to curries whole or grow into larger bulbs resembling speckled unripe tomatoes. You'll even find orange eggplants covered in fine dark hairs. Each one looks different and tastes a little different, so experiment with the eggplants at your own market. You may find you like them better than chocolate.

Chicken in Red Curry with Rice Balls

On the show, I served this chicken in red curry with glutinous rice balls, but it's not necessary to shape the rice into balls. You can skip the first step of the recipe and serve the rice any way you want and with whatever type of rice you want. Glutinous rice just happens to be my favorite. **SERVES 4**

Rice Balls

1 cup warm cooked long-grain rice

1 cup warm cooked glutinous rice

2 tablespoons vegetable oil

3 tablespoons red curry paste (see page 133)

1 pound boneless, skinless chicken, thinly sliced

1/4 cup water

1 cup roll-cut carrots, blanched

1 cup sliced bamboo shoots

2 tablespoons fish sauce

2 teaspoons palm sugar or brown sugar

3 fresh Thai chiles, each cut lengthwise into 4 pieces

4 kaffir lime leaves, julienned

1/2 cup Thai or sweet basil leaves

Thai or sweet basil leaves, thinly sliced, for garnish

1. In a bowl, combine long-grain and glutinous rice. To make each rice ball, wet hands with water and scoop up about 2 tablespoons of the rice mixture, and mold into an oval shape. Place on a serving plate; cover with a damp towel and set aside.

2. Place a wok over high heat until hot. Add oil, swirling to coat sides. Add curry paste and stir-fry until fragrant, about 1 minute.

3. Add chicken and stir-fry until chicken is no longer pink, 2 to 3 minutes. Add water, carrots, bamboo shoots, fish sauce, palm sugar, chiles, and lime leaves. Decrease heat and simmer for 2 minutes. Add basil leaves and cook for 1 minute.

4. Serve curry with rice balls and garnish with thinly sliced basil leaves.

Having a Ball, or Two . . .

Fragrant, long-grain jasmine rice may reign supreme in many parts of Thailand, but it's not the only member of the Thai royal rice family. In northern Thailand, short-grain glutinous rice is the grain of choice. As glutinous rice cooks, its gluten proteins and molecules of a starch called amylopectin get waterlogged. This causes them to swell and become sticky. Northern Thais take advantage of glutinous rice's tendency toward tackiness by steaming it and then rolling it into small balls by hand at the table. They dip these individually into curries, sauces, and soups in much the same way that an American from the southern United States would dip a hot biscuit into a stew. They're tasty, convenient little nuggets, and they make a mouthwatering break from good old long-grain.

Aromatic Duck Breast with Coconut Fried Rice

Foolproof Fried Rice

If I got a nickel every time someone told me it's impossible to make fried rice like the restaurants do, I'd open up my own restaurant and make it for them! That's because making light and fluffy fried rice—yes, just like you get at restaurants—is a snap if you follow a few guidelines. For one, use cooked, cooled rice. If you just scoop the rice out of the steamer, it'll be too warm and moist, leaving you with soggy fried rice that's more like pudding. Use long-grain rice, too. Medium- and short-grain kinds are too sticky to stir and toss around in the wok; you're making stir-fried rice, after all. And before you add cooled, cooked long-grain rice to the wok, separate the grains that have clumped together in the refrigerator; gently break them apart with a fork or, even better, rub them with your lightly moistened fingers.

If you don't have time to marinate the duck in red curry and lemongrass, use a package of Thai aromatic grill sauce. In today's busy Bangkok, many on-the-go Thai families avail themselves of this modern-day convenience. **SERVES 4**

2 (4- to 6-ounce) duck breast halves

1½ tablespoons red curry paste (see page 133)

2 stalks lemongrass (bottom 5 to 6 inches only), finely chopped

1 tablespoon vegetable oil

Coconut Fried Rice

2 tablespoons vegetable oil

1 tablespoon minced lemongrass (bottom 5 to 6 inches only)

½ cup diced carrots, blanched

½ cup sliced asparagus

1 tablespoon oyster-flavored sauce

2 teaspoons sugar

3 cups cold cooked long-grain rice

3 tablespoons unsweetened coconut milk

1 green onion, thinly sliced

2 tablespoons glazed walnuts, (see page 117), for garnish

1. With a knife, make diagonal cuts 1 inch apart across skin of each duck breast half; repeat in opposite direction to create crosshatching. Place duck in a bowl. Combine red curry paste and lemongrass. Spread mixture over duck to coat; cover and refrigerate for 1 hour.

2. Place a wide frying pan over medium heat until hot. Add oil, swirling to coat sides. Place breasts, skin side down, in pan; decrease heat to medium-low, and cook for 8 minutes. Turn breasts and cook for 6 minutes more. The skin should be crisp and the meat still pink. Remove pan from heat.

3. To prepare rice: Place a wok over high heat until hot. Add oil, swirling to coat sides. Add lemongrass and cook, stirring, until fragrant, about 30 seconds. Add carrots, asparagus, oyster sauce, and sugar; cook for 1 minute. Decrease heat to medium; stir in rice, separating grains with a fork. Cook for 2 minutes. Add coconut milk and green onion. Cook, stirring, until heated through.

4. Cut breast meat crosswise into ½-inch slices. Place rice on a serving plate and arrange breast meat on top. Garnish with walnuts, and serve.

Roasted Duck with Red Curry

The duck is simmered in red curry sauce, which is made by first cooking red curry paste with half the amount of coconut milk specified in the recipe. This brings out the natural oils and aroma of the curry paste before the rest of the coconut milk is added. Kaffir lime leaves and medjool dates enrich the sauce's flavor. If you can't find medjool dates, substitute any type of date. After all, who wants to go dateless? (And to save time, buy roasted duck breast at a Chinese market.) **SERVES 2**

1 roasted duck breast

1 cup unsweetened coconut milk

2 tablespoons red curry paste (see page 133)

2 tablespoons sugar

1 tablespoon fish sauce

4 kaffir lime leaves, torn into pieces

6 Chinese long beans, or 24 green beans, cut into 1¹/₂-inch lengths

1 cup cherry tomatoes

1 cup lychees

2 medjool dates, pitted and coarsely chopped

2 baby bok choy, blanched, for garnish (optional)

1. Remove skin from duck breast and discard; scrape off fat. Cut duck into ¹/₂ by 2-inch pieces.

2. Place ¹/₂ cup of the coconut milk in a wok or saucepan over medium heat for 30 seconds. Add curry paste and slowly bring to a boil, stirring constantly, about 1 minute. Add the remaining ¹/₂ cup coconut milk; bring to a boil.

3. Add duck and cook for 2 minutes. Add sugar, fish sauce, and lime leaves; cook for 1 minute. Add beans; cook for 2 minutes. Add cherry tomatoes, lychees, and dates; decrease heat to medium-low and simmer for 1 minute. Transfer to a serving dish and garnish with baby bok choy.

Chile–Garlic Quail over Cabbage

Just like the fine art of the Sukhothai era, these quail are dainty and elegant. What's more, they make deliciously tender counterpoints to a crisp cabbage salad with a simple, tangy dressing. **SERVES 6**

Marinade

4 cloves garlic, crushed

2 tablespoons chopped cilantro leaves

1 tablespoon grated ginger

1 fresh Thai chile, seeded and minced

2 teaspoons red curry paste (see page 133)

2 teaspoons vegetable oil

2 teaspoons soy sauce

2 teaspoons Thai chile sauce

2 teaspoons palm sugar or brown sugar

6 quail

1 cup finely shredded napa cabbage

1/4 teaspoon salt

Dressing

2 tablespoons fresh lime juice

4 fresh red Thai chiles, thinly sliced

1/2 teaspoon sugar

1/4 teaspoon salt

2 tablespoons vegetable oil

2 tablespoons pine nuts

2 tablespoons deep-fried garlic (see page 164)

2 tablespoons deep-fried onion (see page 164)

1 lime, cut into wedges, for garnish

1. To make marinade, in a blender, combine garlic, cilantro, ginger, chile, curry paste, oil, soy sauce, chile sauce, and palm granulated sugar; process until smooth. Split each quail in half by cutting through the breast and backbone. In a large bowl, rub marinade onto quail. Cover and refrigerate for at least 2 hours.

2. Combine cabbage and salt in a bowl; let stand for 15 minutes. Squeeze cabbage to remove excess liquid. Arrange on a platter and set aside.

3. To make dressing, in a bowl combine lime juice, chiles, sugar, and salt. Set aside.

4. Heat a grill pan or a wide frying pan over medium heat. Brush hot pan with 1 tablespoon oil. Lift quail from marinade, drain briefly, brush with the remaining 1 tablespoon oil, and place quail skin side down on pan. Cook, turning and basting occasionally with marinade, until meat near bone is no longer pink when slashed, about 20 minutes. Arrange quail over the cabbage and drizzle with dressing; sprinkle with pine nuts, fried garlic, and fried onion. Place lime wedges around cabbage and serve.

Ground Beef Omelet

If you think omelets are only for breakfast, you're wrong. In Thailand, meats and vegetables are stir-fried and added to eggs to make soft, fluffy omelets. They taste great with a bowl of jasmine rice. **SERVES 4**

Marinade

1 green onion, thinly sliced

1 fresh Thai chile, seeded and thinly sliced

2 tablespoons chicken stock (see page 38)

1 tablespoon fish sauce

1/8 teaspoon white pepper

6 ounces ground beef, pork, or lamb

2 tablespoons vegetable oil

6 eggs, lightly beaten

1. To make marinade, in a bowl combine onion, chile, stock, fish sauce, and pepper. Add beef and mix well; let stand for 10 minutes.

2. Place a wok or nonstick frying pan over high heat until hot. Add 1 tablespoon oil, swirling to coat sides. Add beef and stir-fry until lightly browned and crumbly, about 1 minute. Remove mixture from pan.

3. In the same pan, heat remaining 1 tablespoon oil over medium-high heat; add eggs. Cook, without stirring, until eggs are set around the edges. Return meat to pan, stir toward center, and cook, stirring, until eggs form large, soft, moist curds, about 2 minutes.

4. Slide omelet onto a warm serving plate.

Vanishing Beef?

Ever since the first rice crop was planted in Thailand, the relationship between farmer and water buffalo has been more a partnership than a hierarchy of master and beast of burden. Thai farmers respected their "co-workers," cherishing them as members of their family and celebrating them in paintings and songs. Time marches on, and today the efficiency of modern farm equipment means greater output and lower maintenance costs than what a hungry water buffalo exacts. This has driven many Thai farmers to literally sell their partners to slaughterhouses. In response, the Thai government has initiated a project that encourages farmers to continue providing a role for their buffaloes, in the process preserving a unique part of Thailand's cultural heritage.

Orange You Glad?

If all those pictures you drew as a child with your oversized box of crayons came true, you'd wind up with a scene *almost* as colorful as Thailand. And one of the brightest crayons in the box is the warm orange tinted with saffron and coral that's characteristic of Buddhist monks' robes. Westerners may consider orange a stimulating, "hyper" color, but when it drapes the monks, it reflects their modest serenity. The hue is something of a sacred color in Buddhist cultures, symbolizing monkhood and showing up in such Buddhist rituals as orange candles, golden orange icons, and even the orange tubs that worshipers use to carry donations of food, clothes, and necessities to the monks. In Thailand, choosing orange isn't just a fashion decision; it's an act of devotion.

Buddist monks on their way to prayer.

The Reclining Buddha of Wat Po.

24K Karma

Throughout Thailand, gleaming Buddha statues drip with layers of gold leaf. On a visit to Wat Yai Temple, one of the oldest in the heart of Thailand, in Phitsanoluk, I added my own stamp of gold to the temple's Buddha image, while giving my karma a boast at the same time. For believers in karma, one's deeds in the current life determine the quality of the next, and one good deed is to press delicate leaves of gold sold by temple attendants (the proceeds support temple upkeep) on Buddha statues. Popular spots for pressing include Buddha's mouth (to bring the devotee words of joy), the head (to increase the giver's wisdom), and the heart (for obvious reasons). It's a symbolic gesture of generosity with the real-world benefit of beautifying these holy places.

Beef Curry in Peanut Sauce

Peanut sauce always conjures up thoughts of Thai food. I make my sauce with red curry paste and finely ground roasted peanuts, and serve it with tender flank steak thinly sliced. I've added sugar snap peas to the mix here, but this dish is also delicious without them. **SERVES 4**

1¹/₂ **cups unsweetened coconut milk**

3 **tablespoons red curry paste (see page 133)**

1 **pound beef flank steak, thinly sliced across the grain**

¹/₂ **cup finely ground roasted peanuts**

3 **tablespoons palm sugar or brown sugar**

1 **tablespoon fish sauce**

6 **kaffir lime leaves, julienned**

¹/₄ **cup Thai or sweet basil leaves**

1 **fresh Thai chile, thinly sliced**

1 **cup sugar snap peas, blanched (optional)**

1. Place coconut milk in a wok or saucepan over medium heat for 30 seconds. Add curry paste and slowly bring to a boil, stirring constantly, about 2 minutes. Add beef; cook for about 4 minutes.

2. Add peanuts, palm sugar, and fish sauce; decrease heat to medium-low and simmer for 10 minutes.

3. Add lime and basil leaves, chile, and sugar snap peas; cook for 1 minute more and serve.

Spicy Beef with Tomato and Basil

What's simpler than tender flank steak, stir-fried with tomato wedges and red chiles, and served over a bed of Chinese broccoli? In my book, simplicity in the cooking is simply good cooking. **SERVES 4**

Sauce

2 tablespoons soy sauce

1 tablespoon rice vinegar

1 tablespoon sugar

2 teaspoons sesame oil

2 tablespoons vegetable oil

1/2 cup sliced onion

2 teaspoons minced garlic

2 small dried red chiles, seeded

3/4 pound beef flank steak, thinly sliced across the grain

1/2 cup Thai or sweet basil leaves

2 tomatoes, cut into wedges

1 teaspoon cornstarch dissolved in 2 teaspoons water

8 ounces Chinese broccoli, trimmed, blanched, and cut into 2-inch sections

1. To make sauce, in a bowl combine soy sauce, rice vinegar, sugar, and sesame oil.

2. Place a wok over high heat until hot. Add oil, swirling to coat sides. Add onion, garlic, and chiles; stir-fry until fragrant, about 30 seconds. Add beef and stir-fry until barely pink, 1½ to 2 minutes.

3. Add basil, tomatoes, and sauce; mix well.

4. Add cornstarch solution and cook, stirring, until sauce boils and thickens.

5. Transfer to a platter; arrange broccoli around the beef and serve.

Basil Basics

Calling an herb "Thai" basil is a bit misleading, because Thai cooks—and cooks throughout Southeast Asia—turn to a variety of green, aromatic herbs in the mint family when they're in the market for basil. The most common, sweet basil *(bai horapa)*, has big, fleshy leaves and a strong flavor that calls to mind anise. Few Thai curries, salads, or soups go without it. You may also stumble upon purple basil *(bai krapao)*, with its small, oval leaves that taper at the ends. As its name hints, it's an interesting purple-red color. (It looks fabulous with eggplant!) For a real treat, try to find "hairy" basil *(luk manglak)*. Spot it by the long, slender, light green leaves tipped in a cluster of red seed pods. People in Southeast Asia dry these pods and add them to drinks and desserts for a strong lemony-peppery flavor.

Dry Beef Curry

"Dry" beef curry is made by slowly simmering the curry sauce to reduce it until there's just enough sauce left to cover the beef lightly. This reduction maximizes the intensity of the spice flavors, creating an even tastier dish. **SERVES 4**

Spice Paste

1 tablespoon coriander seeds

2 teaspoons cumin seeds

2¹/₂ tablespoons yellow curry paste (see page 134)

²/₃ cup unsweetened coconut milk

³/₄ pound beef flank steak, thinly sliced across the grain

6 whole fresh Thai chiles

4 kaffir lime leaves, julienned

3 tablespoons palm sugar or brown sugar

2 teaspoons fish sauce

2 teaspoons soy sauce

1. To make spice paste, in a spice grinder finely grind coriander and cumin seeds. Place in a bowl with curry paste; mix well.

2. Place ¹/₃ cup of the coconut milk in a wok or saucepan over medium heat for 30 seconds. Add spice paste mixture and slowly bring to a boil, stirring constantly, about 2 minutes. Add beef and stir until it is no longer pink, about 1 minute.

3. Add the remaining ¹/₃ cup coconut milk; bring to a boil.

4. Add chiles, lime leaves, sugar, fish sauce, and soy sauce. Decrease heat and simmer until sauce thickens enough to lightly coat meat, about 10 minutes.

Daily life on Bangkok's canals.

House with a View

Friends with waterfront property always tell me that it's the only way to live. Well, in parts of Thailand, it really is! In Bangkok, houses supported by stilts line the embankment of the picturesque Chao Phraya River like water cranes balancing on their spindly legs. Keeping a low profile doesn't cut it around here, what with the annual floods washing away anything that's not sitting well above the high-water mark. Even so, I think I could get used to this kind of life on the waterways. Just one afternoon spent catching the reflection of everyday life (commerce, travel, leisure, ceremony) as it floated by on Thailand's "River of Kings" gave me a surprising peace of mind so rarely found in busy cosmopolitan cities.

Spicy Beef Curry with Squash

This dish is flavored with six kaffir lime leaves. The lime leaves add a very tart flavor to the sauce and add complexity to the spicy red curry paste. **SERVES 4**

3/4 **pound kabocha squash, pumpkin, or yam**

1/4 **cup coconut cream**

2 **tablespoons red curry paste (see page 133)**

1/2 **pound beef flank steak, cut into** 3/4**-inch cubes**

3/4 **cup unsweetened coconut milk**

6 **kaffir lime leaves, torn into pieces**

11/2 **tablespoons fish sauce**

1 **tablespoon palm sugar or brown sugar**

2 **fresh red Thai chiles, seeded and thinly sliced**

Thai or sweet basil sprigs, for garnish

1. Peel squash and cut into 1-inch cubes. Place in a saucepan with 1 inch of water and boil until barely tender, about 10 minutes; drain.

2. For coconut cream: Open a can of unsweetened coconut milk (do not shake it first) and spoon the thick cream off the top. Stir remaining coconut milk in can to blend.

3. Place 1/4 cup coconut cream and curry paste in a wok or saucepan over medium heat and slowly bring to a boil, stirring constantly, about 30 seconds. Add beef and cook, stirring, for 2 minutes.

4. Add coconut milk and lime leaves; bring to a boil. Add squash, fish sauce, and sugar; cook for 2 minutes. Add chiles and stir for 30 seconds. Transfer to a serving dish and garnish with basil sprigs.

Three Traffic Lights

While I was stuck in all that Bangkok traffic, an idea came to me, and my next dish was born. I pair foods with curry colors—red curry beef, yellow curry shrimp, and green curry chicken. And keeping with the color theme, I stuff them in their respective color of bell pepper. Line them up and you have a traffic light. While this version steams the peppers, you can also bake them for 40 minutes in a 350° oven. **SERVES 2 TO 4**

Beef Filling

1/4 pound ground beef

1 tablespoon red curry paste (see page 133)

1/4 cup diced onion

1 teaspoon minced lemongrass (bottom 5 to 6 inches only)

1 egg, lightly beaten

1 teaspoon cornstarch

2 tablespoons water

Chicken Filling

1/4 pound ground or minced chicken

1 tablespoon green curry paste (see page 133)

1 tablespoon dried shrimp, soaked 20 minutes in warm water, drained, and minced

1 tablespoon chopped Thai or sweet basil leaves

1 egg, lightly beaten

1 teaspoon cornstarch

2 tablespoons water

Shrimp Filling

1/4 pound raw shrimp, shelled, deveined, and finely chopped

1 tablespoon yellow curry paste (see page 134)

1 tablespoon minced cilantro leaves

1 teaspoon minced lemongrass (bottom 5 to 6 inches only)

1/2 teaspoon minced kaffir lime leaves

1 egg, lightly beaten

1 teaspoon cornstarch

2 tablespoons water

1 red bell pepper

1 green bell pepper

1 yellow bell pepper

Dipping Sauce

3 tablespoons soy sauce

1 tablespoon distilled white vinegar

2 teaspoons sugar

2 teaspoons chopped cilantro leaves

2 fresh red Thai chiles, seeded and minced

1. To make beef filling, in a bowl combine ground beef, red curry paste, onion, lemongrass, egg, cornstarch, and water; mix well.

2. To make chicken filling, in a bowl combine chicken, green curry paste, dried shrimp, basil, egg, cornstarch, and water; mix well.

3. To make shrimp filling, in a bowl combine shrimp, yellow curry paste, cilantro, lemongrass, lime leaves, egg, cornstarch, and water; mix well.

4. Cut each bell pepper horizontally so bottom sections make cups 1½ inches high. Remove seeds (save tops for other uses). Trim bottoms slightly, if necessary, so each cup stands upright. Spoon beef filling into red pepper cup, chicken filling into green pepper cup, and shrimp filling into yellow pepper cup. Stand peppers in a heatproof dish.

5. Prepare a wok for steaming (see page 6). Cover and steam bell pepper cups over high heat until a wooden toothpick inserted in the center comes out clean, about 20 minutes.

6. To make dipping sauce, in a bowl combine soy sauce, vinegar, sugar, cilantro, and chiles.

7. Quarter peppers, transfer to a serving plate, and serve with dipping sauce on the side.

Traffic Thai–Ups

Bangkok is a notorious traffic hotspot. Not only does every type of motor vehicle vie for space on the city's narrow streets, but they do so at breakneck speeds and without the help of strictly enforced traffic laws. But it's a sign of Thailand's modernizing times that in late 1999, the nation christened Skytrain, a sleek, German-built rail system that covers a fifteen-mile-loop at a smooth thirty miles per hour, thirty feet above the city's most migraine-inducing traffic snarls. It delivers riders directly to major hotels, department stores, and popular sites like the zoo and convention center. But don't expect smooth sailing on the streets just yet. Skytrain ridership hasn't quite fulfilled expectations, perhaps because of price or because of the hard-to-kick automobile habit. Only time will tell if it's the cure for Bangkok's traffic blues.

Pineapple Thai Fried Rice

Rich soil and a mild climate make Thailand an exotic fruit cornucopia. Many fresh fruits, including pineapples, find their way into Thai cuisine. To create a beautiful pineapple container for the rice, cut a pineapple down the middle vertically, and cut out the flesh. **SERVES 4 TO 6**

1/3 cup dried shrimp

2 tablespoons vegetable oil

1 tablespoon minced garlic

2 (2-ounce) Chinese sausages, cut diagonally into 1/4-inch slices

1/2 cup sliced onion

3 eggs, lightly beaten

4 cups cold cooked long-grain rice

2 tablespoons soy sauce

1 tablespoon fish sauce

1 cup diced fresh pineapple

1/2 pineapple, hollowed out, for serving

1 tomato, cut into 1/4-inch slices, for garnish

1 small cucumber, cut into 1/4-inch slices, for garnish

1 to 2 teaspoons thinly sliced fresh Thai chile, for garnish

1 green onion, thinly sliced, for garnish

1. Soak dried shrimp in warm water to cover until softened, about 20 minutes; drain.

2. Place a wide nonstick frying pan over high heat until hot. Add oil, swirling to coat sides. Add garlic and cook, stirring, until fragrant, about 10 seconds. Add shrimp, sausage, and onion; stir-fry for 1 minute. Add eggs and stir-fry for 30 seconds.

3. Decrease heat to medium; stir in rice, separating grains with a fork. Cook for 2 minutes. Add soy sauce, fish sauce, and pineapple. Cook, stirring, until heated through.

4. To serve, spoon fried rice into pineapple shell and garnish with tomato, cucumber, chile, and green onion. Or place tomato and cucumber slices around the edge of a serving platter, spoon fried rice into the middle of the platter, and sprinkle with chile and green onion.

Pining for Apples

Where does pineapple come from? Well, about two million metric tons of it come from Thailand each year. This is about 20 percent of the world's production, making Thailand the most prolific producer of this sweet-tart fruit. Recently, I visited a pineapple plantation on Phuket, in southern Thailand (the country's pineapple-producing hub), and hunted through its fragrant jungle for the prized pineapples. It wasn't a tough chase, considering that I could smell their bouquet from miles around. All I had to do was follow my nose to spot them crowning the tops of thick stalks, each surrounded by a ring of long, bladelike leaves that protect them from pineapple pirates like myself. But one quick swipe of the harvester's blade, and the juicy prey was mine.

Chicken with Seasoned Rice

Thailand produces some of the best jasmine rice in the world, and what better recipe to showcase this aromatic rice than Chicken with Seasoned Rice? To give the rice an added leafy flavor, I like to throw a pandan leaf in with the stock. **SERVES 4**

4 chicken legs and thighs

6 cups water

1 teaspoon salt

8 cilantro stems, crushed

Seasoned Rice

2 tablespoons vegetable oil

10 cloves garlic, crushed

1 1/2 cups long-grain rice

1 pandan leaf (see page 196; optional),
  tied in a knot

Dipping Sauce

1 tablespoon fermented soybeans or
  ground bean paste

1 tablespoon rice vinegar

1 teaspoon palm sugar or brown sugar

2 slices ginger, each the size of a
  quarter, crushed

1 fresh Thai chile, crushed

Cucumber slices, for garnish

Cilantro sprigs, for garnish

1. Place chicken, water, salt, and cilantro stems in a 3-quart pan and bring to a boil. Decrease heat; cover and simmer over medium-low heat until chicken is no longer pink when cut near bone, 25 to 30 minutes. Turn off heat, cover, and set aside for 20 minutes. Remove chicken and skim froth. Strain stock and reserve for the rice.

2. To make seasoned rice, place a 2-quart pan over high heat until hot. Add oil, swirling to coat sides. Add garlic and stir-fry until fragrant, about 30 seconds. Add rice and stir for 3 minutes. Add 2 1/2 cups of the stock and pandan leaf. Bring to a boil; decrease heat, cover, and simmer until rice is tender and liquid is absorbed, about 20 minutes. Remove pandan leaf.

3. To make dipping sauce, in a bowl stir together soybeans, vinegar, sugar, ginger, and chile. Mix and set aside.

4. To serve, mound rice on a platter. Remove bones from chicken and slice meat. Arrange chicken around rice. Garnish with cucumber slices and cilantro sprigs. Serve with dipping sauce.

Mother Nature's Rice Cooker

When I visited a tribal village in the rural hills of Thailand, I got a demonstration in steaming rice that made even my mom's beat-up old rice pot seem like a high-tech cooking gadget. These crafty cooks turn to the earth for their cooking equipment, and it hands them—what else?—bamboo. And I don't mean the trusty round bamboo steamer basket, either. No, these tribal cooks use something even more traditional: hollow bamboo tubes. First, they place the raw rice inside the tubes. Then they add water and place the contraptions over heat. In no time at all, the rice is cooked perfectly and flavored with the unmistakable essence of bamboo. Who needs gadgetry when you've got easy access to the equipment in Mother Nature's kitchen?

Rice Vermicelli

Thais eat rice vermicelli for breakfast. The noodles are seasoned with spices, and raw vegetables are placed on top. Hot steaming stock is poured over everything. **SERVES 4**

6 ounces firm white fish fillet, such as sea bass or halibut

2 cups water

4 ounces dried rice noodles (about 1/8 inch wide)

Spice Paste

1 stalk lemongrass (bottom 5 to 6 inches only)

3 walnut-size shallots

2 cloves garlic

3 dried red chiles, seeded

1 ounce salted fish, sliced

2 teaspoons chopped galangal

1 teaspoon shrimp paste

1/3 cup water

1/4 pound Chinese long beans or green beans, cut into 1 1/2-inch lengths

1/4 pound savoy cabbage, shredded

3 cups unsweetened coconut milk

2 teaspoons fish sauce

2 teaspoons sugar

1/4 pound fresh bean sprouts

2 hard-cooked eggs, shelled and cut into wedges, for garnish

1. Place fish and water in a small pan. Bring to a boil, decrease heat, and simmer until fish just begins to flake, 6 to 8 minutes. Remove fish, reserving liquid. Flake fish with a fork and set aside. Soak rice noodles in warm water to cover for 15 minutes; drain. Cook noodles in a large pot of boiling water until tender, 3 to 5 minutes. Drain, rinse, drain again.

2. To make spice paste, thinly slice lemongrass. Place in a blender with shallots, garlic, chiles, salted fish, galangal, shrimp paste, and water; process until smooth.

3. Cook beans and cabbage in boiling water until tender-crisp, 2 minutes. Drain, rinse, and drain again. In a 3-quart pan, combine spice paste with 2 cups coconut milk. Bring to a boil; cook for about 1 minute. Add reserved fish liquid and remaining 1 cup coconut milk; bring to a boil and cook for 2 minutes. Decrease heat and simmer for 5 minutes more. Add fish, fish sauce, and sugar; cook for 30 seconds.

4. To serve, arrange noodles, beans, cabbage, and bean sprouts on a platter. Ladle coconut mixture over and garnish with egg wedges.

Mornings in Thailand

The morning commute in Bangkok is like that in any modern, jam-packed metropolis: loud and hurried. Outside of Bangkok, however, the picture is quite different. When I greeted the day in the northern countryside. I rejected the alarm clock in lieu of the chirping birds. I watched the rising sun dapple emerald pools and lily pads, drying last night's dew from the flowers. And I ignored the passing minutes as I lazily nibbled my morning meal (really the best part of waking up). It's a far cry from my usual routine, and I soon had to bid farewell to this leisurely A.M. pace and get filming. But just one quiet Thai morning left me rejuvenated for the rest of the day.

Fried Rice with Cilantro and Basil

Most people in North America associate fried rice with Chinese food, but they also fry rice in Thailand. Long-grain rice is firmer and better for frying. Here the cilantro and basil add a sweet and pungent flavor, making the rice intensely aromatic. **SERVES 4**

2 tablespoons vegetable oil

6 ounces ground pork

4 cloves garlic, minced

1 tablespoon minced ginger

1 tablespoon coarsely chopped fresh Thai chiles

3 cups cold cooked long-grain rice

1 tablespoon fish sauce

1 tablespoon soy sauce

2 teaspoons palm sugar or brown sugar

1 cup Thai basil or sweet basil leaves

2 green onions, chopped

¹⁄₄ cup cilantro leaves

2 tablespoons chicken stock (see page 38; optional)

1. Place a wok over high heat until hot. Add oil, swirling to coat sides. Add pork and stir-fry until lightly browned and crumbly, about 1 minute. Add garlic, ginger, and chiles; cook for 1 minute.

2. Decrease heat to medium; stir in rice, separating grains with a fork; stir-fry for 2 to 3 minutes. Add fish sauce, soy sauce, and palm sugar; stir-fry for 1 minute.

3. Add basil, green onions, and cilantro; stir-fry for 30 seconds. If mixture seems dry, add stock to moisten. Transfer to a platter and serve.

The Cycle of Life

The rhythm of life in Thailand has traditionally moved with the cycles of the rice harvest. In late spring, all able bodies in the rice-growing community joined efforts to prepare the fields for planting the seedlings. During the rainy season that followed—a time Buddhists know as the Rains Retreat—the rains fed the thirsty, newly planted rice, and the farmers patiently waited for it to grow. When the gray skies cleared and the fields drained, the rice was ready to harvest. Cooperation among villages brought them back to the fields to reap the fruits of their labors and allow the cycle to begin anew for the next harvest. Witnessing this age-old dance with nature filled me with respect both for the farmers and for their partnership with Mother Earth. Their faith in the cycle's continuity is the true legacy that they will leave for future generations.

Phad Thai

Go to any Thai restaurant and you are sure to see a plate of phad thai *noodles on every table. With noodles as soft and flavored as these, it's no wonder everybody likes them. Here's one version I developed a liking for; it's from the Regent Hotel in Chiang Mai.* **SERVES 4 TO 6**

2 tablespoons dried shrimp

1 pound dried or fresh flat rice noodles, about 1/4 inch wide

Sauce

1/2 cup chicken stock (see page 38)

1/4 cup sugar

1/4 cup tamarind water (see page 189) or vinegar

2 tablespoons fish sauce

1 tablespoon fresh lime juice

3 tablespoons vegetable oil

2 tablespoons minced cilantro stems

1 tablespoon minced garlic

1 tablespoon chopped shallots

1 teaspoon crushed dried red chiles

2 ounces ground pork

1/4 pound medium raw shrimp, shelled and deveined

4 ounces pressed bean curd, chopped

1/4 cup chopped pickled daikon

2 green onions, chopped

1 egg, beaten

1/2 cup chopped roasted peanuts, for garnish

1 cup fresh bean sprouts, for garnish

1. Soak dried shrimp in warm water to cover until softened, about 20 minutes; drain and chop finely.

2. If using dried rice noodles, soak in warm water to cover until softened, about 15 minutes; drain. If using fresh rice noodles, rinse with cold water to separate.

3. To make sauce, in a bowl combine stock, sugar, tamarind water, fish sauce, and lime juice.

4. Place a wok over high heat until hot. Add oil, swirling to coat sides. Add dried shrimp, cilantro, garlic, shallots, and dried chiles. Cook, stirring, for 1 minute.

5. Crumble in pork and cook for 2 minutes. Add raw shrimp and stir-fry until barely pink, about 1 minute. Add bean curd, daikon, and green onions; stir-fry for 1 minute. Add sauce. Decrease heat and simmer for 3 minutes. Add noodles; toss to coat evenly with sauce. Add egg and stir-fry until cooked, about 1 minute.

6. Place noodle mixture on platter. Garnish with peanuts and bean sprouts, and serve.

Thailand's National Dish

Think back to your first experience of Thai food and chances are it probably involved *phad thai*. *Phad* more or less means "stir-fry" in Thai, so *phad thai* is, quite simply, the classic Thai stir-fry. And even though there are as many recipes for it as there are cooks preparing it, when you break each down into its component parts, you will end up with that same four-part harmony that characterizes Thai cuisine: sweetness from sugar and tamarind water, the latter also contributing a pleasing tartness in concert with any vinegar or lime juice. The ubiquitous fish sauce doles out its dose of saltiness, and a heaping helping of crushed dried red chiles—a sure bet in any recipe—gives this dish the kick that is the essence of Thai cuisine.

Crispy Caramelized Noodles

Among the most popular dishes in Thai restaurants, these noodles are deep-fried for a light and crunchy taste and tossed with a saucy stir-fry. I like to eat these noodles right away while they are still crunchy. **SERVES 4**

Vegetable oil, for deep-frying
3 ounces dried thin rice noodles

Sauce

$1/2$ cup packed brown sugar
$1/3$ cup fresh lime juice
2 tablespoons dark soy sauce
2 tablespoons fish sauce

$1/2$ tablespoon minced shallot
3 ounces boneless, skinless chicken breast, diced
3 ounces raw shrimp, shelled, deveined, and coarsely chopped
1 ounce pressed bean curd, julienned
5 ounces (about 2 cups) fresh bean sprouts

1. In a wok, heat oil for deep-frying to 375°. Deep-fry noodles in small batches until they puff and expand, about 5 seconds. Turn them over to cook the other side, then drain on paper towels. Place noodles in a large bowl.

2. To make sauce, in a small pan, combine sugar, lime juice, soy sauce, and fish sauce; bring to a boil. Immediately decrease heat to low and cook until sauce turns syrupy, about 10 minutes.

3. Drain all but 1 tablespoon oil from wok and place over high heat until hot. Add shallot and stir-fry until fragrant, about 30 seconds. Add chicken and stir-fry for 2 minutes; add shrimp and cook for 30 seconds. Add bean curd; stir-fry for 1 minute more.

4. Toss sauce with noodles and top with chicken mixture. Serve with bean sprouts over top.

Caring for Caramel

The sweet, richly flavored sauce for *mee krop* is what makes it so special—it's a great example of Thai cooks' knack at balancing sweet and savory. And as simple as the sauce is to make, it actually owes its intriguing character to a number of complex chemical reactions. Food scientists still aren't exactly sure what happens when we caramelize sugar, but they do know that melting sugar to a syrupy consistency changes its color and texture, and creates a complex flavor reminiscent of maple syrup and toasted marshmallows. This sort of richness transcends plain old sweet, and you can only get it through the process of caramelization. But be careful to keep an eye on the sugar's temperature; heat the sugar too high and it burns to an acrid, charred mess that isn't fit to eat.

Never Forget the Elephant

Much more than a passive historical symbol adorning the nation's flag and coins, the Thai elephant is an active, contributing member of society. Ever since the days when Thai warriors rode their trusty pachyderms into battle (you can't find a sturdier war-horse), elephants have earned their keep as beasts of burden, carrying everything from teak logs to tourists. And they don't work for peanuts, either! Out of concern over Thai elephants' dwindling numbers, many organizations have founded special sanctuaries to safeguard these four-legged national symbols. I visited one of these parks, and I can vouch that Thai elephants get the plush treatment, something that befits a true cultural icon.

Top: Elephants working in a park near Chiang Mai.
Bottom: Martin thumbing a ride—Thai style.

224

Fresh Rice Noodles with Seafood and Basil

Seafood and sweet basil complement each other perfectly. Pair with fresh rice noodles and you've got perfection all around. Look no further than this masterpiece. It is a meal in itself. **SERVES 4**

½ **pound dried or fresh flat rice noodles, about ¼ inch wide**

Sauce

1 **tablespoon oyster-flavored sauce**

1 **tablespoon soy sauce**

1 **tablespoon Thai roasted chile paste**

¾ **cup water**

¼ **pound medium raw shrimp**

¼ **pound firm white fish fillet, such as sea bass or halibut**

¼ **pound sea scallops**

2 **tablespoons vegetable oil**

1 **tablespoon minced garlic**

6 **asparagus spears cut diagonally into 2-inch lengths**

¼ **cup Thai or sweet basil leaves**

1 **to 2 teaspoons thinly sliced fresh Thai chile**

1. If using dried rice noodles, soak in warm water to cover until softened, about 15 minutes; drain. If using fresh rice noodles, rinse with cold water to separate layers.

2. To make sauce, in a bowl combine oyster sauce, soy sauce, chile paste, and water.

3. Shell and devein shrimp; cut into ½-inch pieces. Cut fish into ½-inch cubes. If scallops are large, cut into quarters.

4. Place a wok over high heat until hot. Add oil, swirling to coat sides. Add garlic and cook, stirring, until fragrant, about 10 seconds. Add shrimp, fish, scallops, and asparagus; stir-fry for 1 minute. Add sauce; cook for 1 minute.

5. Add noodles; stir well to coat them with sauce. Cook for 2 to 3 minutes to heat through. Stir in basil and chile; cook for 30 seconds more. Arrange on a platter and serve.

Noodle It Up

Ah, what wonders Thai cooks work with rice noodles, those examples of culinary alchemy made with just rice flour and water (that's it!). Thais call the fresh noodles *kway tiow,* and maybe I crave them so much because they're just like the sumptuously chewy *chow fun* I grew up on. The way they stay soft in the center but get crispy and caramelized around the edges—my mouth waters just thinking about it. If your mouth is watering too, find plastic-wrapped trays of fresh rice noodles in a range of widths from ribbons to sheets in the refrigerated section of Asian groceries. Use fresh noodles preferably the day of purchase, because they dry and stiffen with time. To soften them before cooking, gently rinse with warm water, which also removes the oily film that keeps these delightfully gooey noodles from sticking.

Bananas in Glutinous Rice

Thai–Style Burritos

Think of black beans and you think of burrito fillings, right? True, black beans may be a star in Mexican and Cuban kitchens, but they're no slouch in Southeast Asian cuisine, either. Only there's a difference: in Asia, black beans as well as red adzuki beans show off their distinctive flavors and textures in sweets and desserts, most often as fillings—nothing beats a sweet red bean paste bun or a Thai dumpling of bananas, black beans, and sticky rice—or in sweet soups and puddings. At Asian markets, you can find cans of Asian-style beans and bean pastes (best for fillings) in a variety of textures from chunky to smooth. Store any unused portion in a sealed container in the refrigerator, where it will keep for several weeks. (Canned Western-style beans and refried black beans are not substitutes, by the way.)

Mix fruits and grains? Why not? Here's something that will "rice" to the occasion. Sticky glutinous rice and black beans are wrapped with banana and jackfruit in a banana leaf package. Since the banana leaf can tear when wrapping, use two pieces to wrap the filling. **SERVES 8**

$1^2/_3$ **cups glutinous rice**

17 (7 by 9-inch) rectangles banana leaf

1 cup coconut cream

$^1/_2$ **cup sugar**

$^1/_2$ **teaspoon salt**

$^1/_3$ **cup cooked black beans**

$^1/_4$ **cup chopped macadamia nuts or walnuts (optional)**

4 small bananas, peeled and cut in half lengthwise

$^1/_2$ **cup drained and sliced canned jackfruit**

1. Soak rice in water to cover for at least 2 hours or overnight. Steam rice (see page 89).

2. Cut 1 banana leaf into $^1/_4$-inch strips to make ties.

3. For coconut cream, open a can of unsweetened coconut milk (do not shake it first) and spoon the thick cream off the top. In a 2-quart saucepan, combine 1 cup coconut cream, sugar, and salt; bring to a boil. Remove from heat and add rice; mix thoroughly. Add black beans and nuts. Let stand for 15 minutes.

4. To assemble each packet: Stack 2 banana leaf rectangles to form a double layer. On top layer of banana leaf, place $^1/_3$ cup rice mixture with half a banana and a slice of jackfruit; wrap with banana leaf and secure with a banana leaf strip. Place packets in a heatproof dish. Prepare a wok for steaming (see page 6). Cover and steam over medium-high heat until heated through, 6 to 8 minutes. Serve warm.

Banana Cones

Bananas are used in many Thai desserts. Here is one of my favorites: chunks of banana mixed with coconut milk and finely chopped nuts, then steamed inside banana leaf cones. The banana leaf adds wonderful aromatic flavor to this hot dessert. **MAKES 8 CONES, SERVES 8**

8 (7-inch-square) pieces banana leaf

Filling

4 ripe bananas, peeled and mashed
1/3 cup unsweetened coconut milk
1/4 cup cornstarch
1/4 cup sugar
1/2 teaspoon salt
3 ounces shredded unsweetened coconut
1/4 cup finely chopped nuts, such as walnuts, hazelnuts, or pecans

1. Roll each banana leaf into the shape of a cone with a 2-inch opening at the top; secure cone with a wooden toothpick and trim top evenly with scissors.

2. To prepare filling, in a bowl combine bananas, coconut milk, cornstarch, sugar, salt, shredded coconut, and nuts; mix well. Spoon 1/4 cup filling into each cone. Place cones, pointed end down, in a 1-quart (or larger) glass measuring cup to hold.

3. Prepare a deep pan for steaming (see page 6). Place measuring cup in the pan; cover and steam cones until filling is firm, 20 to 25 minutes.

4. To serve, unwrap the cones and transfer to a serving platter.

Going Bananas

The banana split may be your favorite use for the banana, but Asian cooks have turned versatile banana leaves into culinary chameleons. The large leaves wrap sweet and savory fillings in preparation for steaming; some say their cooling, slightly minty fragrance and flavor are the perfect foils for rice. Placed at the bottom of a simmering pot of stew, banana leaves not only add their flavorful essence to the dish but also give it a slight green tint and keep it from sticking to the pan. The best banana leaves for long, slow-cooked dishes are young, thin, and yellow; these are strong enough to withstand extended simmering. Older leaves need soaking first to make them pliable. If you can't find fresh banana leaves, Asian markets often sell packages of frozen ones. If they're larger than you need for your recipe, simply trim them down to the appropriate size.

Golden Temple with Tropical Fruits

This dessert is meant to impress! You can construct temples of a more moderate scale by cutting smaller squares and limiting the temple to three layers. Either way, this dessert is a religious experience. **SERVES 4**

1 (16-ounce) package egg roll wrappers
Vegetable oil, for deep-frying

Fruit Filling

3 tablespoons butter
2 mangoes, peeled and diced
1 (20-ounce) can jackfruit, drained and cut into ¹/₂-inch cubes
1 firm banana, peeled and diced
¹/₄ cup banana-flavored liqueur (optional)
2 tablespoons packed brown sugar

2 teaspoons lime zest
1 tablespoon fresh lime juice
1 teaspoon shredded kaffir lime leaf
1 tablespoon toasted shredded coconut
1 tablespoon shredded mint leaves

Mint sprigs, for garnish

1. Cut wrappers to make four 6-inch squares, four 5-inch squares, four 4-inch squares, and four 3-inch squares. Save trimmings for another use.

2. In a wok or 2-quart pan, heat oil for deep-frying to 350°. Deep-fry wrappers, a few pieces at a time, until lightly browned, 10 to 20 seconds on each side. Remove with a slotted spoon; drain on paper towels. Let cool. (Can be placed in a tightly covered container until ready to use, for up to 4 days.)

3. To make fruit filling, melt butter in a wide frying pan over medium-high heat. Add mangoes, jackfruit, and banana; cook for 30 seconds. Add liqueur, brown sugar, lime zest, lime juice, and lime leaf. Cook for 1 minute. Remove from heat and stir in coconut and mint leaves. Let cool.

4. For each serving, place a 6-inch-square wrapper on a large dessert plate; top with a spoonful of fruit. Repeat for second, third, and fourth layers, using successively smaller squares and a spoonful of fruit with each layer. Garnish each serving with a mint sprig.

Jumpin' Jackfruit

If you're ever wandering through the southern Thai jungle and stumble over a football-sized (maybe larger, maybe *much* larger), yellow-green pod covered in short, hard spines, don't assume you've found something from *The X-Files*. You've just stumbled upon one of Southeast Asia's most enticing tropical fruits, the jackfruit. Cut one open and you'll find flesh that looks as if it's from a pineapple. But try a piece—it's not quite as juicy, right? And do you pick up the banana notes and the heady, slightly fermented aroma? They're hard to miss. But ripe, sweet jackfruit is difficult to find here, so when I can't find it fresh, I jump at its canned cousins. You can find them in most Asian groceries. It's not quite as out-of-this-world as fresh, but it's the next best thing.

Coconut Banana Custard

General Custard

Savvy cooks know how to bake their custards to a silken, creamy texture—and they know how to put an end to those unattractive cracks that form on custards no matter how carefully you watch the oven. The secret is in a pan of hot water, known as a *bain-marie*. When you set cups of custard to bake in a *bain-marie,* the boiling water in the pan turns to steam in the oven. That steam moderates the oven temperature, preventing it from getting so high that it gives your custard that "parched earth" look. To avoid risking a burn when carrying a pan full of hot water and custard cups across the kitchen to the oven, simply place the filled cups in the empty pan, and transfer the pan to the oven rack. Pull the rack partway out of the oven, and then pour the hot water into the pan.

Thailand is the land of romance and enchanting beauty. A candlelight dinner under the star-drenched sky is not complete without a sinfully delicious dessert. Coconut banana custard is just the thing to serve. Once the sugar topping begins to melt, it caramelizes quickly, so watch carefully to prevent burning. **SERVES 8**

Custard

5 ripe bananas
2 cups coconut milk
$1/2$ cup sweetened shredded coconut
2 eggs, lightly beaten
$1/2$ cup sugar

About 1 tablespoon butter, at room temperature
About 1 tablespoon sugar, for topping

1. To make custard, peel bananas and cut into chunks. Place in a food processor or blender and purée. Transfer to a bowl and add coconut milk, coconut, eggs, and sugar; mix well.

2. Preheat oven to 350°. Butter eight $1/2$-cup ramekins; pour custard into the ramekins to three-quarters full. Place ramekins in a baking pan and place in the oven; pour hot water into pan to a depth of 1 inch.

3. Bake custards until they no longer jiggle when gently shaken, about 20 minutes. Immediately remove ramekins from hot water and place on a rack to cool.

4. Just before serving, sprinkle sugar evenly over the custards. Turn the oven to broil and place custards at least 4 inches from heat source until sugar caramelizes, about 2 minutes. Serve immediately.

Sweet Tapioca with Coconut Cream

Forget about ice cream. When I crave a cold, sweet treat, I eat tapioca pearls in coconut cream. My favorite treat is also a favorite of many Thais. And just when I thought it didn't get any better than this, I tried the pearls with mango fruit— absolutely delicious. **SERVES 8**

1 cup small (¹/₈-inch) pearl tapioca
4 cups water
1 cup sugar

Coconut Sauce

1 cup unsweetened coconut milk
¹/₂ cup sugar
¹/₈ teaspoon salt
1 teaspoon cornstarch dissolved in 2 teaspoons water

Mint sprigs, for garnish

1. In a heavy 2-quart pan, combine tapioca, water, and sugar. Cook, stirring, over medium heat until sugar dissolves. Increase heat and boil for 1 minute. Decrease heat and simmer, stirring frequently, 10 to 12 minutes, until mixture thickens and tapioca becomes translucent.

2. Divide mixture equally among 8 dessert bowls and let cool, then chill until serving time.

3. To make coconut sauce, in a 1-quart pan, combine coconut milk, sugar, and salt. Cook, stirring occasionally, over medium heat until sugar dissolves and mixture gently boils. Add cornstarch solution and cook until sauce boils and thickens slightly. Cool to room temperature.

4. To serve, pour sauce over tapioca and garnish with mint sprigs.

A Pearl of the Orient

Poor little tapioca. It gets something of a bad rap in the West. But at least in Asia, it receives the respect that I think it deserves. Tapioca starch itself has a finer, waxier texture than cornstarch, but you can use both to thicken sauces; just remember that you don't need as much tapioca starch as you would cornstarch to achieve an equal amount of thickening. But tapioca really shines like a gem when it's processed into pearly balls—from as small as a mustard seed to as large as a plump pea— that, when simmered in puddings, make tongue-tickling desserts. Some recipes call for soaking the pearls beforehand to soften them, so check before you cook.

Martin celebrates the Thai New Year and keeps cool at the same time.

Soaking up Local Culture

Right when the hot, dry season starts wilting Thailand on the vine, Songkran, Thai New Year, and one of the country's most celebrated holidays, comes to the rescue with a cool splash of water. Thais traditionally commemorate the occasion with a quiet ceremony in which younger family members pay respect to elders by pouring water over the elders' hands. But out on the street, revelers take this sedate soaking to new heights, turning Songkran festivities into a free-for-all water fight. You can run, but you can't hide from the hoses, buckets, and even pickup trucks filled with a liquid arsenal. Whether you're out walking or tucked neatly in a car (invariably with windows rolled down), you're fair game for the next splash. So you might as well dress appropriately and just go with the flow.

Lemongrass Tea

In Thailand's hot and humid weather, this light and refreshing tea is a lifesaver and a thirst quencher. I simmer stalks of lemongrass with jasmine tea, but you can use your favorite kind of tea. Sit back and relax with a tall glass of this ice-cold beverage, and let calming images of Thailand drift though your mind..... **SERVES 4**

4 stalks lemongrass, cut into thirds and lightly crushed
4 cups water
3¹/₂ tablespoons palm sugar or brown sugar
2 to 3 teaspoons dried jasmine tea leaves
Ice cubes
Lime wedges, for garnish

1. In a nonreactive pan, bring lemongrass and water to a boil. Decrease heat, cover, and simmer for 10 minutes.

2. Add palm sugar and simmer for 3 minutes. Turn off heat and add tea leaves; let steep for 10 minutes. Strain. Let mixture cool, then refrigerate until ready to use.

3. To serve, place 2 or 3 ice cubes in each glass and fill with tea. Garnish with lime wedges.

Reading Palm

The process used to extract palm sugar (the ingredient mostly responsible for the sweetness in Thai cooking's four-part balance (for more, see page 128) reminds me of an Asian version of New England maple "sugaring off." Workers tap different types of palm trees to drain the sap. They collect the sap and reduce it to a thick syrup before pouring it into tubelike bamboo molds. There it hardens into a thick, sticky, dark-brown cylinder (commonly found in markets) that, when crumbled, releases coarse grains of sweet palm, or as it's sometimes called, "coconut sugar." Its flavor is even richer and more complex than that of brown sugar, which makes the latter a suitable, albeit less intense, substitute when palm sugar is not available.

Sweet Ginger Lime Juice

The Juice Is Loose

You won't find ginger juice next to the bottles of cranapple and Concord grape at your grocery store. You have to make this stuff yourself. It's simple: Start with about 3 tablespoons minced ginger. Place it in a thin, clean piece of cheesecloth or on a clean coffee filter. Wrap the cloth or filter tightly around the ginger, hold it over a measuring cup or bowl, and squeeze firmly to extract the juice. This should yield about 1 tablespoon ginger juice, although the older the hunk of ginger, the less juice it's willing to give up.

Feel like drinking something refreshing with a little kick that'll wake up your taste buds? This Thai home-style sweet ginger limeade is just the ticket. It can be enjoyed warm or chilled. If you don't feel like squeezing fresh lime juice, you can opt for bottled lime juice, but remember to add some more sugar to compensate for the concentrated juice.

MAKES 1 QUART, SERVES 4

6 to 8 fresh limes
3 1/2 cups water
1/2 cup sugar
1/4 teaspoon salt
3 tablespoons ginger juice

1. Slice 1 lime to use for garnish.

2. Grate 1 tablespoon zest from limes. Cut limes in half and squeeze out the juice to make 1/2 cup.

3. In a pan, combine lime zest, water, sugar, and salt. Place over medium heat and cook, stirring, until sugar dissolves; remove from heat. Add ginger juice and lime juice; mix well and strain through a strainer. Pour into a pitcher and refrigerate until chilled.

4. To serve, place a slice of lime in a tall glass and pour juice to the rim.

Glossary of Asian Ingredients

Although you may have some familiarity with the cuisines of Southeast Asia, many of their everyday ingredients may not be staples on your pantry shelf. This glossary doesn't cover everything, but it does include ethnic ingredients used in the recipes in this book. Thanks to the rising popularity of Asian cuisine, adventurous home cooks are now able to find many of these ingredients in their local supermarkets. The next place to look is in Asian markets (especially ones that cater to a specific country or area), which carry good selections of essential ingredients, including sauces and fresh produce. Farmers' markets, which often offer a variety of produce used in Asian cooking, are another good place to look for ingredients.

We've provided recipes for many spice pastes and sauces in this book, but if you're pressed for time, don't worry: many are also available ready-made. Also, many sauces are interchangeable. For example, each country has its own version of fish sauce or shrimp paste, so there's no need to buy another bottle if you've found a brand you like.

Sauces with a greater proportion of whole ingredients are generally thicker and are referred to as "pastes." Both sauces and pastes are found in various-sized bottles and jars. Once opened, store in the refrigerator. Most will keep for several months to a year. Dry seasonings should be stored in tightly sealed containers in a cool, dry place. Most will keep for several months. Before using canned vegetables, drain and rinse them to remove any trace of the salty canning liquid. You can also blanch canned vegetables in boiling water with a pinch of salt to remove any metallic taste before further cooking.

Asian eggplant: see Eggplant.

Asian greens: see bok choy, Chinese broccoli, Chinese long beans, choy sum, garlic chives, napa cabbage, peas (edible-pod).

Bamboo shoots: Available both fresh and canned, the shoots can be found as whole tips, young tips, sliced, or diced. They all have a slightly sweet flavor, but their texture differs. The most tender are the young winter bamboo tips, and the most fibrous are the sliced shoots.

Banana leaf: Used to wrap foods for steaming or grilling in Southeast Asian cuisine. These large leaves are often available frozen in Asian markets. For more details, see sidebars on pages 173 and 227.

Basil, Thai: For more on this flavorful herb, see sidebar on page 209.

Bean curd: see Tofu.

Bean paste, sweetened red: Primarily used as a filling for a variety of sweet dishes, and occasionally found in savory dishes. The paste is made from cooked, mashed, and sweetened adzuki beans. Sold in cans in Asian markets.

Bean sprouts: The most common sprout varieties are soybean and mung bean. The main difference between them is that soybean sprouts have larger heads and a crunchier texture than mung bean sprouts; they can be used interchangeably, however. Try to use them the day they are purchased, but they will last a couple of days if refrigerated.

Bean thread noodles, dried: Made from mung bean starch, these semitransparent noodles come in different lengths and thicknesses. Also known as glass noodles, cellophane noodles, bean threads, or Chinese vermicelli. For more details, see sidebar on page 165.

Beans, Chinese long: see Chinese long beans.

Black mushroom: Dried brownish black shiitake mushroom with a meaty texture. Also known as Chinese black mushroom.

Black beans, salted: These beans lend a distinctly pungent, smoky flavor to food. Also referred to as preserved or fermented black beans. Often used as a seasoning along with garlic, fresh ginger, or chiles. Found in Asian markets packaged in plastic; they should feel soft and look fresh, not dried out. Before using, rinse the beans, pat dry, and crush slightly.

Black bean sauce: Sauce made from salted black beans and rice wine that may contain garlic or hot chiles.

Black fungus (cloud ear): see Wood ear.

Bok choy: An Asian loose-leaf cabbage with thick white stalks and dark green leaves. The stalks have a slightly sharp taste and a crunchy texture, and the leaves are peppery and soft. The smaller varieties, baby bok choy and Shanghai baby bok choy, are sweeter and less stringy than regular bok choy.

Bouillon: A concentrated flavor cube that is dissolved in hot water to create a stock base for use in cooking. Can be found in numerous flavors: chicken, seafood, beef, and vegetable. The products on the market tend to have added salt, so when using bouillon, it's best to taste before adding any additional salt to the recipe.

Candied citrus: For instructions on how to make these candied peels, see sidebar on page 117.

Candied ginger: see Ginger.

Candied walnuts: see Glazed walnuts.

Char siu or barbecue sauce: A thick Chinese sauce made from soybeans, honey, vinegar, tomato paste, chiles, garlic, sugar, and other spices. Commonly used with grilled meat.

Chiles, dried: Numerous fresh chiles are available in dried form, and provide intense heat to dishes. Can be used whole or broken into smaller pieces. They are available year-round and, stored in an airtight container, will last for months. The crushed variety found in most supermarkets is simply chopped dried whole chiles. Wash your hands after handling both dried and fresh chiles, because their oils can burn and irritate your skin and eyes.

Chiles, fresh: Generally, the smaller the chile, the hotter it is. From hottest to mildest, they include the fiery Thai chile (bird's eye), slightly milder serrano, jalapeño, and mild Anaheim. Many of the Chinese recipes call for red or green jalapeño chiles, which are hot but not too hot, and easy to find in markets. Thai chiles, also known as bird's eye or bird pepper chiles, are small, slender green or red chiles widely available in Asian markets. (For more information on Thai chiles, see sidebar on page 191.) Depending on your taste, you can increase or decrease the amount of chile called for in a recipe or substitute milder ones.

Chile sauces: There four main types of chile sauces used in this book's recipes, and most of them are not interchangeable. Chile sauce from China is both an ingredient for cooking and a common table condiment. In Thai cuisine, Chinese chile sauce is used as an ingredient for cooking because it has a stronger pungency to it than Thai chile sauce. Chinese chile sauce comes in two types: fine chile sauce, made of ground chiles, similar to Tabasco sauce, but with a thicker consistency; and that made of crushed chiles, which are coarser, thicker, and often contain added ingredients such as ginger, shallots, and fermented black beans. Chile garlic sauce is simply a regular ground chile sauce with extra minced garlic added. This can be used as an ingredient or as a condiment on the table. Sweet chile sauce comes bottled and has a slightly transparent red color. Its basic ingredients are sugar, red chiles, garlic, vinegar, and salt. It is often used as a condiment, and very rarely used as an ingredient in cooking. It should not be used as a substitute for Thai chile sauce. Thai chile sauce (*nam prik pao*) is very common in Thai cuisine. Also referred to as roasted chile sauce or roasted chile paste. The basic ingredients are roasted garlic and shallots, dried red chiles, dried shrimp, palm sugar, fish sauce, and tamarind juice. Thai chile sauce is different from Chinese chile sauce or sweet chile sauce, and cannot be substituted for them. Its sweet and sour flavor makes it more popular than Chinese chile sauce as a condiment on the table. If unable to locate, substitute chile sauce combined with a pinch of sugar and a dash of vinegar.

Chinese almonds: Seeds of the apricot that come in two varieties: Southern almonds are mild and interchangeable in taste with American almonds; Northern almonds are more bitter. A soup recipe may call for both types. American almonds are known in China as "flatpeach seeds."

Chinese barbecued pork (char siu): Ready-made cooked pork and pork spareribs sold in most Asian markets in the deli section. Cooked with char siu sauce (see separate listing), which gives the meat its pleasantly sweet, rich taste.

Chinese black vinegar: This vinegar comes from the fermentation of a mixture of rice, wheat, and millet or sorghum. It's sold in Asian markets (sometimes under the name "Chinkiang vinegar"). If you can't find it, balsamic vinegar is a good substitute, though you may want to reduce the amount of sugar, if any, in your recipe.

Chinese broccoli: Different from the broccoli found in most grocery stores, this variety has thin, dusty green stems, deep green leaves, and tiny white flowers, all of which are edible. When cooked, the vegetable will have a slightly bittersweet taste. Look for young, slender stems and leaves without blemishes.

Chinese celery: A delicate celery variety quite different from its American relative, with long, hollow stems and deep green, flavorful leaves.

Chinese chives: see Garlic chives.

Chinese dried seaweed: see Seaweed.

Chinese egg noodles, fresh: These noodles come in a wide variety of widths, sizes, and flavors and are now available in many supermarkets as well as Asian grocery stores. Cook according to package directions.

Chinese five-spice powder: An intensely flavorful, light-brown powder made from ground cinnamon, star anise, fennel, cloves, ginger, licorice, Sichuan peppercorns, and dried tangerine peel. Its strong anise and cinnamon flavor complements braised, roasted, and barbecued meats.

Chinese long beans: Also called yard-long beans because of their extreme length, these legumes look like long, pencil-thin, pale to dark green beans. If your supermarket does not carry them, green beans can be substituted.

Chinese parsley: see Cilantro.

Chinese pea pods: see Peas, edible-pod.

Chinese rice wine: Low-alcohol wine made from fermented glutinous rice and millet. This rich amber liquid is aged from 10 to 100 years to attain its full flavor. Some of the best quality rice wines are produced in Shao Hsing (Shaoxing), located in eastern China.

Chinese sausage (*lop cheong*): Savory-sweet links made primarily with ground pork, pork fat, duck, or beef. They are 4 to 6 inches long, rusty red to brown in color, with a bumpy texture. Can be found in Chinese delis, fresh or in vacuum packages.

Choy sum: An Asian green, also known as bok choy sum. Has the same appearance as small bok choy but it also has small yellow flowers, which are edible. Choy sum should be cooked in the same manner as bok choy.

Chu hou paste: A thick Chinese sauce made of soybeans, garlic, ginger, and sesame seeds; used for braising meats and vegetables.

Cilantro: Known also as Chinese parsley or fresh coriander, it has wide, delicate flat leaves and a distinct, refreshing flavor. The herb is ubiquitous in Southeast Asian cuisine. The Thais use not only the cilantro leaves but also the stems and roots, which are pounded for curry pastes and marinades. Cilantro is widely available in most supermarkets with the roots cut off and discarded. You may have to grow your own if you want to use the roots. Don't confuse it with similar-looking Italian parsley. Also see Coriander seed.

Cloud ear (black fungus): see Wood ear.

Coconut: Southeast Asian curries, stews, and desserts commonly use coconut milk and cream, available in cans. For instructions on extracting coconut cream from can, see page 185. The liquid in the center of a fresh coconut is not coconut milk, but coconut water; it is not used in cooking, but makes a refreshing beverage. Desiccated coconut is sold shredded or flaked, sweetened or unsweetened, in cans or plastic bags. Use unsweetened coconut unless a recipe specifically calls for sweetened coconut.

Coriander seed: The lightly fragrant dried fruit of the cilantro plant (see Cilantro listing). The seeds have a slightly sweet flavor of caraway, lemon, and sage that is completely unlike the flavor of the fresh herb.

Crab: Fresh Dungeness crabs are available from the West Coast of the United States during fall and winter months; the smaller blue crabs from the East Coast are available in the summer and fall. When buying live crabs, refrigerate as quickly as possible and cook and eat them within twenty-four hours.

Cucumber, English: Also known as hothouse cucumber, it can reach more than a foot long. Usually found in markets shrink-wrapped in plastic. It has almost no seeds and a thin, bright green skin that needs no peeling. Japanese cucumbers are similar, but are only about 1 inch in diameter and 8 inches long; they have a crunchy texture and are great for pickling.

Cumin seed: Similar in appearance to caraway seed, this tiny aromatic seed adds pungent flavor to Asian foods such as curries and satay. Many diners first encounter it in Latin American dishes such as chile con carne. Cumin seed is available whole or powdered.

Curry: Curry comes from *kari*, which simply means "sauce" in southern India, where curry most likely originated as a way to preserve food. Curry is a blend of spices as well as a method of cooking found not just in Indian cooking, but also in Malay, Indonesian, Thai, Chinese, and Burmese cuisines. Curry powder is a complex mixture of ground spices that varies from region to region. Turmeric gives it its distinctive yellow color, and its flavor comes from numerous other spices, including chiles, cumin, coriander, cardamom, cloves, cinnamon, and fennel. The basis of Thai curry (*gaeng*) is the highly seasoned red, yellow, or green curry pastes, for which there are recipes in this book. In addition to the recipes, see page 8 (Tools, Techniques, and Tips) for techniques and storage information. If you don't have the time to make them, don't worry; there are all kinds of great premixed curry powders and pastes on the market.

Daikon: A Japanese radish with crisp white flesh and a sweet, peppery taste. Can be found 8 to 14 inches long and 2 to 3 inches in diameter. Pickled yellow daikon, also called takuan, is a bright yellow, robustly flavored, giant radish that, when fresh, measures up to 12 inches in length. It is available in jars and in vacuum packages at most Asian markets.

Dried bean curd sheets: see Tofu.

Dried ginseng root: see Ginseng.

Dried mushrooms: see Black mushroom, Shiitake, Snow fungus, Wood ear.

Dried rice paper wrappers: see Rice paper.

Dried shrimp: Tiny shrimp preserved in brine, and then dried, creating slightly chewy morsels with a strong shellfish taste. They're sold in plastic bags in Asian supermarkets. Before using, soak them in warm water for 20 minutes to soften.

Edible-pod peas: see Peas.

Egg, preserved: see Preserved egg.

Eggplant: Chinese and Japanese eggplants range in size and color. They can be short and pudgy, about 3 inches long, or thin and slender, about 9 inches long. Chinese eggplants are generally white to lavender in color with a sweeter taste than Japanese eggplant, which is light purple to purple-black. They can be used interchangeably in most recipes. Thai eggplant are quite different from the European, Chinese, and Japanese varieties. The taste is similar, but the color, shape, and sizes vary. You can find them white, green, yellow, and purple in all different shapes and sizes in Asian markets (see sidebar, page 199). Regular (European) eggplant makes an excellent substitute.

Egg roll wrappers: Paper-thin wrappers made from wheat flour, eggs, and water; the dough is rolled into thin, flexible sheets that are used to wrap savory fillings. When deep-fried, they turn a golden brown and have a bubbly surface.

Enoki mushroom: Diminutive cultivated fresh mushrooms grown in clumps, with thin, long stems and tiny caps. They have a delicate, mild flavor.

Fermented rice and fermented rice liquid: A byproduct of rice winemaking; the remains of fermented rice and liquid left on the bottom of a vat after the finished wine is removed. The rice, with its liquid, is sold in glass jars in Asian markets. For more information, see page 120.

Fermented soybeans: Soybeans that are packed in tubs, coated with salt, and left to ferment for several months. The beans slowly absorb the salt, shrivel up, and turn black, developing a strong, salty taste. The fermented beans are ground into a paste that is bottled as plain soybean sauce. When other flavorings are added, such as Sichuan peppercorns, chile, garlic, soy sauce, sugar, and spices, several styles of pungent pastes and sauces are produced, including chile bean sauce.

Fish paste: Fish processed into a paste, available ready-made in Asian markets. For directions on how to make your own, see page 26.

Fish sauce: Fermented fish extract used as flavoring agent throughout Southeast Asia and southern China. A thin, amber-colored liquid, fish sauce is as prevalent as soy sauce in Southeast Asian cooking. Its distinct, sharp aroma—like soy sauce melded with fish—mellows with cooking and adds a delicious, slightly salty taste to foods. Known variously as *nam pla* (Thailand), *nuoc cham* (Vietnam), and *patis* (Philippines). For more details, see page 143.

Five-spice powder, Chinese: see Chinese five-spice powder.

Galangal: A rhizome that resembles ginger, with translucent pale yellow skin. For details, see page 192.

Garlic: A member of the onion family. As a guide, 1 garlic clove yields roughly 1 teaspoon minced. Fried garlic, often used as a garnish, can be purchased in Asian markets and some supermarkets. For details on how to make it, see page 164. Pickled garlic is soaked in a brine made from vinegar, sugar, and salt. After pickling, it's used in stir-fries or eaten whole as an accompaniment to curry dishes. The brine can also be used for dipping or as a sauce for other Thai dishes.

Garlic chives: Also known as Chinese chives or *gou choy*, fresh garlic chives are available in the spring and summer. Chinese cooking uses three main varieties of garlic chives: Green garlic chives resemble wide, long blades of grass. Yellow garlic chives are shorter, with more delicate leaves and a faintly onion-garlic flavor. Flowering garlic chives have firm stalks topped with small edible flower buds. Select chives with unopened buds; they are younger and more tender.

Ginger: Fresh ginger is a knobby root with a smooth golden beige skin and a fibrous yellow-green interior. It has a slightly spicy bite and an enticing aroma. **Young ginger,** generally available in the spring, has a smoother, more delicate flavor and less stringy texture. Young ginger needs no peeling. When selecting ginger, find a piece of root that is solid, heavy, and free of wrinkles and mold. One peeled ginger slice the size of a quarter yields about 1 teaspoon minced ginger. To make **ginger juice,** delicious in beverages, see page 234. **Pickled ginger,** cured in brine, then soaked in a sugar-vinegar solution, is used in Chinese cooking; Japanese *red pickled ginger* is somewhat sweeter. **Preserved ginger** is packed in heavy sugar syrup that becomes infused with a mild ginger taste. **Candied ginger** is cooked and sugar-coated pieces of tender young ginger.

Ginkgo nuts: Seeds of the ginkgo tree that have a delicately sweet taste and an orange-yellow color. Most Asian markets sell the fresh nuts in fall and winter. As with most fresh nuts, the ginkgo's hard shell must be removed before eating. Ginkgo nuts can also be found dried or canned. For more details, see page 40.

Ginseng: Aromatic root of a plant in the ivy family. Considered a tonic and restorative by Chinese herbalists, ginseng comes in many forms: powdered, capsules, whole, sliced, and in concentrated extracts. It is generally used to cleanse the blood; it is also used to treat anemia, nervous disorders, excessive sweating, and forgetfulness.

Glazed walnuts: Walnuts coated with sugar syrup, then dried. Available in grocery stores. For information on how to make your own, see page 117.

Glutinous rice: A variety of short-grain rice, also known as sweet or sticky rice. Grains resemble rice-shaped pearls and can be both white or black. When cooked, the rice grains become sticky and translucent. For more information, see sidebar on page 201.

Green onions: Young, immature onions that have been harvested with their green shoots. All parts except the root of the green onion are used in Asian cooking, and in every way, from steaming and stir-frying to garnishing.

Green peppercorn: see Peppercorn.

Green papaya: Unripened green-fleshed papaya that is less sweet and much firmer in texture than its fully ripe counterpart. Used frequently in Thai salads. For details, see page 159.

Hoisin sauce: A robust Chinese sauce made with fermented soybeans, vinegar, garlic, sugar, and spices. Its spicy-sweet flavor complements many dishes, including mu shu variations and Peking duck.

Jackfruit: A very sweet tropical fruit grown mainly in Southeast Asia, South America, and Hawaii. This very large spiny oval or oblong fruit has white or yellowish flesh with a sweet flavor. For details, see page 229.

Japanese-style bread crumbs (panko): Larger and coarser than Western-style bread crumbs, these dried, toasted flakes are perfect for giving a crunchy coating to deep-fried foods. Use in the same manner as bread crumbs. Panko does not taste greasy after frying, and it maintains its crisp texture even after standing awhile.

Jicama: Legume tuber with a tough, brown, leathery skin that surrounds a crunchy and sweet white flesh. Eaten both raw and cooked. Jicama can be used as a substitute for fresh water chestnuts, but it will be a bit more fibrous and bitter. Select small, hard, well-rounded roots that have no blemishes or mold.

Kabocha squash: A dark green globe-shaped winter squash, with pale green stripes, that looks something like a pumpkin and weighs about 3 pounds. The flesh is sweet and nutty textured. For details, see page 32.

Kaffir lime: For details on this small Southeast Asian citrus fruit, see page 163.

Kung pao sauce: Often used as a stir-fry seasoning, this Chinese sauce contains red chiles, sesame oil, soybeans, sweet potato, ginger, garlic, and other spices.

Lemongrass: This indispensable herb gives a distinctive lemon flavor and aroma to Southeast Asian foods. For details, see page 161.

Longan: Round fruit, about the size of a small plum, with red, pink, or yellow skin over sweet translucent flesh somewhat comparable to that of lychee. Longans are available canned, crystallized, dried, and occasionally fresh.

Lop cheong: See Chinese sausage.

Lotus root: This root grows in sausage-like links, that, when sliced, reveal a pattern of lacy holes. Before cooking the root, peel it and slice into rounds. Canned lotus root lacks the crispness and sweetness of the fresh root.

Lotus seed paste: Cooked lotus seeds that are mashed into a paste, something like sweet red bean paste. Used only as a sweet filling in desserts.

Lychee: A small 1- to 2-inch-diameter pink to crimson, fruit with bumpy, leathery peel. When the peel is slipped off, the semitranslucent, juicy flesh is revealed. If fresh lychees are unavailable, canned can be substituted; they save time, too, since they're sold peeled and pitted.

Mustard: Dry mustard powder is widely used in Asian cuisine. The powder is mixed with liquid to create a pungent and hotly spicy condiment for Chinese appetizers. Chinese-, Japanese-, and English-style dry mustards are interchangeable.

Napa cabbage: Two varieties are typically found: short Chinese and tall Japanese. Both have sweet, creamy stalks with ruffled, pale green edges. Either kind can be used as you would regular cabbage, but require less cooking time.

Noodles: see Bean thread noodles, Chinese egg noodles, Rice flour noodles.

Nori: see Seaweed, dried.

Oyster-flavored sauce: A thick, dark brown Chinese sauce made from oyster extract, sugar, soy sauce, and seasonings. Used both as a cooking sauce and as a condiment in Asian cooking. Its sweet-smoky flavor goes well with stir-fries of meat or vegetables. Spicy and vegetarian variations of the sauce are also available.

Oyster mushroom: A delicate shell-shaped fresh mushroom with a subtle, mild flavor.

Palm sugar: For details on this basic sweetener in Southeast Asian cooking, see page 233. Palm sugar is available in solid disks, which need to be crushed before measuring, or as a paste, in jars. It is also sometimes sold under the name coconut sugar.

Pandan leaf: The fragrant leaves of the screwpine add a distinct flavor and green color to Southeast Asian dishes, mainly desserts. See page 196.

Panko: see Japanese-style bread crumbs.

Peanut-flavored sauce (satay sauce): Thai sauce made of ground peanuts, curry paste, and other seasonings. Satay sauce is best for dipping or barbecuing.

Pearl tapioca: see Tapioca.

Peas, edible-pod: Bright green snow peas (Chinese pea pods) have flat pods with a sweet, sugary flavor and crunchy texture. Sugar snaps have thicker pods, similar flavor, and crisp texture.

Peppercorn: The almost-mature berry of the pepper vine. Black pepper comes from nearly ripe berries that are dried in the sun. White pepper comes from fully ripened peppercorns that are also sun dried. Green peppercorns are used in curries without coconut milk and in stir-fried dishes and chile sauces. They are the mildest of the three peppercorns and are available dried or packed in brine. Black peppercorns can be substituted for the green. For details, see sidebar on page 144.

Peppers, hot: see Chiles.

Peppers, sweet: Also known as bell peppers because of their bell-like shape. The peppers have a mild, sweet flavor and juicy flesh. Red peppers are the ripe form of the green pepper. Although red and green peppers are the most common, yellow, orange, purple, and brown bell peppers can also be found.

Pickled daikon: See Daikon.

Pickled garlic: see Garlic.

Pickled sour mustard greens: Chinese mustard greens pickled in brine, usually available in plastic shrink-wrapped packages in Asian markets.

Plum sauce: A sweet-tart sauce made from salted plums, apricots, yams, rice vinegar, chiles, and other spices. The amber-colored, chunky sauce is often served with roast duck, barbecued meats, and fried appetizers.

Portobella mushroom: Fresh, oversized, and fully-grown crimini mushroom. Dark brown in color, with a meaty, earthy flavor.

Potsticker wrappers: Thin circular wrappers made from wheat flour, water, and eggs. They are used to wrap fillings for gyoza, potstickers, and steamed dumplings (*siu mai*). After filling, the wrappers can be deep-fried, pan-fried, steamed, or simmered in soup.

Preserved egg: Sometimes called, 1000-year-old eggs, these eggs are actually preserved for only 100 days at most. Fresh duck eggs are coated with various preservative compounds that permeate the shell and alter the consistency of the egg. After they're preserved, they're shelled, sliced, and served as hors d'oeuvres with slivers of preserved ginger and a vinegar dip.

Preserved ginger: see Ginger.

Red bean paste: see Bean Paste, sweetened red.

Rice: Long-grain rice, such as jasmine rice, is the least starchy of all rice varieties; it cooks up dry and fluffy, with easily separated grains. These characteristics make it superior for fried rice. (For more on jasmine rice, see sidebar on page 156.) Medium-grain rice is a daily staple in Japan and Korea and is also the rice used in sushi. See also Glutinous rice.

Rice cakes (rice-pot crust): The crust that sometimes forms at the bottom of the pot in which rice is cooked. It's then dried in the sun and fried before eating. Rice cakes are eaten as a snack food with dip, somewhat like tortilla chips and salsa. Dried rice-pot crust is available in most Asian markets.

Rice flour: Flour made from glutinous or long-grain rice. Ground glutinous rice flour is most often used to create sweet doughs for *dim sum* and for Chinese

pastries. When boiled, the dough forms a smooth, chewy casing. Deep-frying yields a lightly crisp exterior with a sweet, sticky interior. Ground long-grain rice flour is used to make rice paper, rice noodles, steamed cakes, and other *dim sum* dishes.

Rice flour noodles: Fresh rice flour noodles, made from long-grain rice flour, are soft, flexible, and milky white. Wide, flat noodles are called *kway tiow*. For more information about fresh rice noodles, see page 225. Stiff, brittle dried rice flour noodles are available in a variety of widths and lengths. Thick noodles are called *lai fun*. Rice vermicelli are dried rice noodles approximately 1/8 inch in width.

Rice paper: Round or triangular semitransclucent sheets made from rice flour. Before using, the brittle sheets are softened with water or by placing between dampened towels. Used to wrap savory bundles of meats and vegetables.

Rice vermicelli: see Rice flour noodles.

Rice vinegar: Vinegar made from fermented rice; milder in flavor and sweeter than distilled white vinegar. Chinese and Japanese varieties range from clear or slightly golden in color to rich amber brown. Chinese rice vinegars are generally more sour than the Japanese varieties. Chinese black vinegar (see separate listing) is made from a fermentation of a mixture of rice, wheat, and millet or sorghum.

Rice wine: see Chinese rice wine.

Roasted chile paste: See Chile sauces.

Sa cha sauce: Sauce made from soybean oil, fish, shrimp, onion, garlic, chiles, and spices. Used by the Chinese as a sauce for seafood, as a hot-pot base, or as a stir-fry condiment. Available in jars at most Asian markets.

Sauces: See listings under individual sauce names.

Seaweed, dried: Deep green sheets of Japanese dried seaweed (nori) are used to wrap sushi and shredded for garnishes. Chinese-style dried seaweed is coarser in texture than the more highly processed nori and is sold in round or square bundles in Asian markets. When used for cooking, it should be reconstituted in water. The purple, lacy dried leaves look like purple cellophane, and its sea scent and flavor enhances most dishes made with seafood.

Sesame oil: "Asian sesame oil" is pressed from toasted white sesame seeds. The best oils are labeled as "100 percent pure." Small amounts of this dark amber oil are used to add a nutty taste and aroma to marinades, dressings, and stir-fries. Asian sesame oil is used sparingly as a flavor accent, and should not be confused with the light-colored and more mildly flavored sesame oil made from untoasted seeds, which is used in larger quantities in salad dressings and for sautéing.

Sesame seeds: Can be found in either black or white varieties, they are both used as a flavor accent and as a garnish. Hulled and unhulled white sesame seeds have a sweet, nutty flavor. Black sesame seeds are more bitter in flavor. Toasting intensifies their taste and aroma, especially the white seeds.

Shallots: Asian shallots are generally smaller than the more commonly used Western shallot. Look for bulbs about the size of an unshelled walnut. Fried shallots are used as a garnish; for directions on how to make them, see page 164. Fried shallots also can be purchased in most Asian groceries.

Shaoxing wine: see Chinese rice wine.

Shiitake mushroom: Available both fresh and dried, shiitake mushrooms have brownish-black caps, tan undersides, a rich and meaty texture, and a wild mushroom flavor. Originally from Japan, fresh shiitake are now widely cultivated in the United States.

Shrimp, fresh: Fresh shrimp come in various sizes; when size is relevant to the outcome of the dish, it is listed in the recipe. For instructions on deveining and butterflying shrimp, see page 186. See also Dried shrimp.

Shrimp paste (Thai shrimp paste): This condiment and flavoring agent is made from salted, cured small fish or shrimp that are fermented for several weeks.

Shrimp sauce: A thick and pungent sauce made from salted fermented shrimp; it's an essential ingredient in Chinese and Southeast Asian cooking.

Sichuan peppercorns: Unrelated to black peppercorns, these intense dried rust-colored berries of the prickly ash tree add a woodsy perfume and taste to foods. Toast them in a heavy frying pan over low heat, stirring occasionally, until they become fragrant. Use whole, or crush in a spice grinder into a coarse or fine powder.

Sichuan preserved vegetables: Typically a mixture of Chinese mustard greens, napa cabbage, and turnips that is preserved in salt, ground chiles, and ground Sichuan peppercorns to give them a spicy and salty taste. For more information, see sidebar on page 58.

Snow fungus (white fungus): Resembles a small, hard, round sponge. Its color ranges from golden beige to creamy off-white, which turns silvery white after cooking. Snow fungus is used mainly in sweet dessert soups. It is found dried in plastic bags and must be soaked in warm water to soften before using. The hard core from its underside must be removed after soaking. For more details, see page 68.

Snow peas: see Peas, edible-pod.

Soy sauce: All types of soy sauce are made from naturally fermented soybeans and wheat. The most common variety, **regular soy sauce** gives Chinese dishes their characteristic flavor and rich brown color. **Dark soy sauce** has added molasses. It is thicker, darker, sweeter, and more full bodied. It should be used when a richer flavor and deep mahogany color are desired. **Reduced-sodium soy sauce,** sometimes called "lite soy sauce," contains about 40 percent less sodium than regular soy sauce. It has rich flavor, but a less salty taste. **Thick sweet soy sauce** is very dark brown and thick. Its sweetness comes from palm sugar, and it is also seasoned with garlic and star anise. **Thin soy sauce** is lighter in color, saltier, and thinner than regular soy sauce and is not to be confused with reduced-sodium soy sauce. It is used when little or no color change in the food is desired.

Spring roll wrappers: These paper-thin pancakes are made from a thin batter of wheat flour. The wrappers are square or round, and thinner than egg roll wrappers. When deep-fried, they become crisp and smooth, with a light texture.

Star anise: An inedible 1-inch pod with eight points; within each point is a shiny, mahogany-colored seed. If the whole pod is unavailable, use eight broken points. Star anise adds a distinctive accent of licorice to braising sauces and stews.

Straw mushrooms: Named after the straw they are cultivated on, these mushrooms have a delicate sweetness and a firm, meaty texture. Available in cans, peeled or unpeeled; drain before using.

Sugar snap peas: see Peas, edible-pod.

Sweet and sour sauce: Chinese cooking sauce made from vinegar and sugar, with chiles, ketchup, and ginger added in some versions. Cantonese versions are more fruity in flavor.

Sweet chile sauce: see Chile sauces.

Tamarind: The fibrous, sticky pulp that surrounds the seeds of the tamarind tree has a fruity, sweet-sour flavor that is a distinctive trait in Southeast Asian cooking. Used in curries, chutneys, soups, and stews. Before using, the pulp must be mashed in water, then pressed through a sieve; see instructions on page 189.

Tangerine peel, dried: This brittle, rust-colored peel adds a mellow, citrusy flavor to sauces, soups, and braised dishes. You can buy it in bags in Chinese markets, but it's simple to make: Cut the peel into pieces small enough to spread flat. With a paring knife, remove as much white pith from the inside of the peel as possible. Cut the pieces into smaller strips and set them out to dry until they're firm but still flexible, and very dry. Stored in an airtight container; dried tangerine peel will keep for months.

Tapioca: The white powder is made from the root of the cassava plant. The starch is used as a thickener and can be combined with other flours to make d*im sum* doughs. Tapioca pearls come in various sizes and colors and are used in a variety of dishes; small (1/8-inch) pearls are used in puddings and desserts. For more details see pages 119 and 231.

Taro root: A slightly hairy root with a dark skin and rough texture. The flesh of some varieties turns from white or grayish to light purple when cooked. Cooked taro root has a sweet and nutty flavor and a starchy texture. For more details, see page 80.

Thai basil: For more on this flavorful herb, used widely in Thai cooking, see sidebar on page 209.

Thai chile: see Chiles, fresh.

Thai chile sauce: see Chile sauces.

Thai eggplant: see Eggplant.

Thai roasted chile sauce: see Chile sauces.

Tofu: Also known as bean curd. Tofu is made from soybeans and water and is available in a variety of textures: **soft tofu** has a silky texture and is very light;

regular-firm has a denser structure and slightly springy interior; and **extra-firm** is denser still. Tofu can also be found in sheets measuring about 7 by 21 inches, and in a variety of other forms.

Turmeric: A member of the ginger family, this underground stem imparts a bitter, pungent flavor and bright yellow-orange color to foods. It is a fundamental ingredient in many Indian and Southeast Asian spice blends, especially curry powders. Typically found ground on supermarket spice shelves.

Vegetable oil: Corn oil, canola oil, safflower oil and peanut oil are cooking oils that work well for both stir-frying and deep-frying.

Vinegar: see Chinese black vinegar, Rice vinegar.

Water chestnuts: Fresh water chestnuts, approx 1½ inches in diameter, have a brownish black skin that must be peeled to uncover the tan, slightly starchy, crisp flesh. When buying, select fresh specimens without wrinkles and mold. Canned water chestnuts have a similar texture, but they are not as sweet and must be drained and rinsed to remove the canned flavor.

Wheat starch: Fine-textured, off-white wheat flour with all gluten removed. Frequently used to make doughs for *dim sum* dishes. Steamed wheat starch dough becomes soft, glossy, and opaque white.

White fungus: see Snow fungus

Wine, Chinese rice: see Chinese rice wine.

Wonton wrappers: Made from wheat flour, water, and eggs, wonton wrappers are about 6 inches square and come in two thicknesses: thicker ones are used for deep-frying, pan-frying, or steaming; thinner ones are used in soups. They are used to wrap a variety of fillings, from savory to sweet.

Wood ear (black fungus/cloud ear): An edible fungi that grows on trees. Used not so much for their flavor, which is very bland, but for their crunchy texture and dark color. Like dried mushrooms, they must be soaked, rinsed, and trimmed of any hard woody parts. Fresh black fungus, which doesn't require soaking, is becoming increasingly available in local supermarkets and gourmet food stores.

Wrappers: see separate listings for Egg roll wrappers, Potsticker wrappers, Spring roll wrappers, and Wonton wrappers.

Television Series Acknowledgments

In addition to all the wonderful, talented people who contributed to the cookbook, a crack team came together to create the *Yan Can Cook: Asian Favorites* series on public television.

If I live a thousand years, I still won't have enough time to thank gayle k. yamada for everything she's done, both as executive producer and series producer. Lori Lane was an ace studio producer, and Chris Cochran, studio director, was a fun-loving, creative genius. My appreciation also goes to Tammy Sumner, unflagging associate producer; Stephanie Jan, food and prop stylist; and Audrey Wells, imaginative set designer. As usual, Ivan Lai's irrepressible sense of humor found its way onto the screen; the engaging and fun scripts are a testament to his ingenious talent and insightful understanding of Asian culture. And many thanks to my tireless multitasking assistants, Jeannie Cuan and Leena Hung.

We taped the studio segments at the studios of KVIE, Channel 6, in Sacramento, CA. I admire and appreciate the efforts of our good friends David Hosley, KVIE's general manager, and Jan Tilmon, the station's executive in charge of production. Their professionalism and skill, along with that of the rest of the KVIE production crew, made shooting the segments a breeze. I can't overstate the importance of KVIE's support and facilities, particularly the commercial kitchen—a dream place for a cooking show production. And since we were there in the dog days of a Sacramento Valley summer, I can't overstate the importance of their air conditioner, either!

Some names you've seen before—and a few new ones, too—were responsible for the show's studio cooking segments. Tina Salter was the indomitable culinary consultant and Sandra Rust, as kitchen manager, kept everything in apple-pie order. Thanks to our esteemed chefs William Chow, Julie Tan Salazar, Scott Demnick, David Skrzypek, Sophie Hou, Eva Kwong, Nickel Lowman, and Frankie Poon. Thanks also to culinary staff members Brenda Dennis, Aaron Guerra, Winnie Lee, Michael Smith, and the dozens of dedicated students from Cosumnes River College's Culinary Arts department who helped us.

The international crew braved weeks of flying and the physiological havoc of hopping from time zone to time zone and from hot to cold climates, all in service to the show. Once again, thanks to Stephanie Jan, my right-hand woman and unflagging personal assistant, on-location production coordinator, and food and prop stylist. She's truly irreplaceable, and I hope she knows how much I appreciate her. On-location team in Hong Kong: James Lingwood, director; Dean Head, director of photography; Steve Chan, audio technician; Mark Norfolk and Joseph Chan, editors. On-location team in Thailand: James Lingwood, director; Brian Kimmel, cameraman; Peter Williams, audio technician; Mark Tang, editor. On-location team in Taiwan: gayle k. yamada, director; Brian Kimmel and Wen Qing Chan, cameramen; Peter Williams, audio technician; Scott Tsuchitani, editor.

Everyone exerted a Herculean effort in doing their duties, and I'm in awe of their perseverance.

Producer's Thanks

Yan Can Cook: Asian Favorites, the television series, is a collaborative effort. We've created a family of more than one hundred fifty people in five countries, combining many skills and varied talents to bring this season to fruition. We're thankful also for technology, because e-mail and the Internet have made a huge difference in the production of our show; now we can listen to music from our composer in Australia or e-mail one of our editors in Hong Kong in spite of time differences!

This year we moved our base of television operations to the California state capital, Sacramento. It is rare to be able to say that everything went smoothly, but everything did! At KVIE, the public television station where we produced *Yan Can Cook,* we were given the utmost consideration, and our every request was honored. We felt as though everyone who worked at the station, whether directly involved or not, cared about the shows. Our support staff and kitchen crew were incredible: creative, hardworking, dependable, and intently focused on producing the best series possible. Teaming the *Yan Can Cook* crew with the people at KVIE was fun, too! So, although it is Martin you see on television, you can see and hear the contributions of every single person who has worked with us.

Traveling around Asia—Hong Kong, Taiwan, and Thailand—we were treated with warmth from everyone we met. Their hospitality was extraordinary.

And, of course, none of this would be possible without two people: Martin and his wife, Sue. Martin's enthusiasm for Asia's cultures and foods make him a true culinary ambassador. That enthusiasm is contagious, whether here in the United States or abroad. Sue is a much-appreciated anchor for her traveling husband.

It is a privilege to be able to bring together and collaborate with so many talented people. Each season is a learning experience. Thank you.

—gayle k. yamada

248

Executive Producer and Series Producer

Thanks to those individuals and companies who donated their time, talent, food, furnishings, and equipment in support of *Asian Favorites,* the eleventh, twelfth, and thirteenth series of *Yan Can Cook.*

Studio Culinary Support

California Asparagus Commission

California Fats Restaurant, Sacramento, CA

Cha-Am Thai Restaurant, Vallejo, CA

Monterey Mushrooms

Thai Me Up Restaurant, San Francisco, CA

Studio Production Support

The BRITA Products Company

The GLAD Company

Del Monte Meat Co.

Economy Restaurant Fixtures, San Francisco, CA

Eddie's Restaurant, Sacramento, CA

Greenleaf Wholesale Floral Company

KitchenAid

Mansour's Oriental Rug Gallery, Sacramento, CA

Man-U Imports, San Mateo, CA

Michael Himovtiz Gallery, Sacramento, CA

Mikuni Japanese Restaurant, Sacramento, CA

The New Louis Florist, Sacramento, CA

OXO International

Pottery Barn

The Radisson Hotel, Sacramento, CA

Raley's Food Markets

Royal Hawaiian Seafood

William Glen, Sacramento, CA

Williams-Sonoma

Wing Sing Chong Co., Inc.

Thanks to Sponsors and International Friends

Yan Can Cook: Asian Favorites is made possible by the generosity of these partners.

The best ingredients make the best meals, and the same goes for producing a cooking show and a cookbook. I'd like to express my deepest gratitude to the companies on these pages, whose generous support has made the eleventh, twelfth, and thirteenth series of *Yan Can Cook* possible. They are the true key ingredients in my recipe for success.

Lee Kum Kee
Maker of Oriental sauces since 1888.
Lee Kum Kee, the inventor of oyster-flavored sauce and over sixty other Oriental sauces, is proud to be the leader of authentic Oriental sauces.

Circulon Style
Cooking solutions by design.
Circulon Style is the first COLORED hard anodized nonstick cookware. It features a patented Hi-Low system of grooves and bold enamel exteriors to add color to your kitchen. The pan lids are topped with a unique "S" lid handle that stays cool during cooking.

GE Monogram
For the kitchen of your dreams—the GE Monogram Collection. It incorporates the best of both European and American design into a superior series of professional, freestanding, and built-in appliances. Their pristine exterior, whether in stainless steel or customized to match your cabinets, is overshadowed only by the superb performance of each and every appliance.

Aroma Housewares
Aroma Housewares is a leading manufacturer with a full line of quality kitchenware appliances, dedicated to fulfilling the needs of America's home kitchens.

Melissa's (World Specialty Produce)
The freshest ideas in produce and specialty foods.
Prepare yourself for the unexpected and the extraordinary. Melissa's brings the best of the world's fresh exotic and organic fruits and vegetables, specialty foods, and authentic international ingredients to supermarkets and specialty stores throughout the U.S. With Melissa's, a culinary adventure awaits you.

Diamond of California
No wonder Diamond of California is the world leader in culinary and in-shell nuts. They produce the highest-quality, best-tasting nuts, perfect not only for Asian cuisine, but for all foods. Diamond is proud to be the Official Olympic Nut Supplier of the 2000/2002/2004 U.S. Olympic Team.

Messermeister
Purveyor of high-quality professional chef's knives.
Messermeister has been providing an extensive, innovative selection of quality cutlery since 1866. The new "Meridian elite" forged knife line is rated the sharpest and best-quality professional knife available on the market. Messermeister is also the manufacturer of Martin Yan's Chinese Chef's Knife.

Wegmans Food Markets, Inc.
Wegmans makes great meals easy.
Wegmans Food Markets, Inc. is a sixty-one-store supermarket chain with locations in New York, Pennsylvania, and New Jersey. The family-owned company was founded in 1916. Wegmans is recognized as an industry leader and innovator and is also known for its strong commitment to the communities where it operates stores.

THE BOLD LOOK OF KOHLER.

Kohler
The bold look of Kohler.
A global leader in kitchen and bath design for over 127 years, Kohler has a long-standing tradition in adhering to a singular level of quality. A pioneer of new styles and colors and innovative technologies, Kohler's well-designed, reliable products enhance your lifestyle and perform for as long as you own your home.

Asian Home Gourmet
Asian Home Gourmet natural SpicePastes© are made from fresh herbs and spices. They have no added MSG, preservatives, or artificial colors. Cooking Asian dishes is so easy with Asian Home Gourmet's wide range of natural SpicePastes©.

Argo Cornstarch and Kingsford's Cornstarch
For easy, authentic stir-fry that's simply delicious.
Argo, the leading U.S. cornstarch, and Kingsford's cornstarch, in the West, are the trusted and foolproof thickeners for tasty sauces, gravies, puddings, and pies. Discover the many uses of Argo and Kingsford's at www.cornstarch.com.

AsianConnections.com
The network to the best of the East and the West!
Get connected to a global network of people and find great recipes, shopping, travel, business, feng shui, horoscope, entertainment, and more! Visit Asian-Connections' network: AsianChefs.com, ChinaConnections.com, StudioLA.com, and the AsianSinglesNetwork.com. Go to where many of the world's top chefs go! AsiaKitchen.com—the largest Asian food store on the Web.

A centre for involvement in asian food, culinary skills and craftware.

at-sunrice
A center dedicated to Pan-Asian cuisine. Gourmet travelers savor two weeks of gastronomical delights in two exotic Asian countries. Culinary students participate in two-week, hands-on courses with possible six-month internships.
Visit www.at-sunrice.com;
E-mail zeke@at-sunrice.com.

Dermaguard, Inc.
DermaGuard Inc. is a privately held, minority-owned-and-operated company and the exclusive manufacturer and distributor of SafeShield™, an antimicrobial waterproof barrier moisturizing lotion that kills many bacteria and certain viruses for up to four hours. Dermaguard has its principal office on historic St. Charles Avenue in the "Garden District" of New Orleans.

Hong Kong Tourism Board
www.discoverhongkong.com

Tourism Bureau, ROC (Taiwan)
www.tbroc.gov.tw

Tourism Authority of Thailand
www.tat.or.th

Index

Yan Can Cook

Visit www.yancancook.com to find culinary tips, Chef Yan's favorite recipes and tools, as well as his library of books. You can also ask questions or request that your favorite recipe be added to the website.